Restoring the American Dream

Restoring the American Dream

Providing Community Colleges with the Resources They Need

The Report of The Century Foundation Working Group
on Community College Financial Resources

With background papers by
Bruce Baker *and* Jesse Levin
Anthony P. Carnevale, Artem Gulish, *and* Jeff Strohl
Richard D. Kahlenberg, Robert Shireman, Kimberly Quick, *and* Tariq Habash

THE CENTURY
FOUNDATION

New York • The Century Foundation Press

This volume was published with the generous support of the William T. Grant Foundation.

Library of Congress Cataloguing-in-Publication Data Available from the publisher upon request.

Manufactured in the United States of America
Cover design by Jonnea Herman
Text design by Cynthia Stock

Contents

Members of the Working Group

Thomas Bailey (Columbia University)

Bruce Baker (Rutgers University)

Brooks Bowden (North Carolina State University)

Anthony P. Carnevale (Georgetown University)

Debbie Cochrane (The Institute for College Access and Success)

Michelle Cooper (Institute for Higher Education Policy)

Russ Deaton (Tennessee Board of Regents)

Wil Del Pilar (Education Trust)

David Deming (Harvard University)

Sara Goldrick-Rab (Temple University)

Harry Holzer (Georgetown University)

Tammy Kolbe (University of Vermont)

Jesse Levin (American Institutes for Research)

Bridget Terry Long (Harvard University)

Tatiana Melguizo (University of Southern California)

Gail Mellow (LaGuardia Community College)

Andrew Nichols (Education Trust)

George Pernsteiner (State Higher Education Executive Officers)

Ken Redd (National Association of College and University Business Officers)

Jennifer Rice (University of Maryland)

Robert Toutkoushian (University of Georgia)

Richard D. Kahlenberg (The Century Foundation), *Executive Director*

Report of the Working Group

Executive Summary

I n the United States, where social mobility has been considered a birth-right, community colleges are essential to that promise. Located in hundreds of communities throughout the country, near where people live and work, two-year colleges are meant to be America's quintessential institutions for the aspiring middle class. While elite four-year colleges boast of the proportion of students they reject, community colleges take pride, as one leader suggested, in taking the "top 100 percent of students."

But America's 1,000 community colleges, which educate 9 million students, are routinely under-resourced and often fall short of their promise. Only 38 percent of students entering community college complete a degree or certificate within six years. While 81 percent of students entering community college say they aspire to eventually transfer and receive a four-year degree, only 15 percent do so after six years.

Part of the responsibility lies with K–12 institutions, which do not adequately prepare students for college, and part of the fault lies with the two-year sector, which often fails to provide enough structure and guidance to undergraduates. And part of the fault must be laid at the feet of four-year colleges and universities, which make transferring from community colleges difficult to understand and challenging to achieve. But the lion's share of the blame lies with policymakers who systematically shortchange community colleges financially, giving two-year institutions the fewest resources to educate those students who tend to have the greatest needs.

New data in this report show that, while just one in five students at the most competitive and highly competitive four-year colleges came from the bottom half of the socioeconomic distribution in 2013, the majority of community college students did. Researchers have long recognized that disadvantaged students need more resources to succeed than those who have enjoyed many advantages, and yet state budgets have starved community colleges of the funds they need to succeed.

In fiscal year 2013, private four-year research institutions spent five times as much per full time equivalent student annually ($72,000) as did community colleges ($14,000). Some of that difference is explained by the differing research functions of institutions, but when one excludes research expenses and focuses on education and related expenses, private research universities still spend three times as much as community colleges. Public research universities spend 60 percent more than community colleges.

Inadequate funding of community colleges is deeply troubling given that careful research has found "significant causal impacts" of spending on degree completion. Scholars looking at community colleges between 1990 and 2013 found that a 10 percent spending increase boosted awards and certificates by 15 percent. When students complete an associate's degree, they will see their lifetime earnings increase on average by more than $300,000.

What can be done? In this report, we recommend that states immediately begin to increase community college funding in order to boost opportunities for students. We also call for the creation of a new federal–state partnership for community colleges in which states must agree to do their part in order to qualify for new federal investments in two-year institutions.

Our mid-term recommendation is that federal and state policymakers—and foundation officials—support a new body of research that will establish, for the first time, what it costs to provide a strong community college education. Such studies are commonplace in public K–12 education, where for forty years, researchers have sought to establish what level of funding is required to achieve adequate outcomes and how much additional funding should be targeted to achieve good results for disadvantaged students in particular. These studies also seek to provide guidance on where money should be invested to achieve the greatest bang for the buck.

Part of the reason researchers have not conducted comparable studies at the community college level is that there are special challenges to doing so not found at the K–12 level. For example, the first step in estimating costs is to identify with some precision the desired outcome. In K–12 schooling, researchers often calculate the cost of achieving a certain level of proficiency on standardized tests or higher education completion. But in higher education, such tests of learning outcomes are not widely available, and the ultimate goal students typically have is not only to graduate, but also to acquire skills that significantly and cost-effectively raise earnings and, wherever possible, allow a worker to earn a decent living. Likewise, community colleges offer a widely variety of programs—from nursing to welding—that are not offered at a typical high school. The costs of providing those different types of programs may vary more widely than the cost of providing a traditional high school education.

As a working group, we analyzed and debated these types of thorny questions, and in this report now offer a set of eight recommendations that, taken together, constitute a framework for how researchers can best estimate the cost of a community college education. While acknowledging the complexities, we ultimately believe such a study can and should be undertaken.

Today, policymakers are making decisions about where, and how much, to invest in community colleges without information about what really is needed to achieve the outcomes they seek. Much better research could greatly improve those decisions, substantially boost the life chances of community college students, and jumpstart social mobility in America.

Report of the Working Group

I n the United States, parents have expected their children to grow up to be better off as a matter of course. Social mobility allows a society to tap into the talents of disadvantaged populations in a way that benefits everyone. Vertical mobility permits individuals of all backgrounds the opportunity for an enriching and financially stable life. And forward economic momentum greases the wheels of a smoothly functioning multiracial democracy.

Research finds, however, that social mobility in the United States is on the decline, and polls find that fewer and fewer Americans believe their children will see improved life prospects.[1] When social mobility breaks down, some Americans look for scapegoats, and society's most vulnerable members—immigrants, African Americans, the poor, and religious minorities—suffer. When America loses its optimism, it becomes an uglier place. When fewer Americans have the chance to advance economically, human potential is wasted and society is poorer.

For generations, public education in America has been a driving force for social mobility, beginning with creation of elementary schools, then secondary schools. Now, at a time when the economy demands higher levels of skills among workers, community colleges have become especially critical institutions of social mobility. Whereas a high school diploma and a union card used to provide access to the middle class, today, researchers find, "80 percent of good jobs that support middle-class lifestyles" require some postsecondary education.[2] Two-year colleges, located in hundreds of communities throughout the country, near where people live and work, and open to the "top 100 percent of students," are meant to be America's quintessential institutions for the aspiring middle class and those seeking to avoid downward mobility.[3]

Yet too many of America's community colleges are underfunded and have failed to deliver on their promise. The country's 1,000 public two-year institutions serving 9 million undergraduates are routinely under-resourced, and overburdened.[4] While individual community college leaders are doing extraordinary work, the sector as a whole is not producing the results the country needs. Only 38 percent of students entering community college complete a degree or certificate within six years. While 81 percent of students entering community college say they aspire to eventually transfer and receive a four-year degree, only 15 percent do so after six years.[5]

Research outlined in this report suggests that one central impediment to success is a lack of resources. Society asks community colleges to educate those students who are most likely to face significant disadvantages, and to do so with relatively few dollars. This much we know.

But precisely *how much* funding do community colleges need to succeed? Astonishingly, researchers have conducted almost no empirical research on this question. At the K–12 level, scholars have engaged in dozens of studies to establish the level of funding required to provide an "adequate" level of education. These studies have spurred K–12 finance reforms that have generally led to improved outcomes for students.[6]

The Century Foundation, with the support of the William T. Grant Foundation, created this Working Group on Community College Financial Resources to think about ways to apply K–12 costing-out methodologies to community colleges. The purpose of this report is to establish—for the first time—a framework for how a study could be conducted to estimate the true costs of a strong community college education. (For a list of working group members, see page vi.)

This report proceeds in three parts. The first lays out the stakes—why it is important to establish the true cost of a community college education and provide two-year institutions with the resources they need. The second part examines the four key steps that K–12 costing-out studies take;

outlines four critical differences between pre-collegiate and community college education; and delineates eight concrete recommendations that provide a framework for how this research should be conducted in the future. The third part of the report articulates a plan for how policy leaders could use new empirical evidence provided by a community college costing-out study to inform policymaking.

The Stakes: Why It Is Important to Establish the True Cost of an Adequate Community College Education

The Declining American Dream

Americans are increasingly pessimistic about the prospects of the next generation.[7] According to a 2017 Pew Research Center survey, 58 percent of Americans said today's children will grow up to be financially worse off than their parents, compared with just 37 percent who predicted those children will be better off.[8]

Americans are right to be concerned. According to research by Harvard University's Raj Chetty, the proportion of American children making more than their parents (in inflation-adjusted dollars) has declined, from more than 90 percent of those who were born in 1940 to about 50 percent of those born in 1984.[9] (See Figure 1, page 10.)

Research also finds that relative mobility—the probability that a child born into the bottom fifth of the income distribution will at some point reach the top fifth—is much less likely in the United States than in many other nations. In fact, such social mobility is almost twice as likely to occur in Canada as the United States, according to Chetty's research.[10] (See Figure 2, page 10.)

Community Colleges Can Help Remedy Low Levels of Mobility if Two-Year Institutions Are Properly Resourced

For seventy years, policymakers have viewed public community colleges as a critical driver of upward mobility in the United States. The 1947 Truman

Figure 1. Percentage of U.S. Children Making More Than Their Parents, by Child's Birth Year, 1940–84

Source: Raj Chetty et al., "The Fading American Dream: Trends in Absolute Income Mobility Since 1940," NBER Working Paper No. 22910, December 2016, rev. March 2017, https://www.nber.org/papers/w22910.

Figure 2. Relative Mobility in Advanced Countries

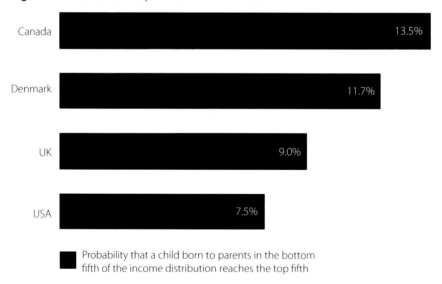

Probability that a child born to parents in the bottom fifth of the income distribution reaches the top fifth

Source: Richard V. Reeves and Eleanor Krause, "Raj Chetty in 14 charts: Big findings on opportunity and mobility we should all know," Brookings Institution, January 11, 2018, https://www.brookings.edu/blog/social-mobility-memos/2018/01/11/raj-chetty-in-14-charts-big-findings-on-opportunity-and-mobility-we-should-know/.

Commission on Higher Education envisioned community colleges as key institutions in reaching the goal of equal opportunity for all Americans. The commission renamed "junior colleges," which had been around since 1901, as "community colleges" to emphasize their vast geographic reach and their special mission in supporting individual communities.[11] Perhaps because of their community focus—and their accessibility to a broad cross-section of students—community colleges command greater support in public opinion surveys than do four-year institutions.[12]

The public is right to believe that community colleges can contribute to upward mobility in the nation. At the same time, too many students at community colleges are not finding their way to a degree or certificate. According the National Student Clearinghouse Research Center, six years after entering community college, only 22.8 percent of students have completed a two-year degree or certificate (and no more), and another 14.7 percent have completed a four-year degree. (See Figure 3.) The vast majority—62.5 percent—have not received a degree of any type after six years (15.2 percent are still enrolled, but 47.3 percent are no longer enrolled).[13]

Figure 3. Six-Year Outcomes for Community College Students

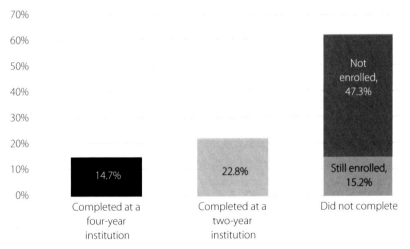

Source: Doug Shapiro et al., "Completing College: A National View of Student Completion Rates—Fall 2011 Cohort," National Student Clearinghouse Research Center, December 2017, Appendix C, Table 39, https://nscresearchcenter. org/signaturereport14/.

Low levels of completion surely reflect in part the academic preparation levels found, on average, among community college students.[14] But careful research that controls for incoming academic preparation and demographic factors finds that students intending to pursue a four-year degree face substantially reduced chances of earning such a degree when they begin at a two-year rather than a four-year institution. Kent State economist C. Lockwood Reynolds, for example, estimated, after applying appropriate controls, that beginning at a two-year college reduces one's ultimate chances of receiving a bachelor's degree by 30 percentage points.[15] This differential may reflect the difficulties that can arise when students transfer from a community college to a four-year institution; but the reduced chances of attaining a bachelor's degree may well be a product of the issue to which we now turn: the relatively low levels of funding found, on average, in the two-year sector.

Community College Resources Do Not Equal the Challenge

Researchers have identified three broad paths for improving outcomes for community college students: (1) providing better academic support to students at the K–12 level so that fewer students are in need of remedial classes; (2) improving efficiency at the community college level through adoption of best practices, such as guided pathways that add greater structure and guidance to the student experience;[16] and (3) providing adequate financial resources. We support all three approaches, but in this report, we focus particularly on the third path, which is too often ignored.

The absolute differences in spending levels between two-year and four-year institutions is remarkable, even accounting for the different functions of research universities and two-year institutions devoted primarily to instruction. According to a 2016 report from the American Institutes of Research (AIR), private research universities spend five times as much per student per year ($71,597) as community colleges do ($14,090), and public research universities almost three times as much ($39,783).[17] (See Figure 4.)

Figure 4. Per-Pupil Total Operation Expenditures, FY 2013

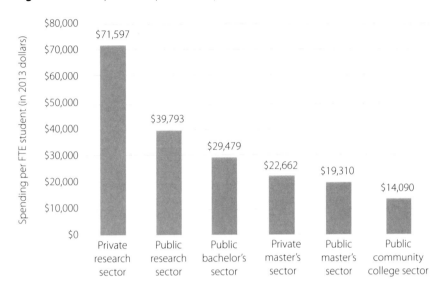

Source: Donna M. Desrochers and Steven Hurlburt, "Trends in College Spending 2003 to 2013," Delta Cost Project and the American Institutes of Research, January 2016, 24–27.

Of course, some of the spending differentials are related to the fact that research universities are tasked with conducting research as well as educating students, but AIR's data show that when one excludes research expenses and focuses on educational instruction, spending inequalities remain.[18] For example, private research universities still spend more than three times as much as public community colleges on "education and related" spending, and public research universities spend 60 percent more ($17,252 at public research universities versus $10,804 at public community colleges).[19] (See Figure 5, page 14.)

To make matters worse, these inequalities in spending occur despite the fact that community colleges tend to educate students with *greater* educational needs than students at four-year institutions. According to new research from Georgetown University's Center for Education and the Workforce, community college students are far more likely to be socioeconomically disadvantaged than students in four-year colleges, especially

Figure 5. Average Education and Related Spending per FTE Student, 2013

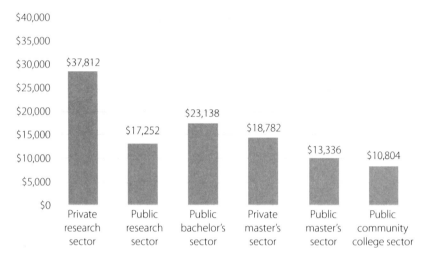

Source: Donna M. Desrochers and Steven Hurlburt, "Trends in College Spending 2003 to 2013," Delta Cost Project and the American Institutes of Research, January 2016, 24–27.

the most selective four-year institutions. While just one in five students in the most competitive and highly competitive four-year colleges came from the bottom half of the socioeconomic distribution of the population in 2013, for example, the majority of students in community colleges did. (See Figure 6.) As discussed further below, researchers have long recognized that to achieve comparable outcomes, students with greater needs require greater resources, not fewer.

Another way to consider the socioeconomic distribution is to examine the destinations of college-going students within each socioeconomic quartile. As Figure 7 indicates, the majority (58 percent) of students in the bottom socioeconomic quartile in 2013 enrolled at community colleges, compared with just 25 percent of students from the top socioeconomic quartile.

Funding Matters in Outcomes at Community Colleges

The lower levels of spending in community colleges—coupled with the greater needs, on average, in community college student bodies—is

Figure 6. Socioeconomic Distribution at Colleges, by Selectivity, 2013

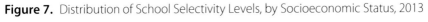

Source: Georgetown University Center on Education and Workforce, unpublished analysis (2018) of High School Longitudinal Study (2009) and Barron's Admissions Competitive Index Data Files, 1972–2014.

Figure 7. Distribution of School Selectivity Levels, by Socioeconomic Status, 2013

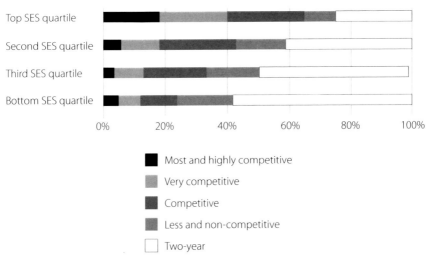

Source: Georgetown University Center on Education and Workforce, unpublished analysis (2018) of High School Longitudinal Study (2009) and Barron's Admissions Competitive Index Data Files, 1972–2014.

important because research suggests that greater resources are connected to better outcomes for students in higher education.[20] In the four-year college sector, for example, John Bound of the University of Michigan, Michael Lovenheim of Cornell, and Sarah Turner of the University of Virginia found in an important 2010 study that declining completion rates over time were due primarily to declines in resources per student.[21] The research on the importance of resources in four-year colleges dovetails with a wide body of research suggesting resources matter at the K–12 level.[22] In a February 2018 study of California's K–12 funding increases, for example, Rucker Johnson of the University of California–Berkeley, and Sean Tanner of WestEd, looking at the effects of the Local Control Funding Formula (LCFF), "found strongly significant impacts of LCFF-induced increases in district revenue on average high school graduation rates for all children." In particular, they found that "a $1,000 increase in district per-pupil revenue from the state experienced in grades 10–12 leads to a 5.3 percentage-point increase in high school graduation rates, on average, among all children."[23]

Similar results have been found in the community college sector. Among the most important recent studies on this topic is one conducted by David Deming of Harvard University and Christopher Walters of University of California–Berkeley for the National Bureau of Economic Research in August 2017. The researchers examined the impact of postsecondary spending between 1990 and 2013 and found "positive and statistically significant causal impacts of spending on degree completion."[24] The authors concluded that spending had even larger impacts in two-year institutions than four-year institutions.[25] Specifically, Deming and Walters found that a 10 percent increase in spending in a given year resulted in increased awards of certificates and degrees in the following two years of 14.5 and 14.6 percent, respectively.[26] The authors did not explore the precise reasons that spending had positive outcomes but suggested it was possible that increased course offerings, shorter waiting lists, better student guidance, and smaller class sizes produced the improved results.[27]

In addition, there is evidence that certain investments are particularly likely to be worthwhile:[28]

- *Full-time faculty.* Much—though not all—relevant research finds that having more full-time faculty on staff leads to improved outcomes for students.[29] Yet today, community colleges frequently rely on inexpensive adjuncts and other part-time instructors. Only 31 percent of faculty members at public community colleges are full-time, compared with 42 percent at public research universities and 50 percent at private research universities. (Graduate assistants are counted as part-time in this analysis.)[30] Investing in more full-time community college faculty could result in improved outcomes for students.

- *Extra tutoring, small class size, intensive advising, and generous financial aid.* There is strong evidence that investing in extra tutoring, small class sizes, intensive advising, and generous financial aid at community colleges can have big payoffs. At a typical community college, classes are crowded and student–adviser ratios can be as high as 1,500 to 1.[31] But at the City University of New York's Accelerated Study in Associate Programs (ASAP), students are provided with the tutoring, class size, advising, and effective financial aid more typical of wealthy four-year colleges. These supports, provided within a highly structured environment in which students must attend classes full time, have been found in a randomized trial conducted by the nonprofit research institute MDRC to nearly double the three-year graduation rates of students (to 40 percent, compared with a control group's 22 percent). The program cost 60 percent more per student—about $16,300 more per pupil over three years—yet by boosting results, it actually reduced the amount spent for each college *degree awarded* by more than 10 percent.[32] More generally, research also finds that investments in smaller class sizes in community colleges, more counselors, and more full-time faculty can improve student outcomes.[33]

- *A variety of high-impact practices that require resources.* The Center for Community College Student Engagement has found a positive relationship between thirteen "high-impact" practices and positive student outcomes: orientation; accelerated developmental education; first year experiences; student success courses; learning communities; academic goal setting and planning; experiential learning beyond the classroom; tutoring; supplemental instruction; proper assessment and placement; registration before classes start; alerts and interventions; and structured group learning experiences.[34] Numerous other studies find positive results from redesigned developmental education, academic support services, and other interventions.[35]

The long-term benefits to society of increased community college completion are substantial. Setting aside the considerable benefits to individuals who can see their chances of flourishing increase by completing a community college degree, the returns to the general taxpayer are very large.

Take, for example, a taxpayer cost–benefit analysis of CUNY's ASAP program. In a 2018 study in the *Journal of Higher Education,* Columbia University's Henry M. Levin and Emma Garcia of the Economic Policy Institute and Georgetown University found that for each additional $1 invested in ASAP, the return to the taxpayer was $3 to $4.[36]

Levin and Garcia estimate the lifetime earnings of an associate's degree holder to be $964,500 on average, compared with $630,300 for a high school graduate, for a net gain of $324,100.[37] Based on those estimates, they calculate that an associate's degree recipient will pay $165,400 more in taxes over her lifetime and will cost taxpayers $40,100 less in health expenditures, welfare and public assistance, and criminal justice costs. The total public benefit over a lifetime is $205,500. The institutional cost of ASAP per graduate for the fall 2007 cohort was $59,300, yielding about $3.50 to the taxpayer for every $1.00 invested.[38] (See Figure 8.) Although the analysis focused on ASAP's ability to boost completion rates, the underlying

Figure 8. Public Investment and Return of Accelerated Study
in Associate's Programs

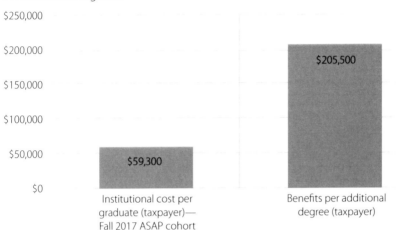

Source: Henry M. Levin and Emma Garcia, "Accelerating Community College Graduation Rates: A Benefit-Cost Analysis," *Journal of Higher Education* 89, no. 1 (2018), 15, Table 8.

measurements of the benefits of raising community college completion apply to any program that does so.

The Need for More Research on Funding Levels

Because there is strong evidence that current community college funding levels are too low to permit colleges and their students to achieve what policymakers desire and expect, and that certain investments are likely to increase outcomes, we recommend short-, medium- and long-term strategies for reform.

In the short term, state and federal policymakers should begin to increase funding for community colleges to improve opportunities for students. While the precise level of funding community colleges need to adequately meet their goals is yet to be determined, the evidentiary basis for the returns to certain increased public investment is strong, so legislators need not wait to act. (In the section "Translating Empirical Evidence into Policy" starting on page 49 of this report, we outline specific recommendations for a new federal–state partnership to boost community college funding.)

In the medium term, federal and state legislators can begin to implement a strategy of supporting rigorous research to help guide the amount and types of investments to be made. Legislators are now in a difficult position, having to make decisions about higher education investments without sufficient research guidance. There is shockingly little research on a basic question: What level of funding could produce adequate community college education outcomes? The dearth of research is particularly remarkable given the extensive body of research that has been conducted in the K–12 arena on the same question.

For almost four decades, researchers have studied the question of how much funding is necessary to produce an adequate elementary and secondary education, including an appropriate funding premium to address the needs of low-income students.[39] A 2008 review of thirteen studies found that the cost of educating socioeconomically disadvantaged students ranged from 22.5 percent to 167.5 percent more than the cost of educating students with no extra needs.[40] In a 2015 analysis, the Education Trust said a 40 percent premium for educating these students should be considered "conservative," given research finding that it costs twice as much to educate low-income students to the same standards as more-affluent students.[41]

Today, at the state level, thirty-seven K–12 funding formulas recognize that students with greater needs deserve greater resources.[42] (See Figure 9.) Research on the level of resources needed for community colleges—and accompanying public policy responses—are by comparison in their infancy.

Finally, in the long run, we recommend that policymakers use the evidence of these research-based efforts to guide future funding decisions, in all likelihood increasing support for community colleges and their students.

Framework for Estimating Adequate Funding for American Community Colleges

We believe it is crucial that scholarship on costs at the community college level catch up with that for similar K–12 research. Federal and state

Figure 9. K–12 State Funding for Low-Income Students or Compensatory Education

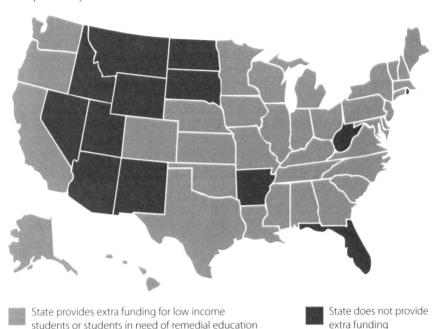

State provides extra funding for low income students or students in need of remedial education	State does not provide extra funding

Source: Deborah A. Verstegen, "How Do States Pay for Schools? An Update of a 50-State Survey of Finance Policies and Programs," Association for Education Finance and Policy Annual Conference, San Antonio, Texas, March 15, 2014, 8.

policymakers and foundation officials should commission research to estimate the true costs of community college education. The task is complex, but after carefully considering and discussing the challenges, we have concluded that it is both possible and necessary for researchers to undertake such a study.

In this section, we delve into some of the issues researchers will face and make recommendations for a framework of how to proceed. We begin by outlining four common steps that researchers take when approximating the true costs of an adequate K–12 education. We next identify four key differences between the K–12 and community college sectors that will require scholars to adjust their methodology. We then review a few preliminary attempts to estimate costs in higher education. Finally, this section culminates in an eight-part framework for conducting studies that estimate the costs of a community college education.

Costing-Out Studies in Elementary and Secondary Education

Since at least the early 1980s, scholars and consultants have been engaged in efforts to estimate the costs of providing adequate educational programs and services toward achieving adequate educational outcomes for children. The pace of progress on estimating the costs of adequate K–12 education accelerated with the proliferation of state accountability systems and outcome measures from the 1990s forward, coupled with increased use of those outcome measures in the context of litigation challenging the adequacy of public school funding under state constitutions. Those legal challenges forced the issues of (a) defining state constitutional obligations, (b) identifying measures of student outcomes which might be used to indicate equity and adequacy, and (c) developing reliable and valid methods for determining the costs associated with meeting measurable outcome goals. Even with improved empirical evidence, and even in the presence of judicial orders, the process by which state school spending levels and distributions are determined remains political, complicated and imperfect.

In this section, we outline four major steps in conducting cost analyses, drawn from decades of experiences in elementary and secondary education.

Step 1. Identifying Desired Outcomes

In order to estimate costs, the first step is to identify with some precision the desired outcome. As Bruce Baker and Jesse Levin explain in their background paper for this working group report, much of the recent interest in estimating the costs of meeting specific educational outcome standards in elementary and secondary education stems from the role of state courts in determining whether adequacy requirements of state constitutions have

Four Steps in Costing Out a K–12 Education

Step 1: Researchers in collaboration with policymakers and other key constituents identify the desired outcomes of the education system, a prerequisite for determining costs.

Step 2: Researchers in collaboration with policymakers and other key constituents identify the relevant unit of analysis for estimating those costs, which might focus on aggregations of institutions (states or school districts), specific institutions or organizations (schools, service providers, and so on), or programs and/or services within those institutions.

Step 3: Researchers determine the appropriate methods for best identifying the costs associated with the desired outcomes, given the units of analysis.

Step 4: Researchers identify the key cost drivers (including student disadvantage) that influence the costs of achieving the desired outcomes, across settings, institutions, programs, and services, and the students they serve.

been met.[43] In recent decades, several states' high courts have determined that their state constitution's education article requires the legislature to provide sufficient funding to meet some minimum standard. In a handful of cases, state legislatures—either prior to, or in response to, legal challenges and court orders—have engaged outside consultants to estimate the costs of meeting those standards and provide guidance on state school finance systems. Specifically, the consultants are hired to provide guidance on how to make those systems compliant with constitutional requirements, as articulated in court orders. (Similar state constitutional obligations arguably extend to remedial courses in community colleges to the extent that material was supposed to be taught in K–12 schooling.)[44]

As Baker and Levin explain, constitutional requirements are often stated in vague terms, and judicial rulings regarding constitutional requirements are at times only marginally more precise. Neither is sufficient for making the leap to establishing an empirical framework and setting up an analysis to determine costs of meeting those requirements. Typically, the

responsibility for specifying measurable outcomes and standards falls on
state legislatures and/or state boards of education and departments of education. State courts may prod legislators to make use of standards, which
they have already legislated. Further, in the absence of judicial intervention, state policymakers may work with external consultants to operationalize state standards and set goals for cost analyses.

Elementary and secondary education standards and accountability
systems tend to be based primarily on (a) standardized assessments of
reading and math from grades three to eight, and sometimes grades ten
and/or eleven, and (b) other measures, such as four-year high school graduation rates. Standardized assessments often have assigned "cut-scores"
that declare whether each student's performance is "proficient" (meeting
basic standards) or not, and in some states, students must pass a common
high school exam in order to receive a diploma. Increasingly, states have
also adopted measures of test score growth, and in some cases test score
growth conditional on student need (comparing students of similar backgrounds and needs). These systems of measures and indicators, though
limited, often serve to provide convenient benchmarks for judicial analysis
and for empirical estimation of "costs."

Step 2. Identify the Relevant Units of Analysis

After identifying outcome goals, researchers must determine the appropriate unit of analysis. K–12 education systems largely strive to provide a
common educational program, often with the dominant purpose of preparing students for their next level of education. As a result, cost analyses
can focus on institutions as a whole—schools or districts—as their unit of
analysis, with a singular set of goals, measured academic standards, and
outcomes. Typically, at the K–12 level, researchers set aside distinctions
having to do with high school vocational programs and other specialized schools (for example, magnet schools, standalone special education
schools, and so on), even though those schools have more varied goals and
corresponding programming.

In most cases in elementary and secondary education, cost analyses focus on state mandated outcomes and constitutional obligations, which are achieved, in turn, by local public school districts. However, the unit of analysis may vary depending on the costing-out method chosen (see Step 3, below). Most *input-oriented* cost analyses—those that tally up the resources needed for delivering specific programs and services—focus on *schools* within districts, and then add administrative overhead costs to determine district unit costs. Most *outcome-oriented* approaches, by contrast, focus on the *district* as the unit of analysis, where the district and its board of education are primarily responsible for financial management of local public schools, and where revenue arrives and expenditure allocations are determined. However, increasingly, even cost modeling approaches are including school-level analyses, in part to begin to attempt to reconcile findings between input and outcome-oriented methods through hybrid approaches. It is also feasible to take these approaches to the next lower level of exploring the costs of specific programs and services within institutions. Input-oriented approaches require as much to arrive at institution-level costs.

Step 3. Determining Appropriate Costing-Out Methods

In addition to identifying goals and the appropriate unit of analysis, researchers must identify the cost analysis method that best suits the policy objective—that is, that best enables estimation of the full costs of meeting the collectively agreed upon outcome goals. Selection of methods may depend in part on the measurability of (and available measures of) those outcome goals. As alluded to above, method types can neatly be categorized as *outcome-oriented* and *input-oriented* approaches.

- Outcome-oriented analyses start with data on both student outcomes and the specific programs and services used by institutions to generate the outcomes. The costs of attaining these outcomes across different site settings—defined by characteristics such as student needs and size of operation—are arrived at using statistical estimation techniques referred to as *cost functions*.

- Input-oriented analyses first identify the staffing, materials, supplies and equipment, physical space, and other elements (inputs) required to provide educational programs and services capable of producing the desired outcomes in a variety of settings (again, defined by characteristics such as student needs, size of operation, and so on). The inputs are then costed out and applied to calculate the costs of providing programming and services across different sites.

Outcome-oriented analysis can only be applied where outcome goals have been measured quantitatively over time, and where adequate data exist on expenditures, cost, and student need factors. However, even where these data are limited but still sufficient, cost modeling can be used in conjunction with input-oriented methods to develop a fuller picture of cost-efficient deployment of resources, programs, and services. In the best-case scenario, as discussed in the Baker and Levin background paper, data are sufficiently rich enough to do extensive cost modeling and to combine and reconcile those findings with input-oriented estimates of institutional costs.

Combining the two approaches may be ideal, because it would provide the right information, where it is needed: outcome-oriented analyses provide information to *legislators* about the *amount* of money required to achieve a given set of goals, while input-oriented approaches give *school leaders* guidance on *where* to invest resources.

Step 4. Identifying Cost Drivers (Including Student Disadvantage)

An important fourth component of the K–12 analysis involves identifying cost factors that may vary from school to school (depending on, for example, the size of the school or its geographic location) and depending on such factors as the proportion of students who are disadvantaged. As discussed by Baker and Levin in their background paper, which factors

influence the costs of achieving desired outcomes are relatively well understood in K–12 education, but our knowledge of those factors continues to
evolve. We know those factors to fall into two distinct groups—student
need factors, and other exogenous cost factors. Further, some student need
factors operate at the level of the individual student and have specific rem-
edies in terms of programs and services, while other student need factors
operate at the level of the collective student population. For example, a
student with a specific disability or language barrier might need very specific supports, whereas an institution serving a generally higher poverty
student population, from less educated households, might require more
generalized resource intensive interventions (expanded early childhood
programs, smaller class sizes, and so on). Finding the best measures to
characterize need and to identify other exogenous cost pressures (competitive wage variation, economies of scale, population sparsity, and so on) is
an important step for either input-oriented or outcome-oriented analysis.

Differences between the K–12 Sector and Community Colleges

The four steps employed in K–12 costing-out exercises can provide a foundation for beginning to think through how such research could be conducted at the community college level. But there are critical differences
between the sectors that will affect the analysis. In seeking to apply K–12
methodologies to community colleges, four fundamental distinctions
between postsecondary education and K–12 education are particularly
important. Each of these four differences presents unique challenges for
estimating the cost of providing an adequate community college education, as detailed below.

Difference 1. Higher Education Involves More Choice on the Part of Students

At the K–12 level, attendance is mandatory and students have less choice
of programs to pursue. With higher education, students have choice of
whether or not to pursue postsecondary education, at which institution to

pursue such education, and greater choice about which programs to pursue should they decide to enroll in community college.

Unlike K–12 education, higher education is not compulsory. An adequate K–12 education system must provide sufficient programs and services for all children to achieve desired outcomes. In higher education, we must also consider access to institutions as a potential outcome of providing more adequate programs and services. That is, who comes, who stays, and who completes? An adequate postsecondary education system is one that provides greater access to more diverse student populations than presently exists, and provides all who enter with equal opportunity to persist and complete.

It is insufficient to measure success rates of only those students who presently access higher education. Higher education institutions that are less accessible, academically, financially, or geographically, may end up serving more advantaged student populations to begin with, and thus may appear more successful by virtue of who they serve rather than the quality of programs and services they provide.

Difference 2. Higher Education Has Fewer Standardized
Tests as Measures of Academic Success

While K–12 education defines outcomes largely by test scores and graduation, higher education does not have widespread testing, requiring researchers to identify different outcome goals.

Unlike K–12 education, community colleges do not have a standard way of assessing learning gains. Outcome measures and data systems in K–12 education proliferated throughout the 1990s and 2000s, enabling statistical analysis of those outcomes, factors affecting those outcomes, and the costs of meeting those outcomes across varied settings and children. Commonly collected and reported outcome measures include state standardized assessments, originally in reading and math (grades three to eight), and later encompassing science and social studies, and extending to high school exams. Most recently, many states have moved toward assessments of common standards, increasing the possibility of estimating costs across multiple states concurrently. States also collect school and district (institution level) data on graduation rates, attendance rates, and, in some cases, college attendance and persistence.

Because the goals of postsecondary education are varied, there do not exist similar common assessments of knowledge and skills. In fact, one purpose of the intermediate measures of knowledge and skills collected in the K–12 system is to be predictive of success in core courses at the postsecondary level. But success in more specialized postsecondary degree and certificate programs is perhaps better measured by outcomes that occur later in life, after postsecondary schooling has been completed—such as achieving relatively greater success in the labor market. In turn, to the extent we cannot measure directly or consistently those outcomes occurring after postsecondary schooling, we must seek intermediate measures within the postsecondary system that may be predictive of those outcomes. (We discuss proposed outcome measures at length below.)

Difference 3. Higher Education Has More Varied Programming
and Program-Specific Costs within Institutions

Whereas K–12 has comparatively far more uniform programming and cost structures within schools, higher education has greater variation within colleges for different credentials and within different academic disciplines. These credentials and programs differ in costs and goals so researchers will have to sort through whether the appropriate unit of analysis should be the college department, the degree or certificate program, or some combination of these.

At the K–12 level, schools are often an obvious level of analysis, but community colleges typically offer a variety of programs that raise questions about the appropriate unit of analysis. Unlike K–12, where most students in a school have roughly common goals (such as developing reading and math skills), within community colleges, students have varying goals. Some seek degrees, others certificates. Some seek specialized skills in programs such as nursing, while others seek general education skills that may prepare them to transfer to a four-year institution. The student choices and varied pathways involved in postsecondary education systems increase the complexity of evaluating costs of achieving desired outcomes for these systems. But it also provides unique opportunities to better understand how students' choices, coupled with institutional structures and supports, affect outcomes.

Difference 4. Higher Education Has Fewer Essential Needs
Programs in Place That Provide Supports Known to Improve Student
Outcomes, Especially for Marginalized Student Populations

For minors in the K–12 system, federal, state, and local policy provides for breakfast and lunch (free and reduced meals programs), health care (the Child Health Insurance Program, known as CHIP), and transportation (free bus service for students who cannot walk to school). Analogous higher education programs are sometimes built into financial aid programs but are often not well developed.

Unlike K–12 education, where supports for nutrition, health, textbooks, and transportation are considered essential programs, at the community college level, those supports, while vitally important, are frequently not provided to students.

In elementary and secondary education, we have come to realize that the provision of an equitable and adequate system for all eligible children requires the provision of more than merely academic programs. Children must be transported to those programs, including students who do not have family supports to provide transportation. Children must be well fed in order to be successful in school, and thus we provide subsidized lunches and breakfast for children from low-income families. In many cases, state and local systems provide additional supports, including physical and mental health screenings, after-school programs, and a variety of parent and community supports. Some of these "supplemental" or "wrap-around" services come about with increased knowledge and awareness that these supports contribute efficiently to student success on measured outcomes. At the K–12 level, taxpayers also provide textbook materials free of charge.

It is similarly the case that college-aged students (traditional or nontraditional) have inequitable access to transportation, and may also lack food and/or housing security. These are essential elements to student success. Adults too must get to school (and/or have sufficient technology to log in online), be well fed, and have housing security to ensure their persistence and completion of programs. In addition, they must be able to afford materials and supplies (textbooks). Sometimes supports for textbooks, meal plans, and housing are incorporated into financial aid programs, particularly at four-year residential colleges, but community college students often lack access to these types of assistance. As discussed further below, since these supports have not historically been broadly and uniformly provided within the public higher education system, identifying the cost of doing so at public expense is necessary.

Early Efforts to Apply Costing-Out Methods to Higher Education and Community Colleges

Perhaps because of the complexity of applying K–12 costing-out techniques to higher education, few such studies have been conducted to date. Instead, community college studies tend to focus on existing levels of *expenditures* rather than on their *costs* to achieve a given objective. As Baker and Levin's background paper emphasizes, expenditure studies are more straightforward because they do not require a measure of outcome goals as cost studies necessarily do. Expenditure studies merely characterize existing expenditures of institutions, given whatever outcomes they presently achieve. That said, expenditure data could be used in combination with outcome data, and data on school contexts and students, to infer the specific costs associated with achieving current outcome levels, and to extrapolate costs associated with achieving different outcome levels.

In this section, we begin with a discussion of existing expenditure studies, then review two early efforts to begin to assess costs.

Expenditure Studies

Researchers have conducted several expenditure studies on postsecondary institutions in general and community colleges in particular, using national data sources either directly from the Integrated Postsecondary Education Data System (IPEDS), or as compiled for the Delta Cost Project.[45] Most recently, Tammy Kolbe and Bruce Baker conducted two studies of the levels, distribution, and trends in community college expenditures by state.

The first study evaluates the level and progressiveness of total spending and instructional spending per pupil for community colleges by state. Specifically, Kolbe and Baker explore whether and to what extent community colleges in counties with lower-income populations spend the same (flat), less (regressive), or more (progressive) per pupil than community colleges in higher-income counties. The study establishes a baseline for understanding present spending levels across states, and for knowing which states have generally more progressive versus regressive spending.

The second expenditure study benchmarks the level and progressiveness of spending in state community college systems against K–12 spending.[46] As with the first, the results vary widely across states and provide a baseline for understanding state policy and contextual differences. In addition, the findings allow for a comparison of the level of commitment to community colleges relative to elementary and secondary education systems, for which a broader collection of comparative studies exists. Like the first study, this study considers only existing spending, toward existing outcomes (that is, it does not attempt to calculate the costs of providing educational adequacy). Both analyses confirm that most existing community college systems do not systematically provide additional funding to community colleges in lower-income settings. Many are neutral at best, and still many others are significantly regressive.

The Real Cost Project (2003)

One notable example of "cost" analysis applied to a community college system is the Real Cost Project, conducted on behalf of the California Community College system in 2003.[47] The Real Cost Project was similar to early elementary and secondary education cost studies, which, instead of focusing on measured student outcomes, focused on programs and services, including additional supports that were presumed (preferably based on research) to lead to desirable outcomes. The approach lays out prototypical institutions based on a collection of best practices. Those prototypical institutions may be developed through consensus-building activities with focus groups of informed professionals, and/or expert knowledge of research-based practices.

The Real Cost Project involved creating similar prototype institutions, as described here:

> The prototype is not the median college, but it is also not a baseline institution which has only those characteristics shared by all colleges. That approach would tend to understate the important local context of rural and urban colleges, and obscure one of the purposes of the Real Cost Project—to capture the unique cost structure associated with the diverse student population of the California Community Colleges. So while the prototype does not describe any actual college perfectly, it is a reasonable representation of typical demographics, generally as reflected in statewide enrollment patterns. As a result, the prototype college looks like California in its relative composition of academic preparation, ethnicity . . . and gender, disability, income status and public assistance, and part-time/fulltime status.[48]

In addition, the resources prescribed for the prototype were driven by a set of quality indicators, albeit not necessarily outcome measures:

> These Quality Indicators represent an integrated approach to quality student learning and achievement. Group learning, team teaching, learning communities, intensive writing across the curriculum, and individualized interaction between faculty and students are possible at the prototype college because of the combination of smaller classes, a shift in faculty time allocation toward students, extensive professional development and training in pedagogical strategies, and a substantial change in the curriculum. Every student desiring to transfer to a baccalaureate university would have a meaningful transfer and educational plan—more than merely a ministerial signature on a form. These are essential attributes of a quality education for the broad diversity of students at the California Community Colleges.[49]

Using a number of quality indicators (such as class size, high-quality faculty and staff, need for counseling and health services, equipment, and technology), the group derived a cost estimate of $9,200 per full-time equivalent student—considerably higher than the actual amount spent around the time (2003), which was less than $5,000.[50]

Baker/Morphew Resource Cost Modeling (RCM, 2007)

In a 2007 analysis, Bruce Baker and Christopher Morphew developed the conceptual thinking around applying cost modeling to higher education by tackling an important complexity: that unlike K–12 education, where course taking is largely prescribed, college students have greater choice in course selection. Specifically, the authors examined how "resource cost modeling"—an input-oriented costing-out approach used at the K–12 level—could apply to higher education, given the varying course-taking pathways students pursue to earning their degrees.[51]

The authors point out that if we are to look at outcome measures such as program or degree completion, one must consider not only the way in which institutions organize their resources, but also the varied ways in which students access those resources toward degree completion. For example, students completing a program in mathematics navigate their way through general education courses as well as math courses, drawing on resources across units within institutions, not merely the higher-level unit offering the degree or credential. Among those students pursuing degrees in math, there may be a handful of most common pathways (which represent resource consumption patterns) to completion. Students may also access varied additional supports— academic, residential, and so on—as they navigate their way toward program completion. A comprehensive and precise estimate of the costs associated with program completion must account for the ways in which students access resources along the way. That is, cost estimates must take into account student pathways to program completion by considering all of the costs associated with providing access to those specific pathways and associated resources. The study provided an important advance in how K–12 techniques could apply to the very different world of higher education.

Framework for Applying K–12 Methods to Community Colleges

The earlier efforts at costing out a college education provide a basis upon which researchers can build in order to try something that is unprecedented: a full-fledged study to estimate the costs of an adequate community college education. Our goal is to advance the thinking on this question by providing a *framework* for applying cost estimation methods from elementary and secondary education to community colleges, recognizing the distinctions between the two.

Below, we identify eight key decision points that researchers will face in applying well-established K–12 analysis principles to the community college sector. For each challenge, we make recommendations providing our best advice on how to proceed.

Eight Issues in Applying K–12 Methods to Community Colleges

1. In beginning to define goals, how should researchers address the non-mandatory nature of attendance in higher education? Because students are not required by law to attend community college, how do we define goals in a way that incorporates access?

2. In further defining goals, what is the best way to articulate adequate outcomes? Should researchers consider intermediate goals, such as completion, ultimate goals such as labor market outcomes, or some combination of the two?

3. In defining goals even further, how should researchers assess the appropriate level of success to be costed out? Not every high school student in a state is likely to complete a community college degree or certificate or higher, for example, so how should the appropriate degree of success sought be determined?

4. How should researchers capture costs across different educational units (program-level versus institution-level costs)?

5. Should researchers employ an input-oriented or an output-oriented analysis, or a hybrid approach?

6. What adjustments to the prototypical community college costs should be made for institutions with higher student need factors? Should need measures include economic disadvantage, academic preparedness from high school, first generation college status, nontraditional/adult learner status, race, and/or other factors?

7. How should researchers account for student needs such as food, housing, transportation, and childcare?

8. What adjustments should researchers make to the cost of a prototypical community college education for other variations in cost related to region, scale, program, and the like?

Issue 1: *In beginning to define goals, how should researchers address the non-mandatory nature of attendance in higher education? Because students are not required by law to attend community college, how do we define goals in a way that incorporates access?*

In K–12 education, schooling is typically compulsory for students through age sixteen, so an outcome metric—such as high school completion—starts with a base of students that is universal. In the community college sector, by contrast, attendance is not mandatory, so a measure that looked at completion rates would not tell us whether a college is doing a good job of providing access to students (by recruiting them, offering courses that are in demand at convenient times, and so on). Indeed, a system that defined outcomes strictly in terms of proportion of beginning students who complete could provide a perverse incentive of encouraging community colleges to recruit only the most prepared students, screening out those with less preparation.

Recommendation 1: *Any evaluation to determine the costs of providing an adequate system of community colleges must include, as one of many outcome measures, indicators of the population served, and ideally should capture the breadth and equity of access.* One might consider, for example, the needs for postsecondary education across economic, geographic, racial, and ethnic groups, and the system's equity of access. And one might evaluate the extent to which the population served sufficiently represents disadvantaged student populations in the relevant service region.

To calculate the cost associated with a particular goal requires that researchers define the outcome measures and the levels denoting accomplishment of the goal. In this case, to determine the types and quantities of resources necessary to successfully recruit and serve a particular population of students requires that one first define the target population. To this end, a key step would be to perform a descriptive analysis of the composition of enrollment with respect to student characteristics (for example, low-income status, first-generation college enrollee, ethnic minority, and so on) across college campuses throughout the state.

Recruitment targets would then be set across the groups, which would be included as part of the goal definition. Note that results of the descriptive analysis would be used as a baseline. That is, the chosen targets may not be simply to achieve the average composition of enrolling students, but rather to significantly improve recruitment among student groups who are currently underrepresented.

Costs of the efforts involved in an expanded targeted recruitment effort, as well as the different and possibly additional supports necessary to adequately serve the new composition of enrolling students, could then be calculated through an input-oriented method, such as professional judgment.

Issue 2: *In further defining goals, should researchers consider intermediate metrics, such as completion, or ultimate goals, such as labor market outcomes, or some combination of the two?*

Among the thorniest issues researchers face in applying K–12 costing-out techniques is articulating a clear set of goals for adequate outcomes. K–12 cost analyses have the convenience of falling back on short-run academic outcomes as their goal, as those outcomes are predictive of success at the next stage of their education. Many community college programs are career-specific, and thus the desired outcomes are employment and income. Should researchers consider labor market outcomes as the appropriate measure, intermediate measures such as retention and completion and transfer, or some combination of the two?

In their background report for the working group, Anthony Carnevale, Jeff Strohl, and Artem Gulish of Georgetown University make the argument that economic adequacy is a necessary condition to achieve educational adequacy. In making this argument, they suggest that labor market outcomes are the most appropriate metric. Because delivering economic self-sufficiency is critical, they argue, a community college education should help students attain skills that will enable them to earn a living. In American society, where government provides few supports to those not in the labor market, human flourishing requires that individuals be economically self-sufficient. Merely providing resources to allow students to *complete* a community college certificate or degree is an insufficient measure of success, Carnevale and colleagues argue, because completion does not guarantee adequate labor market outcomes.

What level of labor market success is necessary to allow for human flourishing in contemporary American society? Carnevale and colleagues operationalize their approach by suggesting a two-part test for economic self-sufficiency: (1) "a program must leave its graduates earning more than $35,000 per year ten years after they have completed it"; and (2) "over that ten-year period, that program also must provide its graduates with a sufficient earnings premium, compared to the earnings of workers with only a high-school diploma, to cover the program's total cost to the student."[52] This second requirement typically translates into a minimum salary of $42,000.[53] The authors say adjustments to these requirements should be made to account for cost of living variations by region, and that race and gender discrimination in the workplace, and society's need for people to enter the intellectual and caring professions, should be considered in using earnings outcome metrics.

Carnevale and colleagues argue this two-part standard provides the minimum economic self-sufficiency necessary for human flourishing because it allows for entry into the bottom rungs of the middle class. A $35,000 salary for a full-time worker generally translates into a $50,000 income for a household. They further note that because there are so many different costs associated with achieving completion outcomes in different programs, it is not possible, using a completion metric, to estimate a single cost for a community college education.

We think this approach has many strengths. Monitoring these data makes sense, and the use of the measures as minimal thresholds could be appropriate in some circumstances. But as Carnevale and colleagues themselves note, a number of complications arise with operationalizing a stand-alone labor market outcome goal.

For one thing, the ability to achieve these economic targets is not in the control of the community colleges alone. Linking employment and income to program quality is complicated by regional labor market variations, employment supply and demand, and temporal cycles. These outcomes depend on economic conditions, and labor markets that can fluctuate more rapidly than institutions can adapt.

Moreover, it is questionable whether we would want our community colleges to try to adapt to every cyclical shift in employment demand. Specifically, while earnings growth might be one measure upon which to judge community college performance, it would be undesirable to structure goals such that community colleges are put in the position of determining program offerings based only on their expected labor market returns.[54] This could result in a significant narrowing of program offerings and there is no guarantee that community colleges would do a good job at precisely forecasting returns to specific degrees or credentials.

In addition, the ten-year lag between the observed goal and the programmatic investment complicates the application of this standard.

Moreover, while the $35,000 threshold is appropriate for estimating the costs of an education that is adequate for generating what we broadly consider to be "good jobs," we acknowledge that this threshold is not universally achievable. Indeed, it is based only on those who currently complete community college credentials, who constitute less than 40 percent of all those currently enrolled—and only two-thirds of that group now achieve this standard. (See issue 3 below, discussing appropriate rates of success for which policymakers should strive.) Moreover, if we successfully increase access and enrollment in community college for disadvantaged or low-achieving groups who do not now attend, attainment of the $35,000 goal could fall even lower.

To be clear, the working group approves of all investments in postsecondary education that are cost-efficient and materially improve the lives of all students, even if the subsequent earnings of these students fall short of helping of meeting the $35,000 standard. Policymakers should always consider the public's "return on investment," which examines the increase in earnings generated by education measured against the cost of the investment.[55] For instance, a short-term and low-cost certificate that raises some students' earnings from $10,000 to $15,000 annually might well be cost-efficient and appropriate for those students, especially those who are not in a position to pursue or attain more substantial credentials.

Accordingly, we believe that the attainment of $35,000 in earnings should be considered the relevant standard of an "adequate" education for some substantial part of the community college population, while a somewhat different standard—consistent with cost-efficiency and significant earnings improvements for those with currently low earnings—is acceptable for those not able to attain associate's degrees or the best-paying certificates anytime soon, as long as there are clear pathways to further education. Exactly what these alternative standards should be, and for how many students each standard is appropriate, could be determined by further research.

We are also concerned about the effect of predicating the goals of community colleges on a single result—labor market outcomes. Public opinion research suggests individuals have a wide variety of rationales for pursuing community college.[56] Individuals and the public derive utility from education for reasons other than pecuniary gain (for example, to satisfy one's curiosity in or passion for a subject), and society invests in education in order to produce better citizens and parents, in addition to better workers. In this way, education is similar to other public goods, such as parks, that public dollars regularly support.

Furthermore, potential income varies by the program or degree sought, which in turn is a function of the interests and desires of individual students. It may well be that the expected income for a graduate of a computer technology training program exceeds that for the veterinary technician from the same institution. But the animal lover who truly desires to be a veterinary technician might find little life satisfaction in maintaining and troubleshooting a bank of computer servers in a corporate basement. If the community college will not offer veterinary programs, she may seek that program elsewhere, perhaps through a private online provider who will offer an inferior program. At the very least, the outcome measures must be sensitive to student choices, and must vary by program, degree, certificate, or academic trajectory. A floor of $35,000 to join the middle-class (or $42,000 to equal the total cost of a program) may not cover important trajectories that students desire.

In part for these reasons, as Baker and Levin point out, most existing mechanisms of accountability for community colleges—such as performance-based funding—use proximal measures, such as completion, rather than distal measures, such as labor market outcomes.[57] Such intermediate measures, while imperfect, avoid the complications associated with a labor market outcome measure and are typically associated with improved earnings. At the same time, we agree with Carnevale and colleagues that proximal measures by themselves are not sufficient, because completion of a degree that does not support adequate earnings cannot be considered a benchmark of success. We therefore suggest a third path that brings together proximal and distal outcome measures.

Recommendation 2: *Proximal measures such as successful completion of a program should serve as the primary goal.[58] However, this measure should include a validation check that these proximal measures translate into positive labor market outcomes for students leaving the particular programs and institutions.*

In other words, we recommend bringing together the recommendations in the two background papers by Carnevale, Gulish, and Strohl and by Baker and Levin. Given practical concerns, preliminary attempts to estimate the cost of adequate community college programs should focus on intermediate measurable outcomes, such as access, persistence, and completion toward degrees, certificates, or successful transfer (followed by completion). However, degree and certificate completion measures can be validated by their relation to longer-term economic outcomes.

That is to say, we suggest an approach that takes Baker and Levin's preference for intermediate, proximate outcomes and the preference of Carnevale, Gulish, and Strohl for distal outcomes and meets in the middle. Researchers would provide an estimate for what it costs to achieve a reasonable level of completion in a particular program. That information is important given that completion, whatever the labor market outcomes, can have independent value. Separately—looking at labor market outcomes for graduates of this program across a variety of community colleges over time—researchers would provide an estimate of what it costs to make it likely that graduates in the program will also meet a labor market wage test. Policymakers would have information about costs associated with meeting the completion standard on the one hand, and the labor market standard on the other, and individual states could decide the relative weight to be accorded to each factor at any given point in time.

Issue 3: *In defining goals even further, how should researchers assess the appropriate level of success to be costed out? Not everyone in a state is likely to complete a community college degree or certificate or higher, for example, so how should the appropriate degree of success sought be determined?*

Whether using proximate goals (degree or certificate completion), distal goals (such as a $35,000 annual salary), or some combination, public policy goals do not expect perfection. It is unlikely that 100 percent of state residents will complete a degree or certificate, or that 100 percent of community college graduates will make more than $35,000 a year, so policymakers must set ambitious but realistic goals. Today, for example, 67 percent of community college graduates with an associate's degree make $35,000 a year ten years after graduation,[59] so a public policy goal might be to raise that level above 67 percent, but aim for something less than 100 percent.

How should such goals be set? Researchers could model a particular success rate for associate's degree holders, or provide cost estimates for a range of success rates—75 percent, 85 percent, and 95 percent, for example. Similar percentages would need to be calculated for those earning certificates with reasonable labor market returns.[60] In determining the range, researchers could examine existing success rates as a benchmark, and then look to projections for employer demand of skill levels in the future. Alternatively, policymakers could conduct surveys of stakeholders to determine acceptable success rates. As outlined below, we recommend a combination of approaches.

Recommendation 3: *Researchers should cost out not a single success rate, but instead focus on a range of possible levels of success, guided by research on community needs and public engagement of stakeholders.*[61] In determining what the acceptable range might be, we suggest the definitions of success be informed by solid analysis of existing access and success measures across campuses in a community college system. In addition, this question can be greatly informed through authentic public engagement where individuals with a stake in community college success rates are able to provide input as to what they perceive as an appropriate goal. Public engagement of this sort has been undertaken in K–12 cost studies. For example, in the adequacy studies for New Mexico and New York, researchers held public engagement forums throughout the state to promote input from parents, teachers, business leaders, taxpayers, and other citizens as to what constitutes an adequate education (that is, how the goals should be defined). For the New Mexico study, two surveys were administered to all legislators, superintendents, and principals in the state, and to the general public, respectively.[62] We recommend a similar approach with respect to determining success goals for community colleges.

Issue 4: *How should researchers capture costs across different educational units: at the program level, institution level, or some combination?*

As discussed earlier, in K–12 costing-out studies, the unit of analysis is typically a school district or an individual school because there are common outcome goals and roughly common cost structures for programs. But community colleges are different. Outcomes (especially labor market outcomes) can vary dramatically by programs within community colleges, as can costs associated with different certificate and degree programs (for example, welding versus general education).

At the same time, students do not take courses only in their program of study. As Baker and Morphew suggested in their 2007 study, students pursuing any specific degree or program goal access a distribution of coursework across multiple units (departments) within an institution. Likewise, there are common costs (for example, administration) that run across individual programs, so it is difficult to isolate costs solely by particular programs.

We again recommend a hybrid approach. This method merges the program-level and institution-level analyses through an examination of student pathways.

Recommendation 4: *Because costs vary dramatically by program, and students take some of their classes in different programs, researchers should use transcripts to identify typical pathways and associated costs.* Then, after the program-level cost analysis is completed, researchers can also compute the costs at the institutional level by adding up the participants in various programs and apportioning institutional costs that cut across programs (for example, for student services, campus infrastructure, and so on).

Deeper exploration of student pathways will aid in identifying those resources accessed by certain students in certain contexts that result in their most efficiently completing program requirements. Exploration of resources associated with student pathways through institutions may be supplemented with exploration of the ways in which resources are organized and delivered within and across different types of institutions.

Persistence and completion toward students' degree, certificate, or academic transfer goals must be analyzed from the perspective of the pathways (course selection, sequence) students take through community colleges. Further, one can use student transcript data to identify which pathways frequently taken by students lead to greater success rates and whether the match between pathway and successful outcomes differs by the backgrounds of students.

Issue 5: *Should researchers employ an input-oriented or an output-oriented analysis, or a hybrid approach?*

As discussed earlier, step three of the K–12 costing-out process looks at whether to use an approach that is outcome-oriented, income-oriented, or employs a combination of the two. Outcome-oriented analyses use "cost functions" to see what resources have been necessary at institutions to achieve a given result (such as access and completion). Input-oriented analyses, by contrast, begin by asking experts to identify key ingredients (staffing, materials, supplies and equipment, physical space, and other elements) required to achieve a particular result. These ingredients are then costed out.

Both approaches offer advantages. Outcome-oriented studies provide validation that a given level of expenditure has resulted in certain outcomes, but provide little guidance on where institutions should allocate resources. Input-oriented studies, by contrast, rely on experts to inform where money should be spent but often lack the real-world validation that these expenditures will achieve a given result.

A third approach draws upon elements of the input and output methods. **Recommendation 5:** *Researchers should draw upon the best elements of the output-oriented and input-oriented approaches in an iterative process.* By combining the two approaches, researchers can determine what particular spending levels have been able to produce actual outcomes, but also providing guidance to colleges on what ingredients are most effective.

For outcome-based modeling, we suggest estimating at the program level, the relationship between measured outcomes, expenses associated with resources consumed (via student pathways), contextual cost factors, and student need factors. We also suggest estimating institutional cost models, with consideration of the distribution of students across program types. Outcome-based modeling will aid in setting per-pupil cost targets toward achieving specific persistence and completion rates by program, context and student types.

Outcome-based models can also provide guidance about which community college programs are relatively more efficient and thereby aid the input-oriented investigation into the combination of personnel and non-personnel resources that are used to produce the results. This input analysis, aided by experts, could generate insights for community college leaders into which investments are commonly found at colleges that are highly effective. Those findings, in turn, could be a jumping off point for more rigorous cost-effectiveness analysis of the type done on the City University of New York's ASAP program. As these types of studies accumulate, they might be used to provide for community college leaders a calculator showing price per improvement.

Issue 6: *What adjustments to the prototypical community college costs should be made for institutions with higher student needs? Should need measures include economic disadvantage, academic preparedness from high school, first-generation college status, nontraditional/adult learner status, race, and/or other factors?*

As with K–12 schools, certain community colleges are likely to have additional costs associated with educating high-needs students who are, on average, less likely to complete. Costing-out analysis needs to adjust costs for programs and institutions based on the level of need. Typically, at the K–12 level, costs are adjusted based on factors such as student poverty, academic preparedness, and special education status. In higher education, performance-based funding models typically provide a premium in funding for success with students who are, on average, less likely to complete, such as those eligible for Pell Grants, those who are first-generation college students, and those who are nontraditional/adult learners. Given the well-documented role that racial and ethnic discrimination has played and continues to play in American society, states should also consider using underrepresented minority status as a need factor.

What is the best way to determine what need factors to employ? Our recommendation is to be guided by research.

Recommendation 6: *In order to isolate which need factors are associated with a need for greater funding, researchers should conduct a statistical analysis to determine those factors that most heavily predict reduced outcomes, controlling for other factors. Researchers should review the literature for economic and demographic factors as well as academic preparedness (from high school) and whether the student is a first-generation or nontraditional/*

adult college student, as well as any additional factors that might be identified which lead to decreased likelihood of persistence and completion.

Issue 7: *How should researchers account for student needs
such as food, housing, transportation, and child care?*

A growing body of research suggests that college students—particularly
community college students—face significant needs associated with food,
housing, transportation, and childcare.[63] (Thirty percent of community college students have dependent children.)[64] Just as policymakers have long
recognized that certain elementary and secondary pupils need publicly
supported transportation to get to school, and free breakfast and lunch
while on campus, policymakers need to acknowledge that community colleges, as an extension of elementary and secondary public education, need
to grapple with providing critical supports to disadvantaged individuals.[65]
Four-year residential colleges, likewise, recognize that in order for students
to succeed, all need access to housing, food, and health care. Americans
appreciate this reality. A 2018 Demos poll found that six in ten Americans
agree that full-time public college students who work part-time should not
have to go into debt to pay for "books, groceries, transportation, and rent."[66]

Since housing and food security is so critical to student success, calculating the cost of addressing those needs is a necessary element of the
costing-out work. For some students, existing federal or state aid may be
enough to address student needs. For some needs, costs may be covered
through state appropriations to institutions or through grant aid, while
others may be supplied through other services or means. Lumping all costs
together, however, can provide a very misleading picture of community
college costs in state-to-state comparisons.[67]

Recommendation 7: *Researchers should separate out the costs associated
with direct educational services from equally important costs associated with
students' basic needs.* In this way, policymakers have a complete picture
of what resources are necessary for student success and they can identify
ways that services and resources can be provided and financed.

It is critical to find ways to estimate the costs necessary for student success, even when they may not be delivered directly by community colleges. Providing food and housing security and ensuring accessible transportation are prerequisites for students to be able to engage in a quality higher education experience.

Issue 8: *What adjustments should researchers make to the cost of a prototypical community college education for other variations in cost related to region, scale, program, and the like?*

It is not enough for researchers to identify the costs of delivering an adequate community college education at the typical institution. Costs will vary based on such factors as region (wages necessary to attract staff and faculty), size (economies of scale), program (for example, welding versus general education), and other cost drivers. We recommend following procedures first established in the K–12 setting.

Recommendation 8: *Any cost analysis of community colleges must give thorough consideration to geographic and structural cost factors as well as student need factors (outlined above) that affect the costs of achieving desired outcome goals.* Cost and need factors are reasonably well understood in K–12 cost analysis and many of those factors carry over into community college analysis. For one, regional competitiveness of faculty and staff wages most certainly plays into the estimation of costs. So too does economies of scale, both at the institutional and program level. We recommend adopting these well-established adjustments in K–12 studies to community college sector research.

Translating Empirical Evidence into Policy

Creating the research to establish expenditures necessary to support an adequate community college education should provide a strong basis for reform. However, it is only a preliminary step to implementing the research findings in the real world.

Whenever introducing empirical evidence into policy deliberations, especially where large sums of tax dollars are involved, expectations must be realistic. Cost estimates may inform policy, but they will likely never determine it directly and precisely. As Baker and Levin discuss in their background paper, cost estimates in K–12 education are often used to benchmark whether and to what extent state school finance systems are meeting adequacy requirements. Estimates of the cost of achieving desired outcomes can assist policymakers in *steering* state funding systems in the right direction. Without such evidence, that direction is unknown.

Empirical estimates themselves may be imprecise, based on limited sets of outcomes, or other imperfect or incomplete data. But the evidence should not be disregarded outright for these reasons, because reasonable estimates are most certainly better than none at all. Those estimates can be used to set overall levels of funding and to determine how much more funding is needed for some students, in some programs and institutions, to achieve comparable rates of access, persistence, and completion.

How will policymakers greet studies of the true cost of a community college education? We begin this section by acknowledging the political impediments to reform. We then cite some reasons for optimism and make suggestions for reform to break the logjam on community college funding reform.

Acknowledging the Impediments to Reform

It is important to acknowledge frankly that policymakers seeking to act upon new research on the funding levels needed to promote a strong community college education will face considerable obstacles. Today's system, which underfunds community colleges, is increasingly reliant upon tuition dollars rather than state support, and continues to rely heavily on the wealth of localities—both of which can undercut adequate funding.

As Richard Kahlenberg, Robert Shireman, Kimberly Quick, and Tariq Habash note in a background paper for the working group, the current funding of community colleges is based on a hybrid model that draws a piece from four-year colleges (with some reliance on tuition dollars) and another piece from K–12 education (with some reliance on local appropriations). In some ways, however, this in-between position results in the worst of both worlds. The reliance on local funds is regressive, since wealthier districts supply more funds to community colleges in rich areas; and the reliance on tuition dollars means the burden of funding education can be shifted from the state to the individual—which is precisely what legislators have done in recent years, as the student population has grown more diverse.[68]

Originally, tuition was not a major source of community college funding. Many of the early community colleges—at the time usually referred to as "junior" colleges—began as extensions of K–12 education systems and followed the K–12 model that is 100 percent funded by state and local appropriations. But this relationship has shifted over time. Between the 1999–2000 and 2014–15 academic years, the proportion of state and local funding of two-year colleges declined from 64 percent to 52 percent, and funding through tuition revenue increased from 22 percent to 33 percent.[69]

Today, scaling investments to meet adequate levels of funding for community colleges faces three critical political challenges associated with political power realities, state budget constraints, and declining support for higher education as registered in public opinion research.

First, current institutional funding disparities—both those between four-year universities and community colleges and those among community colleges themselves—result in part from inequitable access to political power.[70] State representatives—who are more likely to have attended or sent their children to four-year institutions—may also be more likely to respond to these schools rather than to community colleges.[71]

Second, state policymakers determining community college funding face budget constraints. States slashed their higher education budgets during the Great Recession, but even today, slow revenue growth—which economists attribute to a number of factors, including state decisions to enact costly tax cuts—poses challenges to meeting adequacy funding goals.

More troubling still, there is evidence that recent state disinvestment in public higher education may be related to the growing demographic diversity of the student population. Although conservatives complain about liberal bias among higher education faculty, Ronald Brownstein of *The Atlantic* makes the case that the changing demographics of the student body seems a more likely explanation for conservative enthusiasm to cut higher education budgets. There has been a "clear determination . . . to shift the burden from the community collectively to families individually precisely as the student body is reaching historic levels of diversity."[72] As the nation's population becomes blacker and browner, this challenge may become even more acute.

Finally, there is some evidence that support of and confidence in institutions of higher education have fallen among Republicans and conservatives. A 2018 New America survey shows that Republican support for funding is waning (even as overall impressions of higher education remain positive). According to a 2017 survey by Pew Research Center, moreover, 58 percent of Republicans and Republican-leaning independents believe that colleges and universities have a negative effect on the way things are going in the country, while just 36 percent say their effect is positive. The Pew survey had found Republicans' attitudes towards college were positive as recently as 2014, when a 54 percent majority of Republicans and Republican-leaners said that colleges were having a positive effect.[73]

Reasons for Optimism and a Path Forward

Although the current funding system—and the political dynamics underlying it—is troubling, we also think there are three reasons to be hopeful for reform.

First, community colleges have not suffered the same decline in popularity that higher education has as a whole. A 2018 Demos poll found that 85 percent of Americans have a favorable view of community colleges, compared with 66 percent who have such a view of private four-year colleges.[74] (See Figure 10.) Adam Harris, writing in *The Atlantic,* noted, "Despite lukewarm feelings about higher education generally, 80 percent of Americans have a positive view of the institution near them—that often means community colleges."[75] Part of the relative popularity of two-year institutions may also have to do with their visible connection to workforce and economic development. Former Republican Tennessee governor Bill Haslam explicitly linked his support for community colleges to his larger "Drive to 55" campaign to boost economic development in the state by increasing to 55 percent the proportion of residents with a post-secondary credential.[76]

Second, new research evidence can sometimes make a difference in public policy circles. For example, after publication of the research cited above finding that the City University of New York's ASAP program's benefits to taxpayers outweigh the costs by more than three to one, policymakers and philanthropists came together to increase funding for ASAP from roughly 1,000 students in 2010 to 25,000 students in 2018–19.[77]

Figure 10. Favorability Rating of Community Colleges versus Four-Year Private Colleges

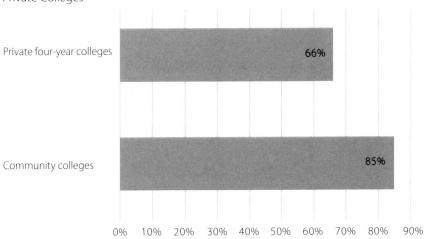

Source: Jonathan Voss, Vice President, Lake Research, Presentation at "Higher Ed 2020: College Affordability Ideas for the Next Congress and Beyond," The Century Foundation, September 26, 2018, https://tcf.org/content/event/higher-ed-2020-college-affordability-ideas-next-congress-beyond/.

New research estimating the costs of an adequate community college education may be particularly persuasive to legislators because efficiency is baked into the methodology. When researchers seek to identify institutions that are already achieving adequate outcomes, the methodology calls on them to identify the most efficient of these institutions in assessing a minimum level of investment required. This feature of the study could be appealing to legislators who want any new financial investment to be applied with high levels of efficiency.

Third, there is reason to believe that the creation of a new federal-state partnership around providing adequate community college funding— grounded in research—could help break the logjam. As Kahlenberg, Shireman, Quick, and Habash note, the federal government has a long history of supporting federal-state partnerships in higher education, going back to the 1862 Morrill Act establishing land grant colleges.[78] Federal-state partnerships are common in a variety of fields, such as unemployment insurance, health care, and K–12 education.[79]

We believe a new federal-state partnership to fund community colleges could create important new opportunities.[80] To begin with, the federal government can be a critical source of new funding for community colleges that changes the state-level funding dynamic. As long as states are constrained to what is seen as a zero-sum game within the realm of education (with four-year colleges, community colleges and K–12 schools competing for their share of a small pie of state resources), the politics of boosting community college funding are challenging. A new influx of federal funds could create a very different political environment.

In addition, a matching funds program in which the federal government provides new dollars only if states agree to increase their own investments can provide a strong incentive for states to commit new resources necessary to support community colleges. In the K–12 arena, federal funding under the Elementary and Secondary Education Act has provided a modest amount of revenue but has given federal policy makers considerable leverage in encouraging states to enact a variety of forward-looking policies.

We are encouraged also by the example of federal–state partnerships in the health care sphere. Medicaid is a voluntary program that all states eventually adopted because of the federal matching funds made available. Likewise, while some conservative governors opposed the expansion of Medicaid funding, most recently under the Affordable Care Act (ACA), it is notable that a number of moderate and conservative governors agreed to take federal money, even though doing so required a modest expansion of state investments. Among the "red" and "purple" states that have adopted Medicaid expansion are Alaska, Arizona, Arkansas, Indiana, Kentucky, Louisiana, Montana, North Dakota, Ohio, and West Virginia. All told, thirty-three states (including Washington, D.C.) have adopted Medicaid expansion programs even though until recently twenty-six states have had Republican control of the executive and legislative branches.[81]

In some ways, a matching funding program for community colleges could be even more attractive to state legislators and governors than Medicaid funding. One key difference, of course, is that Medicaid is an entitlement program whose budgetary commitments are open-ended, while community college funding can be more easily circumscribed and involves a more predictable set of financial commitments. In addition, community college education is not means-tested in the way that Medicaid is, so states may experience relatively greater political pressure from middle-class constituencies to sign onto a federal–state partnership that supports two-year institutions than to those supporting Medicaid. Finally, states have additional political pressure to invest in higher education to keep talented students in-state and avoid a "brain drain," whereas the same pressure to retain low-income families using Medicaid within state borders does not exist.[82]

We also think that a federal–state partnership could be attractive to federal policymakers. Many have grown frustrated that in years past the federal government has substantially increased funding for the Pell Grant program, only to see state public institutions increase tuition as state governments withdraw resources per full-time equivalent student. Federal financial aid expenditures tripled from \$50 billion to over \$150 billion between 1995 and 2015 in constant 2015 dollars, while state appropriations per full-time equivalent student fell in inflation-adjusted dollars by 28 percent.[83] A matching funds program would assure federal policymakers that states would do their part as well.

Conclusion

Community colleges were first created based upon an idea that is both pragmatic and idealistic: that as the economy's need for skills increased, the United States needed a new kind of institution that would help realize the goal of social mobility. Sadly, however, these institutions that disproportionately educate low-income and minority students have been starved of the funding needed to succeed. Policymakers have instructed community colleges to do more with less, even though that cramped point of view stifles the role that community colleges can play in American society.

There is a better way. New evidence demonstrates that money spent wisely on community colleges can yield a payoff to taxpayers that is more than three times the cost.[84] But rigorous research is needed to guide new investments, and to better understand the levels required.

Research on community colleges needs to catch up to elementary and secondary education, where for forty years, scholars have conducted studies on what constitutes adequate funding. This proposed area of research is complex, as we found over several months of discussions on how to apply K–12 costing-out techniques to the community colleges sector. But we believe this report creates a solid framework upon which researchers can build. It is vital that scholars undertake an effort to estimate what some of society's most vulnerable students need in order to realize their potential—and thereby to allow the United States to attain its potential as well. Social mobility is written into the DNA of America, but we are unlikely to make significant progress unless we provide America's community colleges the resources they need.

Notes

1. See, for example, Raj Chetty et al., "The Fading American Dream: Trends in Absolute Income Mobility Since 1940," NBER Working Paper No. 22910, December 2016, rev. March 2017, https://www.nber.org/papers/w22910; Richard V. Reeves and Eleanor Krause, "Raj Chetty in 14 charts: Big findings on opportunity and mobility we should all know," Brookings Institution, January 11, 2018, https://www.brookings.edu/blog/social-mobility-memos/2018/01/11/raj-chetty-in-14-charts-big-findings-on-opportunity-and-mobility-we-should-know/; and Bruce Stokes, "Public divided on prospects for the next generation," Pew Research Center, June 5, 2017, http://www.pewglobal.org/2017/06/05/2-public-divided-on-prospects-for-the-next-generation/.

2. Anthony P. Carnevale, Artem Gulish, and Jeff Strohl, "Educational Adequacy in the Twenty-First Century," The Century Foundation, May 2, 2018, 2, https://tcf.org/content/report/educational-adequacy-twenty-first-century/.

3. Nick Anderson, "'We serve the top 100 percent': California community college chief responds to Trump," *Washington Post,* February 16, 2018 (quoting Eloy Ortiz Oakley, chancellor of the California community college system), https://www.washingtonpost.com/news/grade-point/wp/2018/02/16/we-serve-the-top-100-percent-california-community-college-chief-responds-to-trump/.

4. There are 1,047 public community colleges in the United States. See U.S. Department of Education, "Community College Facts at a Glance," https://www2.ed.gov/about/offices/list/ovae/pi/cclo/ccfacts.html. Unduplicated year-round enrollment shows 9 million undergraduates in public two-year colleges in 2015–16. See "Community College FAQs," Community College Research Center, Teachers College, Columbia University, https://ccrc.tc.columbia.edu/Community-College-FAQs.html. For resource levels, see discussion below.

5. "Community College FAQs," Community College Research Center, Teachers College, Columbia University, https://ccrc.tc.columbia.edu/Community-College-FAQs.html (81 percent of entering community college students aspire to earn a bachelor's degree or higher); Laura Horn and Paul Skomsvold, "Community College Student Outcomes 1994–2009," U.S. Department of Education, Institute of Education Sciences and National Center for Education Statistics, November 2011, Table 1, 2003–04 cohort (81 percent aspire to a bachelor's degree); National Student Clearinghouse Research Center, Signature Report: Completing College: A National View of Student Completion Rates—Fall 2011 Cohort, December 2017, Appendix C, Table 39 (after six years, 23 percent complete at two-year institutions alone and an additional 15 percent complete a four-year degree).

6. See discussion below.

7. See Eleanor Krause and Isabel V. Sawhill, "Seven reasons to worry about the American middle class," Brookings Institution, June 5, 2018 (citing NBC/Wall Street Journal poll finding an increase in pessimism about intergenerational mobility between 2007 and 2014).

8. Bruce Stokes, "Public divided on prospects for the next generation," Pew Research Center, June 5, 2017, http://www.pewglobal.org/2017/06/05/2-public-divided-on-prospects-for-the-next-generation/.

9. Raj Chetty et al., "The Fading American Dream: Trends in Absolute Income Mobility Since 1940," NBER Working Paper No. 22910, December 2016, rev. March 2017, https://www.nber.org/papers/w22910.

10. See first figure in Richard V. Reeves and Eleanor Krause, "Raj Chetty in 14 charts: Big findings on opportunity and mobility we should all know," Brookings Institution, January 11, 2018, https://www.brookings.edu/blog/social-mobility-memos/2018/01/11/raj-chetty-in-14-charts-big-findings-on-opportunity-and-mobility-we-should-know/.

11. Sandy Baum and Charles Kurose, "Community Colleges in Context: Exploring Financing of Two- and Four-Year Institutions," in *Bridging the Higher Education Divide: Strengthening Community Colleges and Restoring the American Dream* (New York: The Century Foundation Press, 2013), 74, https://tcf.org/content/book/bridging-the-higher-education-divide/.

12. See discussion on page 53, Figure 10; Jonathan Voss, presentation at "Higher Ed 2020: College Affordability Ideas for the Next Congress and Beyond," The Century Foundation, September 26, 2018, https://tcf.org/content/event/higher-ed-2020-college-affordability-ideas-next-congress-beyond/.

13. National Student Clearinghouse Research Center, "Completing College: A National View of Student Completion Rates—Fall 2011 Cohort, December 2017," Appendix C, Table 39. This research is consistent with the 2004/2009 Beginning Postsecondary Student Longitudinal Study (BPS), which found that only 34.5 percent of students who started in a two-year college earned a degree or certificate (from their starting institution or another school) within six years (8.5 percent earned certificates, 14.4 percent earned associate's degrees, and 11.6 percent earned bachelor's degrees). See *Bridging the Higher Education Divide*, 30. For a more sanguine assessment, see Kevin Carey, "Revised Data Shows Community Colleges Have Been Underappreciated," *New York Times,* October 31, 2017.

14. According to the Community College Research Center, Teachers College, Columbia University, 68 percent of students beginning at public two-year colleges in 2003–04 took one or more remedial classes in the six years after their initial enrollment. See "Community College FAQs," Community College Research Center, Teachers College, Columbia University, https://ccrc.tc.columbia.edu/Community-College-FAQs.html.

15. C. Lockwood Reynolds, "Where to Attend? Estimating the Effects of Beginning at a Two-Year College," University of Michigan, Ann Arbor, October 25, 2006, cited in William G. Bowen, Matthew M. Chingos, and Michael S. McPherson, *Crossing the Finish Line: Completing College and America's Public Universities* (Princeton, N.J.: Princeton University Press, 2009), 134.

16. See, for example, Thomas Bailey, Shanna Smith Jaggars, and Davis Jenkins, *Redesigning America's Community Colleges: A Clearer Path to Student Success* (Cambridge, Mass.: Harvard University Press, 2015). See also Harry J. Holzer and Sandy Baum, *Making College Work: Pathways to Success for Disadvantaged Students* (Washington, D.C.: Brookings Institution Press, 2017). Others have documented ways to improve the efficiency of developmental education. See Judith Scott-Clayton, Peter M. Crosta and Clive Belfield, "Improving the Targeting of Treatment: Evidence From College Remediation," National Bureau of Economic Research Working Paper, October 2012, https://www.nber.org/

papers/w18457.pdf; and Bridget Terry Long, "Addressing the Academic Barriers to Higher Education," Brookings Institution 2014, https://www.brookings.edu/research/addressing-the-academic-barriers-to-higher-education/.

17. Donna M. Desrochers and Steven Hurlburt, *Trends in College Spending 2003–2013* (Washington D.C.: American Institutes for Research, 2016), 24–27.

18. It is commonly assumed that the first two years of college are less costly than the third and fourth, but Sandy Baum and Charles Kurose find that inequalities in spending between community colleges and four-year institutions remain after one accounts for that difference. See Sandy Baum and Charles Kurose, "Community Colleges in Context: Exploring Financing of Two and Four-Year Institutions," in *Bridging the Higher Education Divide: Strengthening Community Colleges and Restoring the American Dream* (New York: The Century Foundation Press, 2013), 97 and 102.

19. Donna M. Desrochers and Steven Hurlburt, "Trends in College Spending 2003 to 2013," Delta Cost Project and the American Institutes of Research, January 2016, 24–27.

20. Portions of this discussion are drawn from Richard D. Kahlenberg, Robert Shireman, Kimberly Quick, and Tariq Habash, "Policy Strategies for Pursuing Adequate Funding of Community Colleges," The Century Foundation, October 25, 2018, https://tcf.org/content/report/policy-strategies-pursuing-adequate-funding-community-colleges/.

21. See John Bound, Michael F. Lovenheim, and Sarah Turner, "Why Have College Completion Rates Declined? An Analysis of Changing Student Preparation and Collegiate Resources," *American Economic Journal: Applied Economics* 2, no. 3 (2010): 129–57. See also David J. Deming, "Increasing College Completion with a Federal Higher Education Matching Grant," The Hamilton Project, April 2017, 12.

22. See Bruce D. Baker, "How Money Matters for Schools," Learning Policy Institute, December 2017, 14. See also Bruce D. Baker, "Does Money Matter in Education?" Albert Shanker Institute, 2nd edition, 2016, i.

23. Rucker C. Johnson and Sean Tanner, "Money and Freedom: The Impact of California's School Finance Reform," Learning Policy Institute, February 2018, 9.

24. David J. Deming and Christopher R. Walters, "The Impact of Price Caps and Spending Cuts on U.S. Postsecondary Attainment," National Bureau of Economic Research, Working Paper 23736, August 2017, 3.

25. Ibid., Table 4.

26. Ibid., 16.

27. Ibid., p. 21. See also David J. Deming, "Increasing College Completion," 2. See also Kolbe and Baker, 4 (regarding Deming's findings having particular power at the community college level).

28. For an important summary of current research on the benefits of higher education spending, see Stephanie Hall, "How Much Education Are Students Getting for Their Tuition Dollar?" The Century Foundation, February 28, 2019, https://tcf.org/content/report/much-education-students-getting-tuition-dollar/" (suggesting that spending on instruction and student supports is particularly effective).

29. Juan Carlos Calcagno, Thomas Bailey, Davis Jenkins, Gregory Kienzl, and Timothy Leinbach, "Community College Student Success: What Institutional Characteristics Make a

Difference?" *Economics of Education Review* 27 (2008): 632–45, 644. See also Jane Wellman, "Financial Characteristics of broad access public institutions," background paper prepared for the Stanford Conference on Mapping Broad Access Higher Education, December 1–2, 2011, 21–22 (citing three research studies).

30. Donna M. Desrochers and Jane V. Wellman, "Trends in College Spending 1999–2009," Delta Project on Postsecondary Education Costs, Productivity, and Accountability, 2011, 30, http://www.deltacostproject.org/resources/pdf/Trends2011_Final_090711.pdf.

31. Richard D. Kahlenberg, "Community of Equals? Few elites give much thought to community colleges. But they educate 44 percent of our undergraduates—and they need help," *Democracy Journal*, Spring 2014.

32. Susan Dynarski, "How to Improve Graduation Rates at Community Colleges," *New York Times*, March 11, 2015; and Katherine Mangan, "Program's Extra Support for Community-College Students Is Paying Off," *Chronicle of Higher Education*, February 26, 2015.

33. *Bridging the Higher Education Divide*, 35–40. See also David J. Deming, "Increasing College Completion," 6, suggesting "A number of recent high-quality studies find large impacts of student supports and mentoring on persistence and degree completion."

34. "A Matter of Degrees: Practices to Pathways," Center for Community College Student Engagement, University of Texas at Austin, 2014, https://www.ccsse.org/docs/matter_of_degrees_3.pdf.

35. See Carnevale, Gulish, and Strohl, "Educational Adequacy in the Twenty-First Century," 24–25 (citing Judith Scott-Clayton, "The Shapeless River: Does a Lack of Structure Inhibit Students' Progress at Community Colleges?" CCRC Working Paper no. 25, Community College Research Center, 2011; Angela Boatman, "Evaluating Institution Efforts to Streamline Student Remediation: The Causal Effects of Tennessee Developmental Course Redesign Initiative," National Center for Postsecondary Research, 2012; Craig Hayward and Terrence Willett, "Curricular Redesign and Gatekeeper Completion: A Multi-College Evaluation of the California Acceleration Project" The Research and Planning Group for California Community Colleges, 2014; Joshua Angrist, Daniel Lang, and Philip Oreopoulos, "Incentives and services for college achievement: Evidence from a randomized trial," *American Economic Journal: Applied Economics* 1, no. 1 (2009): 136–63; Eric Bettinger and Rachel Baker, "The Effects of Student Coaching in College: An Evaluation of a Randomized Experiment in Student Mentoring," NBER Working Paper 16881, National Bureau of Economic Research, 2011; Alexander K. Mayer, Reshma Patel, Timothy Rudd, and Alyssa Ratledge, "Designing Scholarships to Improve College Success: Final Report on the Performance-Based Scholarship Demonstration," MDRC, 2015; Davis Jenkins, "Get with the Program: Accelerating Community College Students' Entry into and Completion of Programs of Study," CCRC Working Paper no. 32, Community College Research Center, Columbia University, 2011).

36. Henry M. Levin and Emma Garcia, "Accelerating Community College Graduation Rates: A Benefit-Cost Analysis," *Journal of Higher Education* 89, no. 1 (2018): 1–27.

37. Ibid., 10 (present value at age 23 years at 2.5 percent discount rate, 2008–10).

38. Ibid., 11–15. See also Philip Trostel, "It's Not Just the Money: The Benefits of College Education to Individuals and Society," Lumina Issue Papers, October 14, 2015, 9 and 14, https://www.luminafoundation.org/files/resources/its-not-just-the-money.pdf (finding

that the present value of net additional lifetime earnings of a community college associate degree holder of $246,000 in 2012).

39. *Bridging the Higher Education Divide,* 17.

40. *Bridging the Higher Education Divide,* 17.

41. Natasha Ushomirsky and David Williams, "Funding Gaps 2015: Too Many States Still Spend Less on Education Students Who Need the Most," The Education Trust, March 2015, 5.

42. Deborah A. Verstegen, "How Do States Pay for Schools? An Update of a 50-State Survey of Finance Policies and Programs," Association for Education Finance and Policy Annual Conference, San Antonio, Texas, March 15, 2014, 8.

43. Bruce Baker and Jesse Levin, "Estimating the Real Cost of Community College," The Century Foundation, October 23, 2017, https://tcf.org/content/report/estimating-real-cost-community-college/.

44. *Bridging the Higher Education Divide,* 40–41.

45. See websites for the Integrated Postsecondary Education Data System (https://nces.ed.gov/ipeds/) and the Delta Cost Project (https://www.deltacostproject.org/).

46. Tammy Kolbe and Bruce D. Baker, "Fiscal Equity and America's Community Colleges," *Journal of Higher Education,* May 18, 2018.

47. Chancellor's Office, California Community Colleges, "The Real Cost Project: Preliminary Report," September 2003, 9–10, http://californiacommunitycolleges.cccco.edu/Portals/0/Reports/realcost.pdf.

48. "Real Cost Project," 15.

49. "Real Cost Project," 19.

50. "Real Cost Project," 1–2, 15–19.

51. Christopher Morphew and Bruce Baker, "On the Utility of National Datasets and Resource Cost Models for Estimating Faculty Instructional Costs in Higher Education," *Journal of Education Finance* 33, no. 1 (2007): 20-48.

52. Anthony P. Carnevale, Artem Gulish, and Jeff Strohl, "Educational Adequacy in the Twenty-First Century," The Century Foundation, May 2, 2018, 2, https://tcf.org/content/report/educational-adequacy-twenty-first-century/.

53. These figures are in 2016 dollars.

54. For support for the notion that earnings growth could be a measure of community college performance, see Holzer and Baum, *Making College Work,* 175–76.

55. Jacob Mincer, *Schooling, Experience and Earning* (National Bureau of Economic Research, 1974).

56. See, for example, Christine Woff-Eisenberg, "Amplifying Student Voices: The Community College Libraries and Academic Support for Student Success Project," Ithaka S+R and Institute of Museum Sciences and Library Services, 2018, 11–15, https://www.insidehighered.com/sites/default/server_files/media/SR_Report_Amplifying_Student_Voices_CCLASS%20_08132018.pdf.

57. The completion standard applies to students seeking a degree or certificate. Of course, some students take courses at community college in order to attain a new skill without seeking to complete a certificate or degree.

58. When examining completion, we look to goals for the entire population rather than rates for the population in college, for the reasons outlined under Issue 1.

59. Carnevale, Gulish and Strohl, "Educational Adequacy," 2.

60. An expansion of access to community college among those with lower achievement might initially weaken, rather than raise, these success rates.

61. These success levels should be examined both at the institutional and the community-need level. Caution should be taken in judging schools or program based on rates of completion of degrees or certificates, as opposed to the number of completers among the population that needs to be served in the geographic area. An institution may have a reasonable strategy of offering very low-cost access to a broad swath of the local population, giving many adults the opportunity to try out an area of study with an expectation that many may choose not to continue (resulting in a low graduation rate). As long as the courses are affordable, no harm has been done, and many may benefit from the courses they did take. On the other hand, if the broad access consistently fails to produce the degrees and certificates that are appropriate given community needs and the pursuit of equity, or if it leaves former students with debts they cannot repay, then the broad-access strategy should be rethought.

62. See Jay Chambers, T. Parrish, J. Levin, J. Smith, J. Guthrie, R. Seder, and L. Taylor, *The New York Adequacy Study: Determining the Cost of Providing All Children in New York an Adequate Education* (Palo Alto, Calif.: American Institutes for Research, 2004); and Jay Chambers, J. Levin, D. Delancey, and K. Manship, *An Independent Comprehensive Study of the New Mexico Public School Funding Formula: Volume 1—Final Report* (Palo Alto, Calif.: American Institutes for Research, 2008).

63. See, for example, Sara Goldrick-Rab, "It's Hard to Study if You're Hungry," *New York Times,* January 14, 2018, https://www.nytimes.com/2018/01/14/opinion/hunger-college-food-insecurity.html. See also "Food Insecurity: Better Information Could Help Eligible College Students Access Federal Food Assistance Benefits," General Accountability Office, January 9, 2019, https://www.gao.gov/products/GAO-19-95.

64. Harry J. Holzer and Sandy Baum, *Making College Work: Pathways for Success for Disadvantaged Students* (Washington, D.C.: Brookings Institution Press, 2017), 146.

65. See Richard D. Kahlenberg, Robert Shireman, Kimberly Quick and Tariq Habash, "Policy Strategies for Pursuing Adequate Funding of Community Colleges," The Century Foundation, October 25, 2018 https://tcf.org/content/report/policy-strategies-pursuing-adequate-funding-community-colleges/.

66. Jonathan Voss, vice president, Lake Research, presentation at "Higher Ed 2020: College Affordability Ideas for the Next Congress and Beyond," The Century Foundation, September 26, 2018, https://tcf.org/content/event/higher-ed-2020-college-affordability-ideas-next-congress-beyond/.

67. In Vermont, for example, a budgeting process that places social supports in the education budget—a practice not typically used by other states—has led to unfair criticisms that Vermont spends more than other states on education without comparable results.

68. Portions of this discussion are drawn from Richard D. Kahlenberg, Robert Shireman, Kimberly Quick and Tariq Habash, "Policy Strategies for Pursuing Adequate Funding of

Community Colleges," The Century Foundation, October 25, 2018 https://tcf.org/content/report/policy-strategies-pursuing-adequate-funding-community-colleges/.

69. See Kahlenberg, Shireman, Quick and Habash, Figure 5.

70. Nicholas Carnes, *White-Collar Government: The Hidden Role of Class in Economic Policy Making* (Chicago: University of Chicago Press, 2013).

71. National Conference of State Legislatures, Legislator Demographics Survey, "State Legislators 2015 Highest Degree Attained," http://www.ncsl.org/Portals/1/Documents/About_State_Legislatures/Education.pdf. Nationally, the survey found that at least 73 percent of state legislators held a bachelors or advanced degree, with only 4 percent possessing less than a bachelors, and 23 percent missing data. Pew, who helped conduct the survey, also points out that lawmakers with business backgrounds hold the biggest share of seats.

72. Ronald Brownstein, reply to "Letters: Why Have States Cut University Funds?" May 15, 2018. https://www.theatlantic.com/letters/archive/2018/05/letters-american-higher-education-hits-a-dangerous-milestone/560081/.

73. Hannah Fingerhut, "Republicans skeptical of colleges' impact on U.S., but most see benefits for workforce participation," Pew Research Center, July 20, 2017, http://www.pewresearch.org/fact-tank/2017/07/20/republicans-skeptical-of-colleges-impact-on-u-s-but-most-see-benefits-for-workforce-preparation/.

74. Jonathan Voss, vice president, Lake Research, presentation at "Higher Ed 2020: College Affordability Ideas for the Next Congress and Beyond," The Century Foundation, September 26, 2018, https://tcf.org/content/event/higher-ed-2020-college-affordability-ideas-next-congress-beyond/.

75. Adam Harris, "The Higher Education Nearly All Americans Love," *The Atlantic,* May 21, 2018.

76. See Drive to 55 Alliance website, http://driveto55.org/.

77. City University of New York, "Significant Increases in Associate Degree Graduation Rates: CUNY Accelerated Study in Associate Programs (ASAP), March 1, 2017, http://www1.cuny.edu/sites/asap/wp-content/uploads/sites/8/2017/03/ASAP_Program_Overview_Web.pdf.

78. John Michael Lee Jr., and Samaad Wes Keys, "Land-Grant But Unequal: State One-to-One Funding for 1890 Land-Grant Universities," Association of Public and Land Grant Universities, September 2013, 1–2.

79. Jennifer Mishory, "Path to Debt-Free College: A Blueprint for Building a Successful Federal-State Partnership," The Century Foundation, September 26, 2018, 3. For similar programs, see e.g. David Tandberg, Sophia Laderman, and Andy Carlson, "A Federal-State Partnership for True College Affordability," State Higher Education Executive Officers Association, June 2017; David J. Deming, "Increasing College Completion with a Federal Higher Education Match," The Hamilton Project, April 2017, 2; and "Fact Sheet: White House Unveils America's College Promise Proposal," The White House, January 9, 2015, https://obamawhitehouse.archives.gov/the-press-office/2015/01/09/fact-sheet-white-house-unveils-america-s-college-promise-proposal-tuitio.

80. For an earlier call for a federal–state partnership for community colleges, see "Investing in American Education: The American Graduation Initiative," The White House,

https://obamawhitehouse.archives.gov/blog/2009/07/14/investing-education-american-graduation-initiative, and "Transforming America's Community Colleges," The Brooking Institution, May 7, 2009, https://www.brookings.edu/events/transforming-americas-community-colleges-a-federal-policy-proposal-to-expand-opportunity-and-promote-economic-prosperity/.

81. "Status of State Action on the Medicaid Expansion Decision," Henry J. Kaiser Family Foundation, April 27, 2018, https://www.kff.org/health-reform/state-indicator/state-activity-around-expanding-medicaid-under-the-affordable-care-act/?activeTab=map&currentTimeframe=0&selectedDistributions=current-status-of-medicaid-expansion-decision&sortModel=%7B%22colId%22:%22Location%22,%22sort%22:%22asc%22%7D. See also Deming, "Increasing College Completion," 6 (citing the matching program structure as having been "used successfully to boost state Medicaid spending").

82. For discussion of state pressure to avoid "brain drain," see Colleen Campbell, Center for American Progress, remarks at "Higher Ed 2020: College Affordability Ideas for the Next Congress and Beyond," The Century Foundation, September 26, 2018, https://tcf.org/content/event/higher-ed-2020-college-affordability-ideas-next-congress-beyond/.

83. See Deming and Walters, "The Impact of Price Caps," 2.

84. Henry M. Levin and Emma Garcia, "Accelerating Community College Graduation Rates: A Benefit-Cost Analysis," *Journal of Higher Education* 89, no. 1 (2018): 1–27.

Background Papers

Estimating the Real Cost
of Community College

BRUCE BAKER and JESSE LEVIN

Community colleges in the United States play a critical role in promoting social mobility. This is especially the case for first-generation college students, as well as for non-traditional students and career-transitioning adults. Yet, access to equitable, high-quality two-year public colleges remains largely dependent on state- and county-level resources and economic contexts. Individuals have vastly different abilities to pay to advance their education and training, and as things stand, those with the fewest personal resources may be the ones who accrue the greatest benefit from a community college education. Furthermore, community colleges serving those with the greatest needs are likely to be situated in counties and states with the least fiscal capacity to support high-quality programs and services.

State policymakers have begun taking action on the issue of promoting equitable access to higher education with a recent push to extend free public education from the elementary and secondary level to two-year public colleges. For example, Tennessee Governor Bill Haslam approved a plan which would expand on that state's Promise Scholarship model, which offers high school graduates tuition-free access to two-year public colleges. The planned expansion will broaden access to any Tennessee resident who does not already have a college education.[1] In New York, Governor Cuomo and state lawmakers reached a deal to make public two- and four-year public institutions in the state free of tuition for resident students from families with income up to $125,000.[2]

Importantly, the fiscal assumptions to support these plans fail to consider the ongoing costs of providing equitable access to high-quality public higher education systems, instead relying on back-of-the-envelope estimates for subsidizing existing tuition levels for expected participants. The sad fact is that, because of this, government at every level acts with very little knowledge about the actual cost of providing these systems of institutions, how to make them equitably accessible, or even, at the bare minimum, how to provide "adequate" programs and related services. Even in two-year public colleges, which focus primarily on direct instruction, the share of revenue that comes from tuition and fees is about 38 percent in New York and 42 percent in Tennessee of total current fund revenues. While the New York plan promises to maintain the existing state subsidies for higher education, it does not properly account for the real costs of providing and maintaining the system, let alone the goals and broader public interests invested in its success, relying instead solely on the existing tuition subsidy rate and prior state support.

Needless to say, providing equitable access to high quality postsecondary opportunities requires understanding the cost of providing those services. Without that knowledge, government simply cannot provide the funds and establish sustainable tax policies to cover those costs. There is and will likely always be at least some disconnect between state legislative discussions over tax policies, revenue sources, the provision of public goods and services, and the outcome quality expectations of public institutions, in that legislators will tend to (a) spend as little as feasible, holding taxes as low as possible, while (b) demanding, through accountability policies, that publicly supported institutions meet goals, standards and outcomes that far exceed the system's capacity. This is a regrettable tendency, to be sure; but we can counter it, in the case of community colleges, by ensuring that the costs of those goals, standards, and outcomes are based on rigorous and accurate analyses, and not on hazy guesses, or on wishful thinking.

Thankfully, community college systems have well-studied analogues from which much can be learned, and adapted. In particular, scholars and policymakers working in elementary and secondary education have grappled for decades with how to implement appropriate funding mechanisms. Much like community colleges today, PreK–12 state education systems also typically operated under the "three-men-in-a-backroom" negotiation model through the early 1990s, determining state appropriations and formula distributions without any recourse to substantive calculation of costs and need. Now, however, things are very different: over the last quarter-decade, PreK–12 policy makers have introduced a number of conceptual frameworks and empirical evidence into their deliberations over state school finance policies, and their doing so has yielded significant gains in closing the gap between the amount of revenues made available to fund education, how resources are allocated, and what outcomes can reasonably be expected. In this paper, we will examine the methods that these policy makers use, and demonstrate how they can be adapted to make community college truly accessible to everyone.

Before we begin, we must acknowledge that state school finance systems remain far from perfect. Many were frozen or dismantled during the economic collapse in 2009 and haven't been reinstated since, with their current funding remaining at levels lower than they were in 2009.[3] And in other cases, state efforts to implement school finance reform were never fully implemented. For example, New York State, which recently proposed "free college" (and is one of our primary models), has yet to comply with the judicial mandate passed down in *Campaign for Fiscal Equity, Inc. v State* (in 2006) to adequately fund the state's K–12 system—the standards for which have only risen in the years since.[4] Further, New York has continued to ignore the state school finance formula it adopted in 2007 specifically to comply with this order, and continues to maintain one of the least equitable, and most regressive, state school finance systems in the nation.[5]

Similarly, Tennessee, which expanded into tuition-free community college as well, continues to have among the least adequately funded PreK–12 systems in the nation.[6]

But even with these setbacks and shortcomings, the focus on equity and adequacy in PreK–12 education, alongside the related conceptual and methodological developments employed by the policy makers who attend to that sector, can provide us with powerful guidance in mapping out a path toward more equitable and adequate post-secondary education systems. Preliminary analyses applying PreK–12 equity frameworks suggest that state community college systems fail to meet even the most basic equity standards: disparities in general, and instructional spending in particular, remain vast, and have not been rationally tied to variations in local economic conditions or likely student needs.

These are just a taste of the revelations that the methods used in public PreK–12 systems to calculate costs have to offer. In what follows, we trace this thread of inquiry to its end, illustrating the many ways in which policy makers can apply these methods to the community college sector. In PreK–12 education, cost analyses have been used to guide the design of state school finance systems by identifying the costs of achieving state-defined outcome goals and, crucially, by distinguishing, using state aid formulas, state responsibility from local responsibility in financing those costs. Further, PreK–12 policy makers have demonstrated that cost analyses can provide insights for local institutional leaders regarding the productive and efficient allocation of resources given the specific circumstances of the student population being served. In post-secondary education, such analyses may inform both how institutions are funded through state and local resources. Further, in-depth analysis of resource allocation, program and service organization and delivery may provide guidance to institutional leaders.

Much of the hesitancy in the U.S. over providing easier and more equitable access to community college stems from a basic misunderstanding of what doing so would cost. This report recommends approaches that may be able to correct that misunderstanding, and thereby transform that hesitancy into enthusiasm. Extending these opportunities to everyone may not be as difficult, or as costly, as conventional wisdom would suggest.

Conceptions of Equity, Adequacy, and Equal Opportunity

As early as 1979, education researchers Robert Berne and Leanna Stiefel synthesized conceptual frameworks from public policy and finance, as well as evidence drawn from early litigation challenging inequities in state school finance systems, to propose a framework and series of measures for evaluating equity in state school finance systems.[78] This seminal research laid the foundation for subsequent conceptual and empirical developments in measuring equity in PreK–12 education. Berne and Stiefel used two framing questions: (1) "Equity of what?"; and (2) "Equity for whom?" On the "what" side, Berne and Stiefel suggested that equity could be framed in terms of financial inputs to schooling, real resource inputs such as teachers and their qualifications, and, finally, outcomes. But Berne and Stiefel's framework predated (a) judicial application of outcome standards to evaluate school finance systems, and (b) the proliferation of state outcome standards, assessments and accountability systems, first in the 1990s, and then rapidly expanding in the 2000s under the federal mandate of No Child Left Behind. The "who" side typically involved "students" and "taxpayers"—that is, a state school finance system should be based on the fair treatment of taxpayers and yield fair treatment of students.

Drawing on literature from tax policy, Berne and Stiefel (1984) adopted a definition of "fairness" which provided for both "equal treatment of equals" (horizontal equity) and "unequal treatment of unequals" (vertical equity). That is, if two taxpayers are equally situated, their tax treatment (effective rate, burden or effort) should be similar; likewise, if two students have similar needs, their access to educational programs and services or financial inputs should be similar. But, if two taxpayers are differently situated (for example, homeowner versus industrial property owner), then differential taxation might be permissible; and, if two students had substantively different educational needs, requiring different programs and services, then different financial inputs might be needed to achieve equity.

In recent decades, researchers have come to realize the shortcomings of horizontal and vertical equity delineations. First and foremost, horizontal equity itself does not preclude vertical equity, in that equal treatment of equals does not preclude the need for differentiated treatment for some (non-equals). Secondly, vertical equity requires value judgments, and then categorical determinations, as to just who is unequal, and just how unequal must their treatment be in order to be "equitable"? Federal laws (adopted in the 1970s) continue to operate into this model, applying categorical declarations as to who is eligible for differentiated treatment and frequently requiring judicial intervention to determine how much differentiation is required for legal compliance.[9] But most children do not fall under the categories set forth under federal (or state) laws, even though there exist vast differences in needs across those populations of children.

An alternative, unifying approach is to suggest that the treatment, per se, is not the inputs the child receives but the outcomes that are expected of all children under state standards and accountability systems. In this sense, all children under the umbrella of these state policies are similarly situated, in that they are similarly expected to achieve the common outcome standards. Thus, the obligation of the state is to ensure that all children, regardless of their background and where they attend school, have equal opportunity to achieve those common outcome standards.

The provision of equal educational opportunity requires the differentiation of programs and services, including the provision of additional supports. This input (and process) differentiation promotes the equal treatment of similarly situated children, rather than the unequal treatment of unequals. Further, if differentiation of programs and services is required to provide students with an equal opportunity to achieve common outcomes, there exists a more viable legal equity argument on behalf of the most disadvantaged children not separately classified under federal statutes. The conception of equal opportunity to achieve common outcome goals has thus largely replaced vertical equity in the vernacular of PreK–12 equity analysis.[10]

The late 1980s and early 1990s saw a shift in legal strategy regarding state school finance systems away from an emphasis on achieving equal revenues across settings (neutral of property wealth) and toward identifying some benchmark for minimum educational adequacy. Politically, some advocates for this approach viewed it as infeasible for states to raise enough aid to be able to close the spending gap between the poorest and most affluent districts, meaning that achieving fiscal parity would likely require leveling down affluent districts. Focus on a minimum adequacy bar for the poorest districts would alleviate this concern, and potentially garner the political support of affluent communities, who would no longer have anything to lose.[11] Koski and Reich (2006) explain that this approach is problematic, in part because minimum adequacy standards are difficult to define, and also because, when some are provided merely minimally adequate education but others provided education which far exceeds minimum adequacy, the former remain at a disadvantage. Further, the adequacy of the minimum bar is diminished by increasing that gap, because education is to a large extent a positional good, over which individuals compete, based on relative position, for access to higher education and economic prosperity.[12]

Others adopted a more progressive "adequacy" view, which holds that focusing on state standards and accountability systems could force legislators to provide sufficient resources for all children to meet those standards—and that state constitution education articles could be used to enforce this mandate.[13] Under the more progressive alternative, equal opportunity and adequacy goals are combined: the state must provide equal opportunity for all children to achieve "adequate" educational outcomes. For this to succeed, funding must be at a sufficient overall level, and resources, programs and services must be provided to ensure that children with varied needs and backgrounds have the additional supports they need to achieve the mandated outcomes.

It remains important, however, to be able to separate equal opportunity objectives from adequacy objectives, both for legal claims and for empirical analysis. The adequacy bar can be elusive,[14] and state courts are not always willing to declare that adopted assessments and outcome standards measure the state's minimum constitutional obligation. Therefore, the state's ability to support a specific level of "adequacy" may be subject to economic fluctuations.[15] Importantly, at those times when revenues fall short of supporting high outcome standards, equal opportunity should still be preserved. That is, equal opportunity can be achieved for a standard lower than, equal to, or higher than the single "adequacy" standard.[16]

Critical Differences between PreK–12 and Community Colleges

There are a number of critical differences between elementary and secondary education and post-secondary education which influence both how we frame conceptions of equity, equal opportunity, and adequacy, as well as how we approach cost estimation. First, post-secondary education is not compulsory, and so does not generally enjoy state constitutional protection in the way that elementary and secondary education do. Second, because post-secondary education is largely considered a personal choice, and there exist many choices for academic and career paths within that choice set, there are no obvious common outcome goals for post-secondary education.

When evaluating the adequacy of elementary and secondary education systems, state courts often reference the importance of distal outcomes such as "knowledge of economic, social, and political systems to enable the students to make informed choices" or "sufficient training or preparation for advanced training in either academic or vocational fields so as to enable each child to choose and pursue life work intelligently."[17] However, a convenient fallback, and increasingly prevalent standard, for elementary and secondary education is that graduates of a state's secondary schools should be sufficiently prepared for the next stage of their education—or to be "college or career ready." "College readiness" is often reduced to measures of course completion (sometimes with standardized end-of-course assessments), graduation, and scores on those standardized tests presumed predictive of success in introductory college-level coursework.[18]

Outcome expectations for post-secondary education are notably more complex, more difficult to measure and more varied across individuals and institutions, especially where terminal degrees or certificates are involved. There exist few standardized end-of-course assessments, though professional licensure exams are required in some fields. Most importantly, as noted above, students choose widely varied career paths, from culinary training to nursing to air traffic control. Demand for graduates in these fields varies over time and across regions, as do wages, rendering the establishment of common economic outcome measures problematic. Finally, for many public two-year colleges, the dominant outcome is matriculation to four-year colleges, which requires yet another unique set of considerations.

Another difference is the assumption that elementary and secondary education must more comprehensively cover the costs associated with equitable access to adequate programs and services. This often includes the provision of transportation, as well as materials, supplies and equipment. Equity and adequacy are compromised when those costs are passed along to students and their families. In many states it is impermissible to charge students to be transported to school or to purchase their own textbooks, as these are necessary elements of the state's constitutional obligation.

From Conceptions to Costs

In this section we explain how to transition from conceptions of equity, equal educational opportunity, and educational adequacy to the considerations required for accurately estimating the costs of achieving these goals. Perhaps most importantly, estimation of "cost" requires some outcome goal, or some measure of the quality of the product and/or service in question.[19] That is, in performing cost estimation, the researcher must necessarily ask, "the cost of what?" This is entirely consistent with our framing of equal educational opportunity, which asks whether all children have an equal opportunity to achieve some specified set of outcome goals. Thus, the point here is to determine the "costs" associated with achieving the outcome goals in question, and whether and how those "costs" vary across children and settings.

In this section, we begin with a discussion of the complexities associated with setting outcome goals, and how outcome goal-setting may differ in post-secondary education when compared with the goal-setting done for elementary and secondary education systems. Next, we explore (a) cost factors and (b) risk factors, which research on elementary and secondary school systems have shown to collectively affect the "costs" of achieving common outcome goals. Finally, discuss similar types of factors that might affect the cost of providing an equal educational opportunity in the context of post-secondary education.

Toward What Common Outcomes

Moving from conceptions of equal educational opportunity and adequacy to the application of cost estimation requires taking broadly framed outcome goals and reducing them to measures and indicators. In elementary and secondary education, broad outcome declarations, judicial or legislative, such as providing for a "meaningful high school education" or ensuring that all children are "college and career ready," must be operationalized into more practical, tangible measures and indicators. Furthermore, in order to estimate equal educational opportunities, common outcome measures must be established—that is, what common outcome are all students expected to have equal opportunity to achieve? As noted above, most states have adopted standards and measures of accountability that they apply across all of their elementary and secondary school systems. In some cases, state courts have used these standards and measures as the basis for determining broader constitutional requirements.

Elementary and secondary education standards and accountability systems tend to be based primarily on (a) standardized assessments of reading and math from grades 3 to 8, and sometimes 10 and/or 11, and (b) other measures, such as four-year graduation rates. Standardized assessments often have assigned "cut-scores" that declare whether each student's performance is "proficient" (meeting basic standards) or not, and in some states, students must pass a common high school exam in order to receive a diploma. Increasingly, states have also adopted measures of test score growth, and in some cases test score growth conditional on risk factors (comparing students of similar backgrounds and needs).[20] These systems of measures and indicators, though limited, often serve to provide convenient benchmarks for judicial analysis and for empirical estimation of "costs."[21]

Analyses of elementary and secondary education system outcomes often look at system outcomes as a whole—school district outcomes—presuming that a primary goal for all (or at least most) students is post-secondary access, and perhaps more specifically, preparation to undertake traditional undergraduate general education coursework. That is, we often conveniently ignore the role of vocational programs and specialized magnet secondary schools by focusing on a hypothetical "general educa-tion" majority. Rarely if ever have elementary and secondary cost analyses considered whether the arts magnet high school is providing equitable, adequate specialized training for students to productively contribute as creative artists, or whether vocational programs are achieving a sufficient percentage of job placements that result in livable wages. Recent emphasis on "common core standards" and "college and career readiness" for all stu-dents has pushed specialized alternatives further to the margins of second-ary schooling.[22]

As noted above, post-secondary education, unlike elementary and secondary education, is not compulsory for all students, though there is increased interest in ensuring that it is accessible to all students. As we move the conversation from elementary and secondary to post-secondary education systems, we can no-longer sidestep issues of student choice and specialization. While economic outcomes have some influence on how students choose their courses and programs, they remain secondary to "beliefs about course enjoyment and grades."[23] This complicates our options for outcome measures, since the outcomes of uncommon choices and aspirations made by students in post-secondary education vary. However, the logic behind the "general education" outcome orientation in elementary and secondary education is that providing equal opportunity to access and success in post-secondary education will provide students more equitable access to economic and civic participation in modern society. That is, it is presumed that having a "meaningful high school education,"[24] for example, prepares one to attend and complete college, which is increasingly necessary for achieving gainful employment in a modern economy.

Our primary interest in this paper is the translation of cost analysis approaches from elementary and secondary education to two-year public colleges, or community colleges. In some cases, two-year degrees are terminal degrees leading directly to professional careers, and in other cases, two-year colleges serve in a transitional role to four-year degrees. Many students make the transition to four-year colleges before even completing the two-year degree. A recent report from the National Student Clearinghouse described the following three major patterns for students attending community colleges:

- **College Persistence:** Six out of ten students who begin college at a two-year public institution persist into the second fall term. Of the students who persist, nearly one in five do so at a transfer destination.
- **Transfer and Mobility:** Of all students who began college at two-year public institutions in fall 2008, 24.4 percent transferred to a four-year institution within six years and 15 percent transferred to two-year institutions (lateral transfer), for an overall transfer rate of 39.6 percent.

- **Certificate and Degree Completion:** In the 2016 Signature Report on completion rates, the National Student Clearinghouse Research Center found that 30 percent of the fall 2010 entering cohort of community college students completed their first credential within six years at either the initial institution where they were enrolled or at a different two-year college. In addition, another 9.3 percent completed their first credential at a four-year institution.[25]

That is, for nearly 40 percent of community college students, the eventual outcome is not degree completion and employment but rather transfer to another institution. Community college for many is yet another intermediate step. Further, a related NSC report explained:

- One in ten students who started in two-year public institutions transferred and graduated from a four-year institution without receiving any credential from their starting institution.
- Traditional graduation-rate measures that focus only on completions at the starting institution do not account for this type of outcome, even though it is a well-worn pathway pathway that has been increasing in both incidence and attention in today's resource-constrained policy environment.[26]

Several authors have estimated the long term economic value (distal outcomes) of these shorter term (proximal) outcomes: persistence and completion. For example, several studies find that the completion of associate's degrees leads to positive increases in wages in almost every field, but that the increases vary widely by field.[27] Others have found that certificate completion also leads to economic benefits, but that those benefits tend to be smaller than the benefits for degree completion.[28] More specifically, "the return to credits in many career and technical education (CTE) subfields is significant, positive, and oftentimes strong, while the reverse is true of credits in many non-CTE subfields."[29]

So, as with secondary education, we know that the intermediate outcomes of completion alone are significant. But, the choices of programs, and even of individual courses within programs, strongly influence eventual earnings.[30] Thus, while it might be desirable to find some measures of gainful employment or wages (distal outcomes), it may be more practical to focus initial efforts on studying costs in community colleges in relation to the proximal outcomes—persistence and completion—which are associated with those longer term benefits.

On a related note, Bahr explains that the collective choices of students, given local and regional context, can shape the overall mission of community colleges. Bahr describes five types of community colleges: Community Education Intensive, Transfer Intensive, Workforce Development Intensive, High-Risk Intensive, and Mixed Use.[31] These categories are derived from student behavioral profiles for first-time attendees, identified as drop-in, experimental, noncredit, terminal vocational, transfer, and exploratory. Bahr then investigates "whether the patterns of student use that characterize the five types appear to be primarily a consequence of institutional policies and practices or, conversely, a product of localized community demand and the associated circumstances and choices of the students who attend a given college." Bahr finds that "variation in patterns of student use across institutions appears to be primarily a product of localized community demand," and that "institutions that differ in terms of dominant or disproportionate patterns of student use also differ significantly and systematically on a number of measures of institutional performance."[32] Mixed Use community colleges are relatively balanced in their student profiles; Community Education Intensive institutions are represented by high concentrations of drop-in and non-credit students; Transfer Intensive institutions by high rates of transfer and exploratory students; Workforce Development by high rates of terminal vocational profiles; and High-Risk Intensive by high rates of experimental profiles and relatively low rates of transfer profiles, where students of historically disadvantaged backgrounds are disproportionately represented among experimental profiles. Bahr's typology and methods might prove useful for classifying community college types for purposes of comparing costs, where students' collective goals and institutional contexts share similarities.

Cost and Risk Factors

Equal opportunity requires that students, regardless of their personal and educational backgrounds, have equalized chances to succeed on the proximal or distal outcomes in question. Two broad categories of factors affect the "costs" of providing equal educational opportunity: (1) cost factors, i.e. input price levels and other geographic pressures, and (2) risk factors, i.e. characteristics related to individual or collective student needs.[33] One view of educational equity—which falls short of equal opportunity—is that all students should be provided not merely with equal dollar inputs to their schooling but with equitable real resources. The "real resources" of schooling are the people (human resources including faculty and staff), space (capital assets), and the materials, supplies and equipment that go into the provision of educational services (direct instruction and all related supports). Real resource equity is affected by input price variation and by other geographic cost pressures. In contrast, student background characteristics affect the extent to which real resources—programs and services—must be differentiated in order to provide students with equal opportunity to achieve outcome goals.

Figure 1 lays out the relationship between cost pressures, risk factors and outcome goals, as realized through institutional spending on program and service delivery. The amount that must be spent by an institution toward achieving some common outcome goals depends on these cost factors and on student characteristics. An important additional feature of this figure is the delineation between spending and cost. Institutions might spend on things not directly associated with achieving the measured outcomes. That is, an institution might spend more than it would cost at a minimum to achieve the desired outcomes given existing cost pressures and risk factors.

Figure 1. Cost and Risk Factors

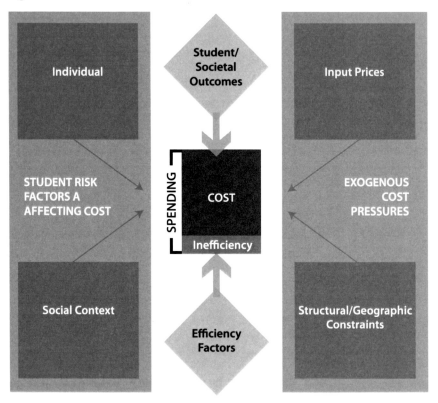

That margin of spending above cost might be characterized as "ineffi-ciency," but in this case, "inefficiency" takes on a broad meaning, including spending on programs and services which may be valued but not mea-sured as primary goals/objectives. For example, institutional expenditures may include expenditures on community-based programs and events, such as athletics and the arts, which may marginally, if at all, contribute to student persistence and completions. This is not to suggest, however, that these expenditures are unnecessary or inappropriate. Rather, they are simply not captured by the outcomes being measured because they serve a different, but still valuable, purpose.

Providing equitable real resources across all locations in a system requires addressing differences in the prices of those resources from one location to another, as well as other potential geographic and structural constraints on delivering those resources. For example, recruiting and retaining faculty of comparable qualifications may require different wages in Garden City, Kansas when compared with Kansas City, Kansas. Similarly, the prices of construction, utilities and other materials, supplies, and equipment may differ. These are what we call "input price" differences. Most studies of elementary and secondary education costs focus on variation in the competitive wages of teachers, usually by comparing teacher wages to those of similarly educated, same-age workers in the same labor market.[34]

Other geographic factors might also affect the costs of providing comparable programs and services. For example, to provide a comparable array of program options in a low-population area may mean having fewer students enrolled in some programs, leading to higher per-pupil costs.[35] Rural secondary schools face a similar constraint with respect to the provision of advanced courses, and even rural elementary schools may be required to operate suboptimal class sizes. These costs, to the extent that they are by necessity rather than choice (i.e., the choice to operate a small school in a population-dense area), should be considered in cost estimation and aid formulas. Transportation costs are also affected by the relative sparsity of student populations, and are necessary to address to ensure equitable access.

The upper portion of Table 1 (page 84) lists price pressures and geographic cost factors commonly cited in elementary and secondary education cost analyses alongside potential cost factors for consideration in post-secondary cost analysis. In elementary and secondary education, two approaches have been taken to address variation in teacher wages. In the first, the comparable wage index approach, the goal, as noted above, is to index the variation in wages across labor markets for individual in non-teaching professions who have similar education levels (and similar ages) to those working in teaching professions. The premise behind this approach is that to the extent that non-teaching wages vary from one labor market to the next, so too will teacher wages have to vary in order to remain similarly competitive (whether equal or not to non-teacher wages). Similar approaches are clearly applicable for community college faculty.

The alternative sometimes applied in elementary and secondary education analysis is to attempt a more fine-grained indexing that additionally takes into account localized working conditions and preferences, in order to level the playing field for teacher recruitment and retention across local districts within labor markets. This approach—the *hedonic wage model*[36]—faces the challenge of precisely identifying those *compensating differentials*, or the higher compensation rates required to hire and retain staff in staff roles and settings that are perceived to be more demanding and/or less pleasant.[37] This approach may also be less applicable to community

Table 1. Cost and Risk Factors

Factors		Pre-K through 12	Community College
Input Price Pressures (to achieve real resource equity)	Personnel and Non-Personnel	Macro (labor market entrants): Comparative Wage Index[38] Micro (sorting across jurisdictions/schools): Hedonic Wage Model[39]	Wages[40]
Geographic Structural Constraints (to achieve real resource equity)		Economies of scale[41] Grade ranges[42] Specialized programs/ schools Capital stock[43]	Scale[44] Program type[45]
Risk Factors & Costs of Risk Mitigation (to achieve equal educational opportunity)	Collective/Population	Poverty[46] Persistent poverty[47] (Poverty density) Race[48]	Family income First-generation Academic preparation[49] (course rigor, peer composition)
	Individual	Language proficiency[50] Disability[51]	

colleges, as it is less likely that there are, or will be, several community colleges operating within a single labor market, competing for the same pool of potential faculty.

Analyses of elementary and secondary education costs also typically include measures of total enrollment size, indicators of grade ranges served, and, in some cases, indicators of specialized programming. Similar issues may be applicable to community colleges, where Bahr's typology mentioned above may prove useful for institutional type classification.

For student risk factors, the idea is that certain measurable attributes of individual students, or collectively of the population served by an institution, may be predictive of outcomes, including risk of failure on the outcomes selected for measurement. Further, it is assumed that appropriate interventions—which come with additional costs—can mitigate these risks. Table 1 lists commonly cited risk factors from elementary and secondary education cost analysis, as well as potential risk factors based on research on post-secondary education outcomes. Analyses of the costs of achieving common outcome goals in elementary and secondary education use a variety of poverty and socioeconomic indices to characterize the student populations served by schools and districts. Measures of poverty and socioeconomic status measures serve to broadly characterize risk and capture the costs associated with schoolwide strategies thought to mitigate those risks, including provision of smaller class sizes, early childhood programs, and the need for compensating differentials for teacher recruitment and retention, to name a few. Cost analyses in elementary and secondary education also commonly include measures of the proportions of the student population with disabilities (preferably by severity of disabilities), and of those who are English-language learners. These "risk" factors are associated with specific program and resource interventions for the targeted student population, whereby the premise is that these interventions are necessary to provide equal opportunity to succeed on the common outcome goals.

Literature on community college outcomes—typically measured as intermediate outcomes of persistence and completion—addresses similar factors. Family income, generational status,[52] "non-traditional" (adult) learners, and prior academic preparation each play a role in the prepared-ness of students to persist and complete their programs of study, and in the types of services, supports and modifications to instructional programs and courses that might improve persistence and completion rates for high-risk students. Language barriers and disability status, and other possible factors, including whether a student is an adult learner, likely also warrant consideration.[53]

The problem of under-preparedness—and lack of rigorous secondary curricular options—raises a systemwide concern (PreK–16). Taking com-munity colleges as independent of elementary and secondary education, under-preparedness is a "cost factor" outside of the control of community colleges. Similarly, the under-preparedness of three- and four-year olds is a risk and cost factor for elementary schools. Under-preparedness for col-lege is controllable (not exogenous) within the larger system, however, and should be addressed earlier in the pipeline, with sufficient resources tar-geted according to student backgrounds and needs. This is especially true of the types of disparities in preparedness identified by Flores and colleagues, where graduates of predominantly minority high schools had less access to advanced coursework.[54] That is, the inequities of the elementary and sec-ondary system disproportionately affect high-risk students, the additional costs of which are passed on to the post-secondary education level.

Methods of Cost Estimation

The purpose of this paper is to consider methods used in cost estimation at the PreK–12 schooling level in order to establish a framework that will allow us to estimate the costs of achieving some common set of outcome goals for students in community college. This section will specifically explore the frameworks necessary to estimate the costs of providing equal opportunity to community college students to achieve a common set of outcome goals, regardless of students' personal backgrounds or where they attend. As noted in the previous section, this discussion requires identifying and accounting for the various "risk" and "cost" factors that mediate the relationship between institutional resources and student outcomes.

In this section, we summarize and classify methods used for the estimation of costs for elementary and secondary schools. Specifically, we focus on methods used in recent decades for determining the costs of meeting state standards, where the findings yielded by these methods have often informed either judicial deliberations over the adequacy of state public elementary and secondary school finance systems, or legislative deliberations regarding appropriate reforms to those systems, or both.

Frameworks from PreK–12

Cost estimation applied to elementary and secondary education has typically fallen into two categories:

- *Input-oriented* analyses identify the staffing, materials, supplies and equipment, physical space, and other elements required to provide specific educational programs and services. Those programs and services may be identified as typically yielding certain educational outcomes for specific student populations when applied in certain settings.
- *Outcome-oriented* analyses start with measuring student outcomes as generated by the specific programs and services offered by institutions. They can then explore either the aggregate spending on those programs and services that yield specific outcomes, or explore in greater depth the allocation of spending on specific inputs.

The primary methodological distinction here is whether one starts from an input perspective or from one that designates specific outcome measures. One approach works forward, toward actual or desired outcomes, starting with inputs; the other backwards, from outcomes achieved. Ideally, both work in concert, providing iterative feedback to one another. Regardless, any measure of "cost" must consider the outcomes to be achieved through any given level of expenditure and resource allocation.

Input-Oriented Cost Analysis

Setting aside for the moment the modern proprietary jargon of costing-out studies, there really exists just one basic method for input-oriented analysis, which since the late 1970s has been given two names: the Ingredients Method and Resource Cost Modeling (RCM); we will refer to it as the latter.

RCM involves three basic steps:

- Identifying the various resources, or "ingredients," necessary to implement a set of educational programs and services (where an entire school or district, or statewide system for that matter, would be a comprehensive package of programs and services);
- Determining the input price for those ingredients or resources (considering competitive wages, other market prices, etc.); and
- Combining the necessary resource quantities with their corresponding prices to calculate a total cost estimate (Resource Quantities × Price = Cost).

Resource cost modeling was applied by Jay Chambers and colleagues in both Illinois and Alaska in the early 1980s to determine the statewide costs of providing the desired (implicitly "adequate") level of programs and services, long before its use in the context of school finance adequacy litigation in Wyoming in 1995.

A distinction between the input-oriented studies conducted prior to modern emphasis on outcome standards and assessments is that those studies focused on tallying the resource needs of education systems designed to provide a set of curricular requirements, programs and services intended to be available to all children. Modern analyses instead begin with goals statements—or the outcomes the system is intended to achieve—and then require consultants and/or expert panels to identify the inputs needed to achieve those goals. Nonetheless, the empirical method is still one of tallying inputs, attaching prices and summing costs.

RCM can be used to evaluate:

- Resources currently allocated to actual programs and services (geared toward measurably achieving specific outcomes);
- Resources needed for providing specific programs and services where they are not currently being provided; and
- Resources hypothetically needed to achieve some specific set of outcome goals—as defined by both depth and breadth.

In the first case, where actual existing resources are involved, one must thoroughly quantify those inputs, determine their prices, and sum their costs. If seeking findings that are generalizable, one must explore how input prices (from teacher wages to pencils and paper) vary across the sites where the programs and services are implemented, and whether context (economies of scale, grade ranges) affects how inputs are organized in ways consequential to cost estimates.

In the second case, where hypothetical (or not-yet-existing) outcome goals are involved, a number of approaches can be taken—including organizing panels of informed constituents, including professionals and researchers—to hypothesize the resource requirements for achieving desired outcomes with specific populations of children educated in particular settings. Competing consultants have attached names including Professional Judgment (PJ) and Evidence-Based (EB) to the methods they prefer for identifying the quantities of resources or ingredients. Professional Judgment involves convening focus groups to propose resource quantities for hypothetical schools defined by varying levels of school needs, scale of operations, and geographic setting to achieve specific outcomes, while Evidence-Based methods involve the compilation of published research into model schools presumed adequate regardless of context because of their reliance on published research where the findings are assumed to be externally generalizable.

One should expect a well-designed input-oriented resource cost analysis to engage informed constituents in a context-specific process that also makes available sufficient information (perhaps through prompts and advanced reading) on related "evidence." Put bluntly, these two methods should not be applied exclusively in isolation from one another. Even under the best application, the result of this process is a hypothesis of the resource needs required to fulfill the desired outcome goals. Where RCM is applied to programs and services already associated with certain actual, measured outcomes, that hypothesis is certainly more informed, though not yet formally tested in alternative settings.

Outcome-Oriented Cost Analysis

The primary tool of outcome-oriented cost analysis is the Education Cost Function (ECF).[55] Cost functions typically focus on the outcome-producing organizational unit, or decision making unit (DMU) as a whole—in this case, schools or districts—evaluating the relationship between aggregate spending and outcomes, given the conditions under which the outcomes are produced. The conditions regularly include economies of scale (higher unit production costs of very small organizational units), variations in labor costs, and, in the case of education, characteristics of the student populations which may require greater or fewer resources to achieve common outcome goals.

Identifying statistical relationships between resources and outcomes under varied conditions requires high-quality and sufficiently broad measures of desired outcomes, inputs, and conditions, as well as a sufficient number of organizational units that exhibit sufficient variation in the conditions under which they operate. Much can be learned from the variation that presently exists across our local public, charter, and private schools regarding the production of student outcomes, the aggregate spending, and the specific programs and services associated with those outcomes.

That said, cost functions have often been used in educational adequacy analysis as a seemingly black-box tool for projecting the required spending targets associated with certain educational outcomes. Such an approach provides no useful insights into how resources (staffing, programs and services, etc.) are organized within schools and districts at those spending levels and achieving those targets. We argue that this is an unfortunate, reductionist use of the method.

As an alternative to the black-box spending prediction approach, cost functions can be useful for exploring how otherwise similar schools or districts achieve different outcomes with the same level of spending, or the same outcomes with different levels of spending. That is, there exist differences in relative efficiency. Researchers have come to learn that inefficiency found in an ECF context is not exclusively a function of mismanagement and waste, and is often statistically explainable. Inefficient "spending" in a cost function is that portion of spending variation across schools or districts that is not associated with variation in the student outcomes being investigated, after controlling for other factors. The appearance of inefficiency might simply reflect the fact that there have been investments made that, while improving the quality of educational offerings, may not have a measurable impact on the limited outcomes under investigation. It might, for example, have been spent to expand the school's music program, which may be desirable to local constituents. These programs and services may affect other important student outcomes including persistence and completion, and college access, and may even indirectly affect the measured outcomes.

Factors that contribute to this type of measured "inefficiency" are also increasingly well-understood, and include two general categories: fiscal capacity factors and public monitoring factors.[56] For one, local public school districts with greater fiscal capacity—that is, those with a greater ability to raise funds, and who spend more—are more likely to do so, and may spend more in ways that do not directly affect measured student outcomes. But that is not to suggest that all additional spending is frivolous, especially where outcome measurement is limited to basic reading and math achievement. Public monitoring factors often include such measures as the share of school funding coming from state or federal sources, where higher shares of intergovernmental aid are often related to reduced local public involvement (and monitoring).

A thorough ECF model considers spending as a function of (a) measured outcomes, (b) student population characteristics, (c) characteristics of the educational setting (economies of scale, population sparsity, etc.), (d) regional variation in the prices of inputs (such as teacher wages), (e) factors affecting spending that are unassociated with outcomes ("inefficiency" per se), and (f) interactions among all of the above.

Comparing Input and Outcome Methods

Table 2 summarizes our perspectives on education cost analysis as applied to measuring educational adequacy and organizes the methods into input-oriented and outcome-oriented methods, which are subsequently applied to hypothetical or actual spending and outcomes. The third column addresses the method by which information is commonly gathered, such as focus groups, or consultant synthesis of literature. The fourth column adds another dimension: the unit of analysis, which also includes the issue of sampling density. Most focus group activities can only practically address the needs of a limited number of prototypical schools and student populations, whereas cost modeling involves all schools and districts, potentially over multiple years (to capture time dynamics of the system in addition to cross-sectional variation). It can be difficult to fully capture the nuanced differences in cost factors affecting schools and districts across a large, diverse state through only four to six (or even forty) prototypes. Alternatively, one might hybridize traditional PJ approaches with survey techniques to gather information across a wider array of settings, thereby increasing the sampling density).[57]

While all methods have strengths and weaknesses, some of the weaknesses represent critical flaws. For example, where the objective is to determine comprehensive, institutional costs of meeting specific outcome goals across varied contexts, the evidentiary basis for "evidence-based" analyses

Table 2. Approaches to Input and Outcome Oriented Cost Analysis

General Method	Outcome/ Goal Basis	Information Gathering	Unit of Application	Strengths	Weaknesses
Input-Oriented (Ingredients Method or Resource Cost Model)	Hypothetical	Focus Groups (Professional Judgment)	Prototypes (limited set)	Stakeholder involvement. Context sensitive.	Only hypothetical connection to outcomes. Addresses only limited conditions/ settings.
	Hypothetical	Consultant Synthesis (Evidence Based)	Single model (applied across settings)	Limited effort. Ability to use and apply one-size-fits-all model to any situation. Built on empirically validated strategies.	Aggregation of "strategies" to whole school is suspect. Transferability of effective strategies is limited. Not context-sensitive.
	Actual	State data systems that contain school-level information: personnel data, annual financial reports, outcome measures.	Schools/ districts sampled from outcome-based modeling (efficient producers of outcomes under varied conditions)	Grounded in reality (what various schools/ districts actually accomplish and how they organize resources)	Requires rich personnel, fiscal, and outcome data. Potentially infeasible where outcome goal far exceeds actual observed outcomes.
Outcome-Oriented (Cost Function)	Actual	State fiscal data systems that provide accurate district- or school-level spending estimates, including district spending on overhead.	All districts/ schools over multiple years.	Based on estimated statistical relationship between actual outcomes and actual spending. Evaluates distribution across all districts/schools.	Requires rich, high-quality data on personnel, finances and, outcomes. Focuses on limited measured outcomes. Limited insights into the internal resource use/ allocation underlying the cost estimate.

may fall short. While research evidence can be useful for identifying specific interventions which may yield positive outcomes, research evidence
rarely addresses whole institutions or provides evidence on a sufficient
array of interventions, which, if cobbled together, could constitute an
entire institution (inclusive of administrative structures, etc.).[58]

The greatest shortcoming of the arguably more robust RCM process
used in Professional Judgment is that the link between resources and
outcomes is hypothetical (i.e., based solely on professional opinion). The
greatest weaknesses of cost modeling are (a) that predictions may under-
state true costs of comprehensive adequacy where outcome measures are
too narrow, and (b) that like any costing-out method, when desired goals
far exceed those presently achieved, extrapolations may be suspect. Stress-
ing the latter point, cost modeling and other approaches to costing out
are most useful where there exist institutions in the sample or population
which actually perform to expectations and/or meet desired standards.
That is, where the range of variation among existing institutions includes
sufficiently resourced, successful, productive, and efficient institutions as
well as those which are not, the need to extrapolate outside the sample
becomes limited. Given these weaknesses in costing out approaches, there
are a number of ways researchers can explore the validity and reliability
of the costs estimated using input- and output-oriented approaches. For
more on these, please see the Appendix.

Implications for Cost Analysis of Public Two-Year Colleges

So then, what might be the most applicable methods for the study of community college costs? The biggest difference between higher education and
public elementary and secondary education remains that higher education is (a) generally voluntary, (b) involves individual student choices of
outcome goals, and (c) relies on individual student choices of pathways
toward achieving those goals. As noted earlier, consideration of how to deal
with student choice in higher education raises new questions regarding

the sufficiency of prior PreK–12 analyses—specifically, their application to secondary schools, where similar questions of individualization occur.

Input-Oriented Analysis of Resources and Student Pathways

Chambers and colleagues, in a series of 1990s analyses of costs associated with the provision of services for children with disabilities, lay out a useful alternative.[59] Most often in input-oriented education cost analyses we focus on the institutional provision of programs and services.[60] Chambers analyses flip the focus to the student consumption of programs and services. On a daily basis, students with disabilities, through their individualized educational programs, access a mix of special-education and general-education programs and services. Chambers used data on 1,300 individual students with disabilities in Massachusetts to identify the mix of programs and services accessed by students with varied disability classifications, and to attach expenditure estimates to individual programs and services.

Baker and Morphew lay out how this method applies to post-secondary cost analysis in a 2007 article on direct instructional cost variation for undergraduate degrees by field.[61] The authors use data from the transcript component of the Baccalaureate and Beyond Study to characterize the average mix of courses taken toward completion of bachelor's degrees in several fields. They then use data from the National Survey of Postsecondary Faculty to estimate the direct instructor wage expense for each content area credit (given wages at constant faculty attributes and teaching load). Finally, the direct instructional delivery expense estimates are combined with the student credit consumption behaviors to estimate variation in degree completion costs.

More precise and far more comprehensive estimates can be achieved using detailed institutional information systems—perhaps in combination with student transcript data from the National Student Clearinghouse[62]—to capture a larger set of institutions and programs. As with Baker and Morphew's analysis one can determine the typical student pathways, or mix of instructional units (courses and credits) accumulated by students who complete programs of study in specific fields—for instance, perhaps those who successfully transfer to four-year institutions. One can then estimate the direct expenses associated with the delivery of each instructional unit.

The left-hand side of Figure 2 addresses direct expenses associated with the delivery of specific courses (and credits), the core of which is compensation of instructors. Individual instructors can be linked directly with courses delivered, and the portions of their compensation attributed

Figure 2. Estimating Institutional Costs of Delivering Instructional Units

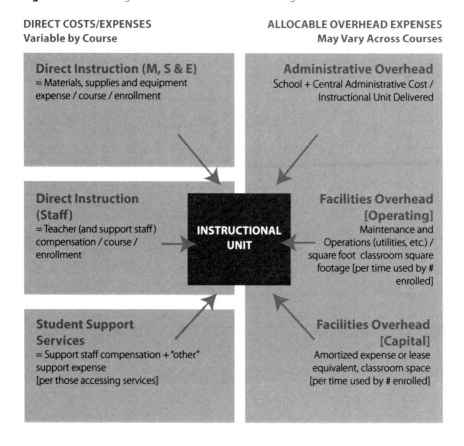

DIRECT COSTS/EXPENSES
Variable by Course

ALLOCABLE OVERHEAD EXPENSES
May Vary Across Courses

Direct Instruction (M, S & E)
= Materials, supplies and equipment
expense / course / enrollment

Administrative Overhead
School + Central Administrative Cost /
Instructional Unit Delivered

**Direct Instruction
(Staff)**
= Teacher (and support staff)
compensation / course /
enrollment

**INSTRUCTIONAL
UNIT**

**Facilities Overhead
[Operating]**
Maintenance and
Operations (utilities, etc.) /
square foot classroom square
footage [per time used by #
enrolled]

**Student Support
Services**
= Support staff compensation + "other"
support expense
[per those accessing services]

**Facilities Overhead
[Capital]**
Amortized expense or lease
equivalent, classroom space
[per time used by # enrolled]

to each individual credit hour of production can be determined. In sufficiently large systems and programs, we can determine average direct instructional expenses for similar course-offerings, to reduce the influence of individual faculty compensation on expense estimates. Ideally, course specific materials, supplies, and equipment can also be identified. As noted previously, however, higher education systems are more likely to pass along these costs to students. These student expenses must be included in the analysis.

The right-hand side of Figure 2 addresses institutional expenses which may be "allocated" to instructional units based on an allocation factor. That is, we must determine an appropriate method for assigning expenses associated with administrative overhead, and plant operations to the delivery of courses and credits. We also must find a way to measure the extent to which students access student and academic support services and determine the expenses associated with those services.

Figure 3 (page 98) presents an alternative perspective on the same task, as viewed from the perspective of plausible data sources. At the bottom of the first panel, we have the direct expenses associated with credits taken by students toward degree completion. These estimates are arrived at through evaluations of student course-taking behavior (from student transcripts, combined with scheduling and enrollment data systems) and personnel data (linking instructors, their qualifications and compensation to courses), which are represented in the second panel of the figure. Overhead expenses can be obtained from detailed institutional expenditure reports drawn from financial information systems and must then be formulaically allocated to courses. Less precise overhead expenses might be drawn from larger sets of institutions using financial data from the Integrated Postsecondary Education Data System (IPEDS).

Importantly, if the goal of these analyses is to provide policy guidance regarding the costs of persistence and completion, we must also be able to estimate additional costs of attendance currently covered by students,

Figure 3. Cost Centers and Information Sources for Determining Unit Costs of Instruction

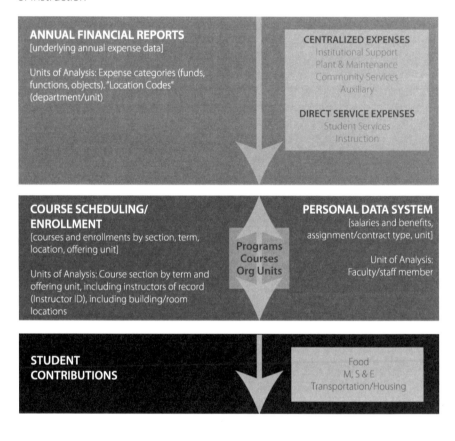

including food (while on site), textbooks and other course materials, and transportation and housing, where applicable.

Expenditure analyses of the type described thus far could be readily carried out on one or a handful of selected community colleges. Romano and colleagues applied similar methods to a New York community college.[63] The major limitation of these analyses, however, is that they merely describe their observations in a single or handful of institutions, given existing outcomes (sufficient or not) of existing populations (diverse or not) in existing contexts and at existing degrees of inefficiency.

From Pathway-Dependent Expenditure Summaries to Cost Estimates

What we have described thus far in this section is an analysis of the institutional "expenses" (not costs) associated with degree completion for one student or a group of students. That is, how much direct expense is attributed, and indirect expense allocated, to the credits consumed by students toward completing certain degree requirements? Taking the step toward cost analysis requires that we more thoroughly parse the relationship between the inputs used to provide the credits and associated spending, and the outcomes attained.

We will now review concepts laid out previously in this paper. Institutions might expend somewhat more than might be minimally necessary to achieve any given level of outcomes:

$$Cost = Expenditure - Inefficiency$$

But that doesn't mean that existing institutional practices and expenditure data aren't useful for distilling "costs." In fact, they may be the only basis— the starting point—from which we can begin to understand costs. To accomplish this task, we must evaluate variations in institutional expenditures as they relate to variations in student outcomes, with consideration for the "risk" and "cost" factors addressed previously and while acknowledging that variations in inefficiency exist. That is, what do existing institutions spend to achieve selected, measured outcomes, taking into account environmental prices and other cost factors, and given who they serve? Or, expressed as a function:

$$Expenditure = f(Outcomes, Risk Factors, Input Prices, Scale, Type, Inefficiency)$$

We can leave it at that, assuming that the remaining spending variations not associated with outcome variations or cost and risk factors constitute inefficiency;[64] or we can explore potential sources of inefficient expenditure, then statistically control for those factors when determining "costs."[65]

Identifying the underlying absolute minimum cost at which any given set of outcomes can be produced is an unattainable goal. But that should not stop us from exploring the variations in expenditures across existing institutions and programs that share similar goals.

Much can be learned from variation in existing institutional production of student outcomes, with consideration for alternative student pathways toward those outcomes. As such, we must find ways to:

- conduct student pathway analyses simultaneously across multiple institutions, including similar programs across multiple institutions and contexts;
- combine these analyses with models of institutional expenditures, including those directly attributable to instructional programs as well as overhead expenses allocable to those programs; and
- identify outcome measures that better capture differences in the quality of outcomes rather than merely the quantity.

The first of these issues can most likely be addressed by applying cost analysis to large state systems, including multiple two-year public institutions offering the same types of programs, certifications and degrees, as well as common employee compensation data systems, common course coding systems and programmatic requirements, common chart of accounts for expenditures, and common measures of student outcomes. Where these conditions are met, one could determine the program within institution expenses associated with achieving common outcome goals, and further explore how those expenses vary from one institution to the next, and across different types of entering students. That is, one could discern whether the presumed risk and cost factors (addressed previously in this report) are associated with different expenses toward achieving common outcomes, and one could then attempt to distill differences in efficiency toward achieving common outcomes, given those risk and cost factors.

Where specific programs of study (within institutions) are the unit of analysis, one can more precisely match the outcome measures to programmatic goals: comparing degree completions across similar fields (with appropriate consideration for nuances),[66] certificate completions across fields,[67] and programs with similarly high rates of transfer.[68] Further, where end-of-course exams and/or professional licensure exams exist, apples-to-apples comparisons of costs in relation to those measures may be made.

A second-best alternative involves applying more traditional cost models to institutions as the unit of analysis, as is usually the case in elementary and secondary education cost modeling. As Bahr has shown, community colleges may be classified by the types of programs and courses of study their students pursue, in part driven by the economic context in which they operate.[69] Modeling institutional expenditures and outcomes, given risk and cost factors, for institutions of similar type (while applying relevant outcome metrics), may also provide useful insights, though with less precision than comparing specific programs across institutions would offer.

Conclusions and Policy Implications

In elementary and secondary education policy, the purpose of estimating costs is to directly inform policy—specifically, to inform the design of state aid formulas so that they provide for equal educational opportunity and educational adequacy. The policy goal to provide equal educational opportunity through state, intermediate (county), and local financing should be similar for community college education. Thus, the purpose of cost analysis in the post-secondary context is similar, but from a starting point where few, if any, systemwide cost analyses of community colleges have yet been conducted, and where cost and risk factors have yet to be fully vetted for their potential inclusion in targeted aid formulas. In translating the work of cost analysis from the elementary and secondary setting to post-secondary settings, we suggest the following guiding principles:

1. Outcome goals must be sensitive to institutional goals and derivative of student choices and economic context.
2. Policies must address all costs associated with successful persistence and completion of quality degree and certificate programs (including transportation, food, materials, supplies, etc.).

3. Policies must provide sufficient resources to mitigate student risk factors, to equalize the likelihood of success regardless of student background factors.

4. Policies must be sufficiently sensitive to regional variations in labor costs, costs associated with dis-economies of scale, and population sparsity.

We acknowledge that we cannot possibly prescribe the resources required for the perfectly efficient post-secondary institution, but that this unattainable objective should not interfere with our pursuit of reasonable estimates based on existing realities. Further, we suspect that producing cost analyses based on the collective professional judgment of scholars, practitioners, and the available research evidence in order to propose the hypothetically ideal community college, while certainly interesting, would be an overwhelming task given the limited body of evidence upon which to draw.

Thorough, well-constructed hybrid cost analyses may provide useful guidance for both state policymakers operating at the higher level at which policy decisions are made, and for institutional leaders closer to where services are actually delivered who are seeking guidance regarding effective resource allocation strategies. In the best case, top-down cost modeling driven by student pathway analysis that uses programs as the unit of analysis, coupled with detailed data on institutional overhead and related service costs, can provide us with (a) accurate and comprehensive estimates of the costs of achieving desired persistence and completion rates by program, and (b) estimates of which programs and institutions seem to be achieving better outcomes more efficiently or effectively. Importantly, this approach provides the opportunity for follow-up (and deep-dive) analyses of how those institutions allocate resources within their programs and distribute student services and institutional supports across programs.

Figure 4 addresses the higher-level policy question of how program-specific cost estimates may inform public policy. Specifically, information on how costs vary across institutions by context and students served, coupled with information on local capacity to raise revenues, can inform the development of state aid formulas for community colleges. These aid formulas may include regional cost adjustment factors, adjustment for costs associated with the delivery of necessary small-scale programs and services (e.g., those in remote rural settings), and weights applied to institutional aid based on student populations served and additional support services necessary for their success. Because community college financing, unlike elementary and secondary financing, also involves direct student support via student financial aid, cost findings may also provide guidance

Figure 4. Informing Higher-Level Post-Secondary Finance Policy

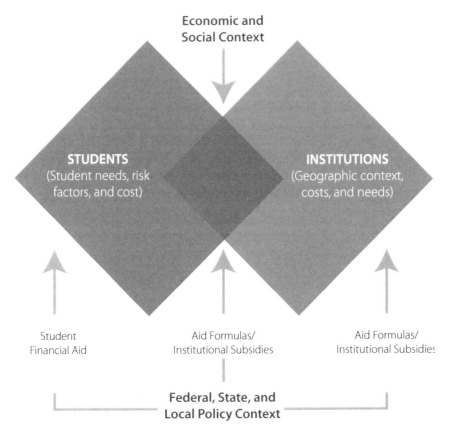

on differentiating student aid by program, institution, and by individual needs and risk factors.

At these early stages, it seems unlikely that convened panels of practitioners or policymakers could engage in developing bottom-up specifications of the resources required to provide adequate, equitable community college education across the array of existing program and institutional types. More speculative yet, it would be extremely difficult for expert practitioners working in isolation to develop improved institutional structures under which adequate community college programs might be provided in an equitable manner. However, we firmly believe that there are many lessons to be learned from examining existing variations across institutions and programs, including from detailed information on how those institutions deploy and compensate full-time and part-time faculty, how student support services are delivered, how faculty supports are organized, and how department and institutional administrative structures are organized. Specific programs and institutions identified as especially productive and efficient with certain students and in certain contexts should therefore be used to generate detailed resource and expenditure profiles which may provide useful guidance for local, institutional leaders, as well as for state policymakers.

Much can and should be learned from the ways in which existing institutions organize their resources, and the manner in which students access those resources, toward achieving their respective institutional and individual goals and broader societal and economic contributions. Some institutions are more effective than others at achieving these goals and some students choose more efficient paths than others. At the intersection are institutional structures that enable and encourage individuals to pursue their most efficient pathways to their desired outcomes.

Cost analyses must be ongoing and cyclical to support policy refinement. As institutions adapt and change in the presence of shared information on costs, those adaptations may influence the next cycle of cost analyses—perhaps revealed as improved efficiency. With institutions like community colleges so highly responsive to local economic contexts, changes to those contexts may also influence cost estimates over time. As the student populations entering community colleges in general, and specific degree and certificate programs in particular, change, so too do the costs of meeting their needs. Finally, as the role community colleges play in society at large changes and as the outcome goals of community colleges evolve, so too do the costs of achieving those goals. The end goal must not merely be to make community college more equally accessible but to provide for a system which ensures that all that enter have equal opportunity to persist, complete and achieve their desired outcomes.

Appendix: Evaluating Reliability and Validity

Far too little attention has been paid to methods for improving reliability and validity in education cost analysis. In this context, we evaluate validity and reliability as follows:

Validity: Does the cost estimate really reflect what goes into producing the desired level, depth, and breadth of educational outcomes?

Reliability: Are the costs measured consistently over time, across methods or when applied by different individuals or teams?

These two must go hand in hand, or at least reliability should be contingent on validity, because a finding can be reliably wrong (i.e. measuring the wrong thing, but consistently). Baker (2006) and Duncombe (2006, 2011) proposed steps to strengthen the reliability and validity of education cost studies, especially when applied in the context of estimating the costs of achieving specific educational outcomes, or educational "adequacy."[70]

Validity takes many forms, the simplest of which is "face validity." That is, on its face, does the estimate measure what it purports to measure? Where the goal is to measure the costs of achieving specific state standards, arguably, the Evidence-Based approach of aggregating research findings on strategies implemented in entirely different settings, and evaluated by entirely different outcomes, fails to achieve face validity. This is not to suggest, however, that context-specific focus group recommendations formulated through a Professional Judgement approach that do not take into account any research evidence are superior. Some hybrid of the two, with additional validation, is warranted.

Predictive validity asks whether the cost estimates are actually predictive of the spending levels required for achieving desired outcomes and should be included in any cost analysis. Baker (2006), Chambers, Levin, and Parrish (2006), and Levin and Chambers (2009) explain that one weak predictive validity check on educational adequacy cost studies is the evaluation of whether those schools and districts identified as having funding shortfalls—that is, those that have less than they need for achieving "adequate" educational outcomes—do in fact achieve less than adequate outcomes, while those having more than adequate resources exceed adequate outcomes, and further, whether the magnitude of the resource deficits or surpluses correlates with the magnitude of the outcome deficits or surpluses.[71] Such checks and balances are especially warranted in focus group-driven RCM analyses, where the association with outcomes is more speculative, or hypothetical. In cases where the relationship between input gaps and outcome gaps is very weak, findings are particularly vulnerable to skeptics, and legitimately so.[72]

For focus group-driven RCM, the hypotheses of resources needed for achieving desired outcomes might be validated by comparison with the resources of actual schools and districts, as estimated via cost function modeling, that actually achieve the desired outcome levels with profiles of spending and resource use that mirror that of the RCM-prescribed model.

Finally, specific to ECF modeling, alternative models should be tested for their ability to accurately predict the spending behavior of districts excluded from the model. With complex statistical models having many variables and moving parts, it is important to identify a model that is sufficiently generalizable. In this case, "sufficiently generalizable" means that the model characterizes well the patterns of relationship among conditions, students, resources, and outcomes, such that the model can be used to predict the spending levels needed to achieve desired outcomes under different conditions.[73]

Alternatives for reliability checks are also relatively straightforward. Exclusively within a focus group-driven RCM format, one might convene independent panels that are provided similar tasks (identifying resources needed to meet a particular set of outcomes X, Y, and Z under specific conditions A, B, and C) and then compare findings across panels. That is, conduct a within-method reliability check. Alternatively, one might evaluate the correlation between findings across the RCM and ECF approaches. But again, reliability is of little concern in the absence of reasonable validity checking.

Notes

1. Adam Tamburin, "House approves Haslam's tuition-free college plan," the *Tennessean*, April 13, 2017, http://www.tennessean.com/story/news/education/2017/04/13/house-approves-haslams-tuition-free-college-plan/100417716/.

2. Scott Jaskin, "New York Adopts Free Tuition," *Inside Higher Ed*, April 10, 2017, https://www.insidehighered.com/news/2017/04/10/new-york-state-reaches-deal-provide-free-tuition-suny-and-cuny-students.

3. Michael Leachman and Chris Mai, "Most states still funding schools less than before the recession," Center on Budget and Policy Priorities, October 14, 2014, https://www.cbpp.org/research/most-states-still-funding-schools-less-than-before-the-recession.

4. Bruce Baker, "School Funding Fairness in New York State: An Update for 2013–14," *Alliance for Quality Education*, January 24, 2014, http://www.aqeny.org/wp-content/uploads/2012/03/School-Funding-Fairness-in-New-York-State-An-Update-for-2013-14.pdf.

5. Bruce Baker et al, "Is School Funding Fair? A National Report Card," *Education Law Center*, January, 2017, http://www.edlawcenter.org/assets/files/pdfs/publications/National_Report_Card_2017.pdf.

6. Ibid.

7. Robert Berne and Leanna Stiefel, "The Equity of School Finance Systems over Time: the Value Judgments Inherent in Evaluation," *Educational Administration Quarterly 15*, no. 2, 1979, 14–34.

8. Robert Berne and Leanna Stiefel, *The Measurement of Equity in School Finance: Conceptual, Methodological and Empirical Dimensions* (Baltimore, MA: Johns Hopkins University Press 1984); Robert Berne and Leanna Stiefel, "Concepts of School Finance Equity:

1970 to the Present," *Equity and Adequacy in Education Finance: Issues and Perspectives* (Washington, D.C.: National Academy Press, 1984), 7–33.

9. Regarding children with disabilities, see: *Endrew F.. v. Douglas County School District RE-1*, 580 U.S. (2017). Regarding children with limited English language proficiency, see: *Issa v. School District of Lancaster*, U.S. 3rd Circuit 16-3528 (2017).

10. Bruce Baker and Preston Green, "Conceptions, measurement and application of educational adequacy standards," *AERA handbook on education policy* (New York: Routledge, 2009), 311–337; Bruce Baker and Preston Green, "Conceptions of equity and adequacy in school finance," *Handbook of Research in Education Finance and Policy*, eds Helen Ladd and Margaret Goertz, (New York: Routledge, 2008), 203–221.

11. William Clune, "The Shift from Equity to Adequacy in School Finance," *Educational Policy 8*, no. 4 (1994): 376–394.

12. William Koski and Rob Reich, "When Adequate Isn't: The Retreat from Equity in Educational Law and Policy and Why It Matters," *Emory Law Journal 56*, no.3 (2007): 545.

13. For example, the Kansas Constitution requires that the legislature "shall make suitable provision for finance of the educational interests of the state." Those educational interests are articulated in standards adopted by the state board of education (which holds independent constitutional authority for the "general supervision of public schools"). Kansas courts have repeatedly held that the legislature's obligation is to provide financing which grants all children equal opportunity to achieve those standards. *Gannon v. State*, 368 P.3d 1024, 303 Kan. 682 (2016); *Gannon v. State*, No. 113, 267 Kan. (June 28, 2016); *Montoy v. State*, 279 Kan. 817, 112 P.3d 923 (2005); *USD NO. 229 v. State*, 256 Kan. 232, 885 P.2d 1170 (1994).

14. Avidan Cover, "Is Adequacy a More Political Question Than Equality: The Effect of Standards-Based Education on Judicial Standards for Education Finance," *Cornell Journal of Law and Public Policy 11*, no. 2 (2002): 403.

15. Michael Rebell, "Safeguarding the right to a sound basic education in times of fiscal constraint," *Albany Law Review 75* (2011): 1855.

16. Bruce Baker and Preston Green, "Conceptions of Equity," 203–221; Bruce Baker and Preston Green, "Conceptions, Measurement and Application," 311–337.

17. *Rose v. Council for Better Educ., Inc.*, 790 S.W.2d 186, 60 Ky. 1289 (1989).

18. Andrew Porter and Morgan Polikoff, "Measuring Academic Readiness for College," *Educational Policy 26*, no. 3 (2012):, 394–417; Peter Conforti, "What Is College and Career Readiness? A Summary of State Definitions," *Pearson Bulletin 22* (2013): 1–4.

19. William Duncombe and John Yinger, "Performance Standards and Educational Cost Indexes: You Can't Have One Without the Other," *Equity and Adequacy in Education Finance: Issues and Perspectives 260* (1999): 261.

20. An emerging body of literature on value-added contributions of post-secondary institutions exists: Ou Liu, "Value-added assessment in higher education: A comparison of two methods," *Higher Education 61*, no. 4 (2010): 445-461; Jesse Cunha and Trey Miller, "Measuring Value-Added in Higher Education: Possibilities and Limitations in the Use of Administrative Data," *Economics of Education Review 42* (2014): 64–77; Ou Liu, "Measuring value-added in higher education: conditions and caveats–results from using

the Measure of Academic Proficiency and Progress (MAPP™),” *Assessment & Evaluation in Higher Education*, 36, no. 1 (2011): 81–94; Richard Shavelson et al, “On the practices and challenges of measuring higher education value added: the case of Colombia,” *Assessment & Evaluation in Higher Education* 41, no. 5 (2016): 695–720.

21. Bruce Baker and Preston Green, “The Politics of School Finance in the New Normal Era,” *Handbook of Education Politics and Policy* (New York: Routledge, 2014), 166.

22. Robert Rothman, “A Common Core of Readiness,” *Educational Leadership* 69, no. 7 (2012): 10–15.

23. Bruce Baker et al, “The Effect of Labor Market Information on Community College Students’ Major Choice,” (presentation, *ASSA Annual Meeting: Major Choices: Students’ Beliefs About Labor Market Outcomes, American Economic Association*, Ann Arbor, MI, April, 2017).

24. *Campaign for Fiscal Equity, Inc. v. State*, 2006 N.Y. Slip Op 8630 (2006).

25. Community Colleges Outcomes Report: the Role of Community Colleges in Post-secondary Success,” *National Student Clearinghouse Research Center*, 2017, https://student-clearinghouse.info/onestop/wp-content/uploads/Comm-Colleges-Outcomes-Report.pdf

26. Doug Shapiro et al, “Completing College: A National View of Student Attainment Rates–Fall 2008 Cohort (Signature Report No. 8),” *National Student Clearinghouse*, 2014, https://nscresearchcenter.org/wp-content/uploads/SignatureReport8.pdf; See also: Susan Dynarski, Steven Hemelt, and Joshua Hyman, “The missing manual: Using National Student Clearinghouse data to track postsecondary outcomes,” *National Bureau of Economic Research*, October, 2013, http://www-personal.umich.edu/~jmhyman/dynarski_hemelt_hyman_missing_manual.pdf

27. Christopher Jepsen, Kenneth Troske, and Paul Coomes, “The Labor-Market Returns to Community College Degrees, Diplomas, and Certificates,” *Journal of Labor Economics 32*, no. 1 (2014): 95–121; Mina Dadgar and Madeline Weiss, “Labor Market Returns to Sub-Baccalaureate Credentials: How Much Does a Community College Degree or Certificate Pay?” *Educational Evaluation and Policy Analysis* 37, no. 4 (2015): 399–418.

28. Peter Bahr, “Labor Market Returns to Community College Awards: Evidence from Michigan. A CAPSEE Working Paper,” *Center for Analysis of Postsecondary Education and Employment*, March, 2015, https://capseecenter.org/wp-content/uploads/2015/03/labor-market-returns-michigan.pdf; Christopher Jepsen, Kenneth Troske, and Paul Coomes, “The labor-market returns,” 95–121.

29. Peter Bahr, “The labor market return in earnings to community college credits and credentials in California” (working paper, Center for the Study of Higher and Postsecondary Education, University of Michigan, 2014).

30. Ibid.

31. Peter Bahr, “Classifying community colleges based on students’ patterns of use,” *Research in Higher Education 54*, no. 4 (2013): 433–460.

32. Ibid; Bruce Ingraham, “Frequent Patterns in California Community College Student Course Sequences” (dissertation, Kalmanovitz School of Education, Saint Mary’s College of California, 2016).

33. William Duncombe and John Yinger, "Measurement of Cost Differentials," *Handbook of Research in Education Finance and Policy*, eds Helen Ladd and Margaret Goertz, (New York: Routledge, 2008), 238–256.

34. Lori Taylor and William Fowler, Jr., "A Comparable Wage Approach to Geographic Cost Adjustment. Research and Development Report," *National Center for Education Statistics*, May, 2006, https://nces.ed.gov/pubs2006/2006321.pdf.

35. Matthew Andrews, William Duncombe, and John Yinger, "Revisiting economies of size in American education: are we any closer to a consensus?" *Economics of Education Review* 21, no. 3 (2002): 245–262.

36. Jay Chambers, "The Hedonic Wage Technique as a Tool for Estimating the Costs of School Personnel: A Theoretical Exposition with Implications for Empirical Analysis," *Journal of Education Finance* 6, no. 3 (1981): 330–354.

37. William Duncombe and Dan Goldhaber, "Adjusting for Geographic Differences in the Cost of Educational Provision in Maryland" (report prepared for the State of Maryland, December 31, 2003).

38. Lori Taylor and William Fowler, Jr., "A Comparable Wage Approach."

39. Jay Chambers, "The Hedonic Wage Technique," 330–354.

40. Christopher Morphew and Bruce Baker, "On the Utility of National Datasets and Resource Cost Models for Estimating Faculty Instructional Costs in Higher Education," *Journal of Education Finance* 33, no. 1 (2007): 20-48.; Susan Twombly and Barbara Townsend, "Community College Faculty What We Know and Need to Know," *Community College Review* 36, no. 1 (2008): 5–24.

41. Matthew Andrews, William Duncombe, and John Yinger, "Revisiting economies of size," 245–262.

42. Jennifer Imazeki, "Grade Dependent Costs of Education: Evidence from Illinois" (draft paper, San Diego State University, 2001).

43. Timothy Gronberg, Dennis Jansen, and Lori Taylor, "The Impact of Facilities on the Cost of Education," *National Tax Journal* 64, no. 1 (2011): 193.

44. Paul Brinkman and Larry Leslie, "Economies of Scale in Higher Education: Sixty Years of Research," *The Review of Higher Education* 10, no. 1 (1986): 1.

45. Christopher Morphew and Bruce Baker, "On the Utility of National Datasets," 20–48.

46. William Duncombe and John Yinger, "How much more does a disadvantaged student cost?" *Economics of Education Review 24*, no. 5 (2005): 513–532.

47. Katherine Michelmore and Susan Dynarski, "The Gap within the Gap: Using Longitudinal Data to Understand Income Differences in Student Achievement," *National Bureau of Economic Research*, July, 2016.

48. Bruce Baker, "Exploring the Sensitivity of Education Costs to Racial Composition of Schools and Race-Neutral Alternative Measures: A cost Function Application to Missouri," *Peabody Journal of Education* 86, no. 1 (2011): 58–83.

49. Gloria Crisp and Chryssa Delgado, "The Impact of Developmental Education on Community College Persistence and Vertical Transfer," *Community College Review* 42, no. 2 (2013): 99–117; Deryl Hatch and Crystal Garcia, "Academic Advising and the

Persistence Intentions of Community College Students in their First Weeks in College," *The Review of Higher Education* 40, no. 3 (2017): 353–390; Carlton Fong, Taylor Acee, and Claire Weinstein, "A Person-Centered Investigation of Achievement Motivation Goals and Correlates of Community College Student Achievement and Persistence," *Journal of College Student Retention: Research, Theory & Practice*, October, 2016, https://doi. org/10.1177/1521025116673374.

50. Oscar Jimenez-Castellanos, Amelia Topper, "The cost of providing an adequate education to English language learners: A review of the literature," *Review of Educational Research* 82, no. 2 (2012): 179–232.

51. Jay Chambers and Jean Wolman, "What Can We Learn from State Data Systems about the Cost of Special Education? A Case Study of Ohio," *Center for Special Education Finance*, John C. Flanagan Center at the American Institutes for Research, September, 1998.

52. Forthcoming work by Toutkoushian suggests that while first-generation students may struggle to complete four-year undergraduate programs, they may perform better (including better than their peers) in some community college settings.

53. "Study by Stella Flores Finds More Than Half of the Racial College Completion Gap Explained by Pre-College Factors," *At a Glance: News from the Steinhardt School of Culture, Education, and Human Development*, April 6, 2017, http://steinhardt.nyu.edu/site/ ataglance/2017/04/study-by-stella-flores-finds-more-than-half-of-the-racial-college-com-pletion-gap-explained-by-pre-college-factors.html; Stella Flores, Toby Park, and Domi-nique Baker, "The Racial College Completion Gap: Evidence from Texas," *The Journal of Higher Education* 88, no. 6 (2017): 1–28.

54. Ibid.

55. For a review of cost function analyses, see: William Duncombe and John Yinger, "Are Education Cost Functions Ready for Prime Time? An Examination of Their Validity and Reliability," *Peabody Journal of Education* 86, no. 1 (2011): 28–57; Timothy Gronberg, Dennis Jansen, and Lori Taylor, "The Adequacy of Educational Cost Functions: Lessons from Texas," *Peabody Journal of Education* 86, no. 1 (2011): 3–27.

56. Lars-Erik Borge, Torberg Falch, and Per Tovmo, "Public sector efficiency: the roles of political and budgetary institutions, fiscal capacity, and democratic participation," *Public Choice* 136, no. 3-4 (2008): 475–495; Shawna Grosskopf et al, "On the Determinants of School District Efficiency: Competition and Monitoring. *Journal of Urban Economics* 49, no. 3 (2001): 453–478.

57. John Sonstelie, "Aligning School Finance With Academic Standards: A Weighted-Student Formula Based on a Survey of Practitioners" (occasional paper, Public Policy Institute of California, March, 2007).

58. Overly confident efforts to suggest otherwise have been met with sharp ridicule. See: Eric Hanushek, "The Confidence Men: Selling Adequacy, Making Millions," *Education Next* 7, no. 3 (2007).

59. Jay Chambers, "The Patterns of Services Provided to Students with Disabilities," *American Institutes for Research in the Behavioral Sciences*, 1998, http://files.eric.ed.gov/ fulltext/ED425568.pdf; Jay Chambers and Jean Wolman, "What Can We Learn from State Data Systems;" Jay Chambers, "Measuring Resources in Education: From Accounting to

the Resource Cost Model Approach" (working paper, US Department of Education, Office of Educational Research and Improvement, National Center for Education Statistics, June, 1999).

60. Jay Chambers, "The Patterns of Services."

61. Christopher Morphew and Bruce Baker, "On the Utility of National Datasets," 20–48.

62. Susan Dynarski, Steven Hemelt, and Joshua Hyman, "The Missing Manual."

63. Richard Romano, Regina Losinger, and Tim Millard, "Measuring the Cost of a College Degree: A Case Study of a SUNY Community College," *Community College Review* 39, no. 3 (2011): 211–234.

64. Tommaso Agasisti and Clive Belfield, "Efficiency in the Community College Sector: Stochastic Frontier Analysis," *Tertiary Education and Management* 23, no. 3 (2017): 1–23. See also: Clive Belfield, "Measuring Efficiency in the Community College Sector. CCRC Working Paper No. 43," *Community College Research Center, Columbia University*, April, 2012, http://files.eric.ed.gov/fulltext/ED531229.pdf.

65. Recall that variations in inefficiency across local government agencies are commonly presumed to be a function of variations in (a) public monitoring, (b) fiscal capacity, and (c) competition density. Inefficiency = f(Public Monitoring, Competition, Fiscal Capacity)

66. Elisa Rassen et al, "Nuances of completion: Improving student outcomes by unpacking the numbers," *Community College Research Center, Columbia University*, April 2013, https://ccrc.tc.columbia.edu/media/k2/attachments/nuances-completion-student-outcomes-cbd.pdf; Thomas Bailey et al, "The Effects of Institutional Factors on the Success of Community College Students," *Community College Research Center, Columbia University*, February, 2005.

67. Di Xu and Madeline Trimble, "What About Certificates? Evidence on the Labor Market Returns to Non-degree Community College Awards in Two States," *Educational Evaluation and Policy Analysis* 38, no. 2 (2016): 272–292.

68. Peter Bahr et al, "A Review and Critique of the Literature on Community College Students' Transition Processes and Outcomes in Four-Year Institutions," *Higher Education: Handbook of Theory and Research* (Netherlands: Springer, 2013), 459–511; Scott Carrell and Michael Kurlaender, "Estimating the Productivity of Community Colleges in Paving the Road to Four-Year College Success," *Productivity in Higher Education* (Chicago: University of Chicago Press, 2017); Davis Jenkins and John Fink, "Tracking Transfer: New Measures of Institutional and State Effectiveness in Helping Community College Students Attain Bachelor's Degrees," *Community College Research Center, Teachers College, Columbia University*, January, 2016.

69. Peter Bahr, "Classifying Community Colleges." The categories of "Community Education Intensive," "Transfer Intensive," "Workforce Development Intensive," "High-Risk Intensive," and "Mixed Use" come from this paper.

70. Bruce Baker, "Evaluating the Reliability, Validity, and Usefulness of Education Cost Studies," *Journal of Education Finance* 32, no. 2 (2006): 170–201.; William Duncombe, "Responding to the Charge of Alchemy: Strategies for Evaluating the Reliability and

Validity of Costing-Out Research," *Journal of Education Finance* 32, no. 3 (2006): 137–169.; William Duncombe and John Yinger, "Are Education Cost Functions Ready," 28–57.

71. Bruce Baker, "Evaluating the Reliability," 170–201.; Jay Chambers, Jesse Levin, and Thomas Parrish, (2006), "Examining the Relationship between Educational Outcomes and Gaps in Funding: An Extension of the New York Adequacy Study," *Peabody Journal of Education*, 81, no. 2 (2006): 1–32.; Jay Chambers and Jesse Levin, "Determining the Cost of Providing an Adequate Education for All Students," *National Education Association*, 2009.

72. Eric Hanushek, "The Alchemy of 'Costing Out' an Adequate Education," presented at *Adequacy Lawsuits: Their Growing Impact on American Education*, Kennedy School of Government, Harvard University, October 13–14, 2005.; Eric Hanushek, "Science Violated: Spending Projections and the 'Costing Out' of an Adequate Education," *Courting Failure: How School Finance Lawsuits Exploit Judges' Good Intentions and Harm Our Children* (Palo Alto, CA: Education Next Books, 2006), 257–312.; Robert Costrell, Eric Hanushek, and Susanna Loeb, "What do cost functions tell us about the cost of an adequate education?" *Peabody Journal of Education* 83, no. 2, (2008): 198–223.

73. One can test the generalizability of alternative cost models by splitting the sample of schools or districts in a state into two groups, fitting a model to one group, and then using it to predict the spending of the other. For an application of this type of validity testing, see: Bruce Baker, "Exploring the Sensitivity of Education Costs." One can either split the sample down the middle, or into a smaller group for prediction checking, using the larger group for model-fitting. This predictive validity check is commonly referred to as the split-cross validation method. Alternatively, one can hold back subsequent years of data for prediction testing and use prior years to fit the model. See William Duncombe, "Responding to the Charge of Alchemy."

Educational Adequacy in the Twenty-First Century

ANTHONY P. CARNEVALE, ARTEM GULISH, and JEFF STROHL

D emocratic societies are rooted in the widely shared belief that all lives have value. As a result, the idea of educational adequacy in a democracy is rooted in the conviction that education's primary mission is to provide knowledge and skills sufficient to allow people to live fully, according to the standards of their time. In a democracy with a market economy—and little support for an extensive social safety net—paid work is essential to individual human flourishing. In the U.S. socio-economic system in particular, individuals are expected to attain a base of self-sufficiency. In this system, individual well-being is primarily a personal responsibility. Education is the preferred method in the United States of providing access to opportunity to attain self-sufficiency.

The goals of education in modern democratic capitalism must strike a pragmatic balance between the intrinsic value of human flourishing and the extrinsic economic value of careers that provide access to broad, middle-class earnings. And while equitable funding for community colleges to achieve adequate outcomes is an important policy objective, it is imperative to clearly and concretely establish the outcomes that post-secondary education is expected to achieve to be considered adequate. Equalized funding does not, in itself, ensure that higher education fulfills its intended role in American democracy. By the same token, we cannot begin determining an appropriate level of funding until we have a clearly defined goal of success.

Educational adequacy has evolved over the decades of American history to become an established responsibility of state governments, following a series of court cases in the United States during the 1970s and 1980s.[1] In the transition from an industrial economy to a post-industrial service economy, the role of education as a bridge to adulthood has grown from universal elementary to secondary schooling and beyond. This happened because technological advancements increased the demand for educated workers, while the nation moved from agriculture through industrialization and into the modern digital economy. The increase in workplace skill requirements over time has transformed the meaning of educational adequacy.

Educational adequacy is a broad concept that includes economic, academic, social, civic, and humanistic aspects, among others. A narrower standard of economic self-sufficiency is a necessary, but not sufficient outcome for higher education to achieve its goals. Individuals cannot live fully in their time if they are living under a bridge. The modern economy now demands a workforce with education and training beyond high school. The day when high school was enough is slipping; today, only three out of ten jobs for high school workers are fulfilling the promise of economic self-sufficiency, and almost solely for men.[2] Clearly, high school is not adequate in a modern economy where over 60 percent of all jobs require at least some postsecondary education beyond high school,[3] as do 80 percent of good jobs that support middle-class lifestyles.[4]

This leads us to argue that a two-year degree is on its way to becoming the minimum education needed to be self-sufficient, and thereby the minimum adequate education must be framed as high school plus two years of college. To help policymakers, colleges, and the public make the right choices, the post-high school education must be accompanied by a new standard for measuring educational adequacy.

We propose a new concrete standard for educational adequacy focused on the demonstrated capacity of postsecondary programs to provide economic self-sufficiency to graduates, based on the earnings of students who complete educational programs. We acknowledge that reality is complex, and so it will be necessary to adjust this standard in applying it to the real world. Nevertheless, we view it as an important starting point.

In order to be educationally adequate, a postsecondary program must provide its graduates with economic self-sufficiency. We propose that, to be recognized as leading to such self-sufficiency, a program must leave its graduates earning more than $35,000 per year ten years after they have completed it. Over that ten-year period, that program also must provide its graduates with a sufficient earnings premium, compared to the earnings of workers with only a high-school diploma, to cover the program's total cost to the student. The program's total cost includes its direct cost, as measured by net price, and its opportunity cost, as measured by the student's forgone earnings during the period that the student was enrolled in the program.

The earnings figure of $35,000 ten years after graduation is not a goal that programs should strive upward to reach, but rather a floor through which they must not fall. It is expected that many graduates will exceed that figure by far, as plenty now do: 67 percent of workers with associate degrees and 85 percent with bachelor's degrees now exceed those earnings after ten years.[5] But, it is also expected that with adequate funding a significant portion of a program's graduates—a precise level to be determined—must not fall below that earnings level, lest the program be deemed not adequate. Furthermore, this figure is based on averages—average cost of living, earnings premiums, and so on—and when applied should be adjusted to take into account regional variations in the labor market; it will need to be adjusted upward in high-cost, high-wage states, and downward in states with low cost of living.

Importantly, the annual earnings figure of $35,000 is also the threshold into the middle class. Americans who devote two years of their lives to postsecondary education, and then spend a decade in the labor market, should at least be able to attain this standard of self-sufficiency; if they cannot, then this raises serious questions about education's role and value in a democratic capitalist society.

As a practical matter, this outcomes-based approach to defining educational adequacy helps create an incentive structure in postsecondary education. For colleges, it offers potential rewards for finding efficiencies in achieving desired outcomes, while leaving them the autonomy to make their own decisions about how to bring about those efficiencies. Several factors—including high levels of variability in educational practice by program and institution, as well as variation in individual student needs—complicate efforts to come up with a single common adequacy cost across programs. But, in order to begin the process of identifying a variety of cost structures associated with different programs, we must begin by identifying a common endpoint of what constitutes success.

Focusing on student earnings-related outcomes tied to economic self-sufficiency creates an incentive mechanism, much like the efficiency drivers seen as the foundation of a perfectly competitive market. In the economic market model, efficiency gains occur because firms are constrained by a market-clearing cost and the desire for profit. In this model, firms take cost to the lowest point achievable, given present technology; internal process is irrelevant, as long as the cost structure is sustainable, given the market-clearing price. Although we acknowledge that higher education is not the same as an unregulated market, we suggest that, for postsecondary education, economic self-sufficiency should serve a similar function as the market-clearing price, setting expectation for programs of study to achieve this goal with a sustainable cost structure and rewarding efficiencies attained in the process.

Of course, setting rigorous goals without providing necessary resources is a recipe for failure, as we have seen at the K–12 level.[6] That is why, in addition to outlining the desired outcomes in this report, The Century Foundation's Working Group on Community College Financial Resources will separately be making recommendations on how best to estimate the level of investment required to meet these goals.

This paper begins with a brief history of the co-evolution of educational adequacy and democratic capitalism. This will help the reader understand how education has gained prominent role the U.S. society and how the notions of what is adequate education changed as the economy and social institutions have evolved. The report then discusses the difficulty of defining education adequacy in a rapidly changing economy and educational system. It then presents a simplified approach to calculating a standard for measuring educational adequacy based on the earnings of graduates, to give the reader a concrete grasp of how these principles can be applied. At the same time, the authors acknowledge the need to deal with numerous complexities if our concept of economic self-sufficiency is to be applied to real world conditions, and understand that policymakers and practitioners will need to make additional adjustments for this model to fit their particular circumstances. This report ends with a discussion about some of the issues that will need to be grappled with, and suggests that the answers to many questions will need to be based on very subjective decisions, or on social consensus.

The Co-Evolution of Educational Adequacy and Democratic Capitalism

Educational adequacy is an amorphous target. It expands in size and changes shape with the growth in social and economic complexity that occurs in democratic capitalism. The idea of educational adequacy is deeply rooted in the original historic tension between democracy and capitalism. The idea that there needs to be some measure of adequacy in the provision of education and social welfare has helped prevent a breakdown in the social contract between democracy and capitalism in the years since the industrial revolution dawned.

During the eighteenth and nineteenth centuries, democratic ideas grew alongside economic markets. Capitalism and democracy were allies in their revolt against the economic and political bondage imposed by feudalism. At the same time, however, they remained in some ways natural antagonists, the tensions between them driven, in part, by irreconcilable ideas. Democratic citizenship presumes equality. Market economies, however, are driven by the economic inequality necessary to motivate work effort, talent, and entrepreneurship, and they inherently produce lopsided accumulations of wealth and investment capital in private hands.

The Nonmonetary Value of General Elementary Education as the Baseline Adequacy Standard

Alfred Marshall was one of the most influential economists of the late-nineteenth century. Speaking at the Cambridge Reform Club in 1873, he offered one of the first arguments attempting to square equality among individuals with the inequality and amoral risk inherent in markets. He argued that capitalism and democracy were antagonists in theory, but also could be allies in practice. He argued further that the contradictions between democracies and markets could be reduced if markets would become the paymaster of a constant expansion in publicly funded education and social services.

"The question," Marshall said, "is not whether all men will ultimately be equal—that they certainly will not—but whether progress may not go on steadily, if slowly, till, by occupation at least, every man is a gentleman . . . [who values] education and leisure more than the 'mere increase of wages and material comforts.'"[7] Marshall's notion of educational adequacy in the early years of democratic capitalism referred to the nonmonetary value of what we now think of as elementary education—the kind of elementary education that encouraged the populace to "steadily accept the private and public duties of citizenship."[8] He assumed that a basic general education would also be a universal common experience for the citizenry, rather than a sorting device for allocating economic opportunity.

In Marshall's day, education had relatively little significance in the economic sorting of the broad mass of society. The vast majority of people learned the specific skills for their occupations in their homes or on the job, not in grade schools, colleges, or universities. Marshall did not foresee that a long revolution in the valuing of human capital would make education—and the access it provides to highly paid occupations—a key basis for determining who accumulates wealth and power. He had no idea that, by the twenty-first century, a massive system of colleges and universities—with varying degrees of selectivity in admissions—would serve to stratify American society by race and class.

The notion of educational adequacy has expanded over time, its growth driven by increasing social and economic complexity.[9] In different national contexts, it has expanded at different rates and taken on different shapes. The history of educational adequacy in the United States parallels the evolution of democratic capitalism in Europe, but with notable differences, particularly concerning the nation's diversity. The European nations have historically been much more demographically homogeneous, which made it easier for their central governments to expand both their welfare states and their education systems.[10]

In the United States, a historical commitment to a general elementary curriculum for youth arose from efforts at the local level, and the education system as a whole generally evolved alongside economic and societal change. To meet the demands of workplaces and broader society, public education on the American continent went from being almost nonexistent in the seventeenth and eighteenth centuries to providing universal access to schools at the elementary level and then the secondary level by the mid-twentieth century. In the twenty-first century, it must now expand to encompass at least two years of postsecondary education.

In the colonial days of the early 1600s, public education primarily consisted of grammar schools for boys. Then, as the needs of the country changed around the middle of nineteenth century, age-based grades were introduced, along with standardization of public school curricula. By 1918, compulsory public schooling had been introduced in each of the forty-eight states.[11]

The movement toward universal high school began in New England, but came to full flower among the nation's most homogenous white, protestant populations, in places such as Iowa and Nebraska.[12] Demographic diversity was often a barrier to the expansion of educational adequacy nationwide, then and now.[13] Voters were never happy to support expansion in the welfare state or education for people who looked different or went to different churches. In addition, the U.S. Constitution, written long before education played a significant social and economic role, lacks any reference to a federal right to education,[14] such as those incorporated in constitutions subsequently drafted by other nations. At the same time, our diversity—and our successive waves of immigration—also acted as a spur, leading to calls for a common elementary curriculum that would have the assimilation of a diverse population as one of its chief goals.

The "common school" in the early United States offered a general academic education devoted to cultural and moral precepts, as well as the three Rs (reading, writing, and arithmetic). Its teachings were deemed adequate in that they were "education for life," not as specific education for work. Training for specific jobs took place in the spaces of everyday life, such as the home or the workplace. In the eighteenth and early nineteenth centuries, new waves of immigration, combined with an abundance of land and chronic labor shortages in towns as well as in the countryside, created powerful incentives for adults to engage in informal learning. For most non-Hispanic white men, our early history provided opportunities for individual striving as boundless as the western frontier. The exploitation of the West made America a boomtown for the fraternity of white men, who joined enthusiastically in the commerce and politics of the time.

The extraordinary vigor of American politics—with voter participation rates generally above 90 percent among the franchised population of white men—helped give rise to the equally extraordinary proliferation of newspapers and spread of literacy in the first half of the nineteenth century. This was America's first information revolution—the new democracy and unfettered capitalism in print. Between 1790 and 1835, while the population grew from 3.9 million to 15 million, the number of newspapers increased eleven-fold, from 106 to 1,258. By 1840, total weekly newspaper circulation in the United States, with a population of 17 million, exceeded that of all Europe, which had 233 million people.[15]

According to historian Robert Wiebe:

> To utilize this network, Americans made themselves literate. With little help from public schools, democratic communication sent literacy rates soaring between 1800 and 1840: from around 75 percent of adult whites to around 95 percent in the north and from around 50 percent to around 80 percent in the south.[16]

The Economic Value of Career-Related Education Becomes a Key Consideration in Defining Adequacy

The notion of adequacy became more complicated as the nation moved toward urbanization and industrialization in the latter half of the nineteenth century. The changes flowed both from the bottom up and from the top down. From the bottom, the elementary school curriculum became more practical, with a shift from character building and godliness toward a stronger emphasis on the more utilitarian three Rs. At the top, the recognition of elite knowledge as economic capital gave us the Morrill Act of 1862, which promoted the modernization of agriculture and industry through science and engineering.[17]

At the elementary level, the new pragmatism balanced basic skills for practical application with character development. At the university level, a new balance arose between knowledge as economic capital and the more abstract liberal-arts curriculum. The Morrill Act sought to promote practical disciplines "without excluding . . . classical studies."[18] The pragmatic turn in the notion of educational adequacy also caused it to assume a new dualism: balancing the interests of the economy and the state with individuals' interest in human flourishing. Over the next century and a half, education became a major determinant of an individual's wages and material comfort. Education institutions promoted human flourishing in a nonmonetary sense, but they also recognized that flourishing in a capitalist economy requires a sufficient education to obtain gainful employment at living wages. This dualistic concept of educational adequacy under democratic capitalism continues to influence our thinking today. In our effort to determine standards for educational adequacy, both theory and practice continue to be haunted by the tension between education intended for life in a democracy, and education intended for work in a capitalist economy. This tension shows up in a number of major debates in education, including arguments that pit the economic value of education against its nonmonetary value; general education against specific education; academic learning against applied learning; and vocationalism against professionalism. These dualities don't align neatly. Both general and specific education, for example, have economic and nonmonetary value. The same is true for the intuitive distinction between applied and academic learning. Each, as John Dewey explains, is complement and substitute along the continuum of human experience.[19]

These tensions can spark acrimonious debates over educational adequacy, because historically what has been at stake are varying degrees of opportunity in a demographically diverse society and class-based market economy. Over the long term, social and economic change has produced demand for education to be increasingly equally distributed, for both its economic and nonmonetary value. The expansion of access to education, however, has always been fraught with questions of social and economic justice, with equity issues tending to arise as the process of change leads to new forms of academic tracking. Periods of expansion of education access in the name of educational adequacy are followed by periods of increased stratification through tracking and variation in quality. As a rule, educational adequacy moves forward while preserving educational tracking for the least advantaged, thereby hindering upward mobility and preserving the intergenerational reproduction of social and economic privilege.

A pivotal moment in the expansion of educational adequacy was the high school movement of the early twentieth century. As the industrial economy started ramping up, vocational education started becoming more widespread. High schools increasingly shifted their focus to providing students with the literacy and numeracy skills needed to take up assembly line jobs in the burgeoning number of factories and plants across the nation.[20] Vocational schools offered additional technical training for more-specialized industrial positions.[21]

In the 1910 school year, only 9 percent of seventeen-year-olds graduated high school. By 1950, that share rose to more than 50 percent.[22] Because of the high school movement, the United States had far exceeded the European systems of democratic capitalism in the provision of general education. Notably, however, the growth of public high schools led to a growing belief that four-year colleges represented the gold standard in educational adequacy. The number of higher-education institutions in the U.S. rose from 977 in 1900 to 1,851 in 1950.[23]

Mostly, the movement toward universal access to high school was a victory for general education, and for much of this time, the purpose of high school was seen as educating students for life and citizenship, rather than as preparation for college. But throughout the history of thinking about educational adequacy, new efforts at stratification followed efforts to provide universal access as surely as night follows day. A milestone in the stratification process came with the federal government's enactment of the Smith-Hughes National Vocational Education Act of 1917, which established vocational education in "agriculture, trades and industry, and homemaking."[24] It isolated vocational education, intended to prepare students for a job following graduation, from the rest of the general education curriculum in most high school settings. In doing so, it isolated working-class and poor youth, and young women consigned to homemaking, from the general curriculum in high school and, as a result, limited access to college and the workforce.

By the end of World War II, the contours of the current adequacy debate were beginning to come into focus. The demand for adult education increased substantially as veterans found themselves having to develop higher skill levels to enter the workforce, a need recognized with the passage of the GI Bill in 1944. Junior, community, and technical colleges stepped up to meet returning veterans' growing education and training needs.[25] After World War II, high school also started becoming a mass institution and increasingly compulsory in all fifty states.[26]

Adequacy for Whom? The Modern Stratification of Educational Adequacy by Class and Demographic Groups

By the end of World War II, a new equilibrium needed to be found in the bargain between capitalism and democracy, and the role of educational adequacy needed to be established as part of that bargain. With fascism defeated, the contest between the victors—the communists on one side and the democratic capitalists on the other—began in earnest, as the Cold War dawned.

In 1949, Thomas Humphrey (T. H.) Marshall (no relation to Alfred), a prominent social scientist whose work focused on the subject of citizenship and related areas of civil, political, and social rights, updated the original bargain between capitalism and democracy in a lecture commemorating Alfred Marshall's classic formulation. T. H. Marshall essentially doubled down on Alfred Marshall's 1873 argument, asserting that the equality implicit in democratic citizenship implied "a modicum of economic welfare and security" sufficient "to share to the full in the social heritage and to live the life of a civilized being according to the standards prevailing in the society."[27] T. H. Marshall went on to explain that the institutions most closely connected with this notion of equality in capitalist economies "are the educational system and the social services."[28]

His lecture was seminal because it became the widely recognized summary argument for the massive expansion in both public education and the welfare state as an alternative to Soviet and Chinese communism after World War II.[29]

T. H. Marshall 's 1949 speech would prove to be prescient. He worried that the education solution to the problem of inequality in market economies had developed flaws since the time of Alfred Marshall's original lecture in 1873. He ruminated over how education's role as a mediating force between citizenship and markets increasingly was compromised by the growing alignment between education and elite occupational preparation. Education made everyone equal as citizens, but those with the most education, especially in lucrative fields of study at the college level, could accumulate wealth and power to a greater degree. T. H. Marshall fretted that industrial society had "been accused of regarding elementary education solely as a means of providing capitalist employers with more valuable workers, and higher education merely as an instrument to increase the power of the nation to compete with its industrial rivals." He continued, "As we all know, education today is closely linked with occupation, and . . . [through] its relations with occupational structure . . . operates as an instrument of social stratification." The impact of a K–20 education becomes especially powerful because it is frontloaded in the life cycle: "The ticket obtained on leaving school or college is for a life journey."[30]

T. H. Marshall foresaw the growing contradiction between education as an equalizer and education as a source of inequality. This contradiction has only become more pronounced over time, with the strengthening of the sequential alignment between access to higher education, choice of field of study, occupational choice, and individual earnings. Over time, education—especially postsecondary education and training—has become a double-edged sword, providing opportunity while also protecting privilege. The postwar postsecondary system was a boon to striving white baby boomers, but it also fostered stratification that reinforced class and racial privilege.

In the postwar era, the notion of educational adequacy fragmented as the United States emerged as a global colossus and the defender of the free world. A single definition of adequacy came to be replaced by an elitist hierarchy of definitions, an increasingly selective higher-education apparatus at its peak. T. H. Marshall was ahead of his time when he worried that educational adequacy was becoming detached from its democratic mission and more "an instrument to increase the power of the nation to compete with its industrial rivals."[31]

During this time, decision-makers agreed that the United States needed college-educated leaders and high school-educated followers, along with a reliable system for producing them. Not surprisingly, Americans tended to agree that society's leaders ought to be self-selected based on merit. James Bryant Conant, then president of Harvard, emerged as the man with the plan for how such selection should occur.[32] Although a Protestant New Englander, he was not from one of the region's better families—he was raised in Dorchester, a working-class Boston neighborhood. He believed talent ought to trump social standing. He wanted to build an education system that mined the nation's best and brightest, wherever they came from, in a way that was both fairer and more efficient than the WASP (White Anglo-Saxon Protestant) old-boy networks that had been in place for two centuries. Determined to find the next Einstein out somewhere behind a plow, he wanted to build a selective education system that elevated those with innate academic talent. His goal was to create a governing class consisting of the best and brightest, one worthy of a world economic power and able to fight the growing threat of communism.[33]

Conant proposed setting aside an educational elite consisting solely of men from wealthy backgrounds and replacing it with an elite drawn from the masses through the identification of academic talent. He called for the education system to develop the new meritocracy. He proposed using the Scholastic Aptitude Test (SAT) to select the best and brightest for admissions to the selective colleges that would prepare them to lead and serve. His vision could be seen as an updated, secular version of the Calvinist urge to build an orderly world run by the elect. In effect, he intended to take the religious notion of the elect and institutionalize it in secular terms, in the form of government by a natural aristocracy.[34]

To construct the new sorting system, Conant proposed reinventing the education pipeline. The nation already had grade schools and high schools in place, even if barely half of students finished high school in the 1940s. He laid out his plan for a new sorting system in his 1959 book, *The American High School Today*, a number-one bestseller. In it, he proposed the creation of comprehensive high schools with two separate tracks: one for the majority of students, who required vocational training, and another for the minority of students with IQs over 115, who would be groomed for selective colleges and leadership positions in the governing meritocracy.[35]

Conant wrote to a prospective staff member, "I wish to identify the schools which are doing a good job in preparing for college the youth with IQs above 115, but at the same time are handling adequately the vocational courses and schools where the academic group is not more than 50 percent."[36] There is little doubt about where he stood on the effects of nature versus nurture. He believed that intelligence was innate, fixed at birth, and one-dimensional. "The percentage of those who had a delayed intellectual awakening," he thought "was too small to bother with."[37]

The new elite may have been narrow, but it was open to talent at a time when the looming Cold War had made the need to find the best and the brightest a national emergency. John Kenneth Galbraith urged Conant to make a "stern attack on home and motherhood" if he hoped to avail the nation of its female talent. Conant replied:

> My case for the recommendations for the academically talented was very largely based on national need. If we were not living in such a grim world, I doubt I should advocate the high school program I recommend in my report. From the academically talented will come the future doctors, engineers, scientists and scholars, as well as . . . business executives. . . . These professional people will be 97% men.[38]

Conant wanted to limit access to selective colleges to high school students in the top 15 to 20 percent in terms of aptitude. He was concerned, however, that minorities and the poor might become easy targets for the communists. He said as much in his 1961 book, *Slums and Suburbs*,[39] in which he proposed liberal and professional education for the best and indoctrination for the rest. He wrote:

> I do not have to remind the reader that the fate of freedom hangs very much in the balance. Our success against the spread of communism in no small measure depends on the successful operation of our own free society. These young people are my chief concern especially when they are pocketed together in large numbers within the confines of the big city slum. . . . What can words like "freedom," "liberty" and "equality of opportunity" mean to these young people? With what kind of zeal and dedication can we expect them to withstand the relentless pressures of communism?[40]

Conant's meritocratic system got a huge boost from the Cold War and from an economy that continued to demand more college education. He proposed his system as a means to fight the communists in the same way his Puritan ancestors promoted literacy as a means to make the scriptures accessible and thereby fend off false prophets and papism. His 1948 best seller, *Education in a Divided World: The Function of the Public Schools in Our Unique Society*,[41] had articulated the establishment view that education was the meritocratic "engine of democracy," critical to an upwardly mobile, well-informed, economically powerful society that ultimately would defeat communism in the global contest of cultures.

In Conant's vision of the comprehensive high school, 80 to 85 percent of students were not college material, and represented the future members of the working class. They needed courses like English, history, and civics, but only to acquaint them with the individualist heritage found at the root of the American Creed, so they would reject the alternative offered by communism. Conant believed these non-college-bound students also needed to be enrolled in vocational programs that would lead them to have economic autonomy and a stake in the capitalist system.

Those in the 15 to 20 percent chosen for the meritocratic elite would continue on to liberal arts colleges for more general education. They then would move on to graduate and professional schools, to hone their ability to apply knowledge.

Conant's vision was not just steeped in an American idea that traces back to the Puritans. It also evoked a Western idea that traces all the way back to Plato's concept of a government by philosopher kings, who alone truly understood the true, the good, and the beautiful. Although a consistent strand in American thought, it is most famously associated with Thomas Jefferson. In 1813, Jefferson wrote to Adams:

> There is a natural aristocracy among men. The grounds of this are virtue and talents. . . The natural aristocracy I consider as the most precious gift of nature for the instruction, the trusts, and the government of society. . . . May we not even say that the form of government is the best which provides the most effectually for a pure selection of these natural aristocracy into offices of governments?[42]

John Adams' return letter was prophetic:

> Your distinction between natural and artificial aristocracy does not appear to me well founded . . . both artificial aristocracy, and monarchy, and civil, military, political and hierarchical despotism have all grown out of the natural aristocracy of virtue and talents. We, to be sure, are far remote from this. Many hundred years must roll away before we shall be corrupted.[43]

The argument between Jefferson and Adams still applies. There is little doubt, however, that Jefferson's perspective became the organizing principle for American education in the latter half of the twentieth century.

The hierarchical concept of educational adequacy has been challenged, primarily because it became the source of race- and class-based tracking.

As the importance of education grew alongside the nation and its industry, people became more mindful that educational inequity existed, with the differences in quality between racially segregated public schools standing as a glaring example. Legal challenges to the segregationists' argument that public schools can be "separate but equal" led to the Supreme Court's 1954 *Brown v. The Board of Education of Topeka* ruling, which stated:

> [E]ducation is perhaps the most important function of state and local governments. Compulsory school attendance laws and the great expenditures for education both demonstrate our recognition of the importance of education to our democratic society. It is required in the performance of our most basic public responsibilities, even service in the armed forces. It is the very foundation of good citizenship. Today it is a principal instrument in awakening the child to cultural values, in preparing him for later professional training, and in helping him to adjust normally to his environment. In these days, it is doubtful that any child may reasonably be expected to succeed in life if he is denied the opportunity of an education.[44]

Yet in continued legal battles over state spending on education, courts have held that no right to educational adequacy exists in the U.S. Constitution. In the U.S. Supreme Court's landmark 1973 *San Antonio v. Rodriguez* decision, the majority of justices made this point clear. The majority opinion explicitly stated: "Education, of course, is not among the rights afforded explicit protection under our Federal Constitution. Nor do we find any basis for saying it is implicitly so protected."[45]

This declaration in *San Antonio v. Rodriguez* stood on the wrong side of history. It starkly opposed the American belief system's reliance on education as the foundation of a functioning and fair democracy.

Although the *Rodriguez* plaintiffs failed, other litigation challenging school financing as inequitable met with some limited success, bringing about increases in minimum spending levels to help close spending gaps.

The success of such challenges was limited, however. By the early 1980s, the defenders of the status quo were prevailing most of the time. They easily beat back general appeals to state constitutions' due-process and equal-protection clauses, appeals easily rejected based on the Supreme Court's reasoning in *San Antonio v. Rodriguez*. The cases had some success in creating spending floors, but no luck in lowering spending ceilings. They suffered from their inability to establish clear links between differences in funding levels and differences in educational outcomes and quality. Financial equity is difficult to define without some sense and measure of sufficiency for a particular purpose.

A turning point came with the Kentucky Supreme Court's 1989 decision in *Rose v. Council for Better Education*. It marked a move away from the narrow focus on equity in K–12 financing and a return to a standard of sufficiency based on educational outcomes and the purposes of K–12 education. In its *Rose v. Council for Better Education* ruling, the Kentucky court invalidated the entire state system of education. The court then went on to hold that an efficient education would be measured by its sufficiency in achieving a broad set of learning and labor market student outcomes after graduating from the K–12 system:

i.   Sufficient oral and written communication skills to enable students to function in a complex and rapidly changing civilization;

ii. Sufficient knowledge of economic, social and political systems to enable the student to make informed choices;

iii. Sufficient understanding of governmental processes to enable the student to understand the issues that affect his or her community, state, and nation;

iv. Sufficient self-knowledge and knowledge of his or her mental and physical wellness;

v.   Sufficient grounding in the arts to enable each student to appreciate his or her cultural and historical heritage;

vi. Sufficient training or preparation for advanced training in either academic or vocational fields so as to enable each child to choose and pursue life work intelligently; and

vii. Sufficient levels of academic or vocational skills to enable public school students to compete favorably with their counterparts in surrounding states, in academics or in the job market.[46]

Beginning with the Kentucky case, the tide turned. Plaintiffs began prevailing in most cases, mainly because the courts' focus was shifted from broad equal-protection and due-process claims to financial equity in complying with specific provisions in state constitutions related to states' obligation to bring about certain educational outcomes. In this new phase of defining educational adequacy, "adequate" meant the achievement of some purpose—and the provision of adequate resources to get there. It presumed educational attainment and achievement attached to some level of functioning in society.

At the national level, the shift in focus from equity in K–12 finance to adequacy in functional outcomes had already begun, with the publication in 1983 of the report *A Nation at Risk*[47] and the standards-based K–12 reform movement that it sparked. The school-finance reform movement that began with the *Rodriguez* case sought to establish quantity-based financial criteria attached to the cost of inputs. The standards-based reform movement, by contrast, has sought at the state and national level to assess educational adequacy using quality-based criteria that focus on the cost of achieving functional outcomes.

The New Adequacy Standard: General Preparation and Career Exposure in K–12 Education Leading to Postsecondary Education and Training for All

As the economy's skill requirements grew in the latter half of the nineteenth century and early twentieth century, K–12 education came to be seen as increasingly important in providing access to gainful employment.

Americans had gradually accepted the idea that education through high school was key to individual flourishing and the proper functioning of a democratic system of government. The growing public support for K–12 education had led the nation to build on compulsory education through high school as a right of the people and the responsibility of the states. By the mid-twentieth century, the United States had a robust system of universal public secondary education and Americans were the most educated people in the world.[48] By 1950, only 6.2 percent of Americans had college degrees[49] and the vast majority of American workers who joined the middle class in the postwar industrial economy did so with a high school diploma or less.

The nation's strong educational achievements during the middle of twentieth century helped fuel the industrial economy and helped the United States cement its status as the most prosperous nation on earth, with robust economic growth and declining levels of inequality.[50] In response to the Soviet Union's 1957 launch of *Sputnik*, the Earth's first artificial satellite, the United States scrambled to strengthen secondary education further. The National Defense Education Act of 1958 provided new funds to improve American schools and to promote postsecondary education, focusing heavily on science and technology.[51] Later, the Elementary and Secondary Education Act (ESEA) of 1965 further solidified federal funding for K–12 education.[52]

James Bryant Conant's hierarchy of educational adequacy, which had held up pretty well through the 1960s, began to fall apart with the decline of the blue-collar economy in the 1970s. Various trends during that decade began transforming an industrial-production economy into a post-industrial, knowledge- and skill-based service economy.[53] As a result of such developments, the share of the workforce employed by production industries—such as manufacturing, construction and natural resources—declined from nearly 50 percent of all workers in 1947 to just 19 percent in 2016. At the same time, the share employed in high-skill service industries—including health care services, consulting and business services, education services, and government services—grew from 28 percent of the workforce in 1947 to 46 percent in 2016.[54] During this period, the share of jobs held by workers with a high school diploma or less dropped to 34 percent, while the share of jobs held by workers with some education or training beyond high school grew to 66 percent.[55] This skill-biased technological change has pushed the college wage premium—the difference between the average annual pay of college graduates and that of high-school graduates—from 40 percent in the 1970s to 67 percent today.[56]

In the 1970s, most American workers had a high school diploma or less, and almost a third were high school dropouts. Most of these high-school graduates and high-school dropouts were in the middle class. Since the 1980s, the difference in lifetime earnings between someone with a college degree and someone with a high-school diploma has doubled to an average difference of $1 million, even as the number of college graduates has quadrupled.[57] This accounts for 70 percent of the increase in earnings inequality since the 1970s. Between 1970 and 2007, the share of high school graduates who reached the middle class declined from 46 percent to 33 percent.[58] Only three out of ten workers with no more than a high school education, mostly men, are still able to reach the middle class.[59]

By the 1980s, skills and the economic competitiveness of American education moved to the forefront of policy discussions. *A Nation at Risk* had sounded an alarm about the urgent need to reform the nation's mediocre education system. The report faulted the system for leaving too many young people without the skills to earn a living, which placed the country in a weak position to compete economically with other nations around the globe. Other countries were quickly overtaking the United States in terms of educational attainment and quality of education.[60]

The national response to *A Nation at Risk* was the signal moment in the shift to a K–12 system that sought to provide general education for all, and the shift to the view that postsecondary education represented a legitimate standard of adequacy. Helping it capture attention, *A Nation at*

Risk contained breathless prose and a narrative that paralleled Conant's nationalist call to arms:

> Our nation is at risk. Our once unchallenged preeminence in commerce, industry, science, and technological innovation is being overtaken by competitors throughout the world . . . [W]hat is at risk is the promise first made on this continent . . . that all children . . . can hope to attain . . . gainful employment.[61]

The shift to a new social and economic standard of educational adequacy pegged to some form of postsecondary education and training, rather than just a high-school diploma, spelled the end of traditional vocational education in high school. The "college for all" mantra overtook the American high school curriculum. Following the publication of A Nation at Risk, high-school curriculums universally became more academically rigorous, featuring more course requirements in math, science, and the liberal arts. Home economics and vocational education fell by the wayside.

A *Nation at Risk* recommended that states strengthen their high school graduation requirements to include the "Five New Basics": four years of English, three years each of mathematics, science, and social studies, and half a year of computer studies.[62] The new model tends to focus on academic requirements and career exposure through a limited number of Career and Technical Education (CTE) courses, as well as experiences such as internships. The new high school claims to make students "college and career ready," but there is very little relationship between high school curriculums and college majors, let alone career pathways.

In the 1990s, policymakers increasingly concentrated on strengthening the connection between education and jobs by connecting classroom academic learning with work-based professional learning. School-to-work initiatives designed to strengthen the pathway from secondary education to employment increasingly gained momentum, and were at the core of the School-to-Work Opportunities Act of 1994.[63]

In the decades since the publication of *A Nation at Risk*, such trends have only become starker. Compared to 1982, the share of high school students now who take the Five New Basics requirements is five times higher, encompassing nearly a quarter of all students.[64] On the other hand, the share of students who take at least three career-related courses has fallen from roughly a third to about a fifth of high school students.[65] Of the roughly twenty-seven required high school credits, twenty-one credits are dedicated to academic requirements.[66] High schools, once looked to for the preparation of the vast majority of students for the jobs not requiring a college degree, are now responsible primarily for preparing people for college. American colleges have become the de facto workforce development system. They are expected to provide students career preparation, either through a mix of specific and general education, or through programs that focus narrowly on specific education and culminate in certificates, industry-based certifications, or other vocational credentials. Little career preparation takes place in today's high school, and youth employment programs account for just pennies out of every $100 America spends on educating and training young people.

In the twenty-first century, the policy conversation has shifted from envisioning two pathways, "college or careers," to envisioning an increasingly interconnected concept, "college and careers."[67] Education and training beyond high school is regarded now as essential for individuals to secure an economically viable career with which they can support themselves and their families.[68] College increasingly is being viewed as one of the few pathways for individuals to gain job-related skills that lead to employment and competitive, family-sustaining wages.

The college-for-all rhetoric has conditioned the public to believe that high school is no longer an acceptable minimum for an adequate education. Economic change has cemented this consensus in place. The 2005 National Education Summit on High Schools recognized this reality when it stated, "It is no longer enough to ensure that all students are proficient at each grade level. It is time for every student to graduate both proficient and prepared for the real demands of work and postsecondary learning."[69]

The 2006 Commission on the Future of Higher Education, commonly known as the Spellings Commission, finally arrived at the inevitable end game of education reform by endorsing postsecondary education for all. It argued: "[E]veryone needs a postsecondary education. Indeed, we have seen ample evidence that access to postsecondary education is increasingly vital to an individual's economic security."[70]

President Obama's administration followed suit with his first address to a joint session of Congress, when he said, "I ask every American to commit to at least one year or more of higher education or career training. This can be community college or a four-year school; vocational training or an apprenticeship."[71]

As was the case of the shift from grade school to high school in the twentieth century, the twenty-first century shift from high school to postsecondary education and training has resulted in greater access to higher levels of education. Regretfully, in an echo of the past, the latest expansion of access has been followed by stratification and tracking. The nation advocates access to postsecondary education and training "for all," but it increasingly relegates less-advantaged students to overcrowded, underfunded, open-access two-year and four-year colleges, along with the nondegreed sector. The consequences, as measured by social and economic outcomes, are predictably negative.[72]

In another echo of the past, the twenty-first century shift in the adequacy standard—from high school to postsecondary education and training—has produced a great divide between the advocates of degrees and the advocates of a more specific, career-focused approach. In the evolution of educational adequacy, social and economic justice issues have constantly come up. These issues have centered on access to higher levels of educational attainment and the mix of general and specific education among the more and less advantaged. As a rule, progress has been marked by a dynamic in which our society's advantaged members lead the way in terms of overall access to the richest mix of general and specific education at the bachelor's degree level and to specific graduate education in elite fields of study.

The nation's past shift from universal attainment of grade school to universal attainment of high school initially relegated the less advantaged to vocational preparation and the advantaged to college. Similarly, the current shift from universal high school to universal postsecondary access relegates the least advantaged to sub-baccalaureate education and training, with an emphasis on vocational preparation for middle-wage jobs.

At this early juncture, it is probably safe to say that there is still a theoretical and aspirational consensus on postsecondary adequacy—it is centered on the mix of general and specific education typical of American two-year and four-year degrees, and holds the bachelor's degree as the gold standard. The call for more postsecondary education demands that degrees have both economic and non-economic value. The public tends to agree with experts' views on this front. Most want degrees for themselves or their children. Growing numbers agree that a high-school diploma is no longer sufficient to meet a twenty-first century standard for human capital development in modern economics, or to flourish in a more diverse, complex, turbulent world.[73] It has become commonplace to assert that the bachelor's degree is more and more the gold standard for the transition from youthful dependency to adult independence as a worker and as a fully empowered individual and citizen. Others, who shy away from calling for a bachelor's degree for all, nonetheless, call for at least an associate's degree for all, suggesting that "fourteen has become the new twelve" in our thinking about the minimum number of years of education needed.[74] The associate's degree has growing support in the political arena, because it is seen as having legitimacy, with the preferred mix of general and specific education characteristic of American degrees. Also, to some extent, it provides a pathway to the bachelor's degree.

This distinctive commitment to the mix of general and specific education is the liberal education, which is the characteristic signature of

American college degrees. Both the two-year and four-year college degrees at the core of the American system are composed of fields of study. Classes in those fields of study represent 30 to 40 percent of the academic credits in the curriculum for each credential and another 60 to 70 percent of credits in the curriculum are in general education across a broad variety of fields. This preferred hybrid of specific and general education is a typical element of two-year and four-year college degrees in the American post-secondary education system. As the Association of American Colleges and Universities points out, it represents:

> An approach to college learning that seeks to empower individuals and prepare them to deal with complexity, diversity, and change. This approach emphasizes broad knowledge of the wider world (e.g., science, culture, and society) as well as in-depth achievement in at least one specific field of study.[75]

The argument for the hybrid of "general and specific education for all" rests on two pillars. The first is the idea that a combination of general and specific coursework provides nonmonetary benefits in areas such as health and political participation, and also makes one a fully rounded, holistically educated, flourishing individual.[76]

The second pillar is research that shows there is an optimal mix of general and specific education that provides greater economic value than either general or specific education alone, because it prepares students both to enter the labor market and to adapt their skills in response to changing demands.[77] General education adds economic value by enabling people to adapt to changing technologies and demands for new skills. Taken together, the benefits of mixing general and specific education accrue to both the individual, by widening opportunities, and the economy as a whole, by enhancing flexibility and empowering technological adoption.[78]

At the same time as liberal education has become more attractive because of economic change, more specific career-related education has increased in value as well. The doubling of the wage premium for the average bachelor's degree is not the only dramatic trend since the 1980s. The variation in earnings by postsecondary field of study has more than quadrupled during that time. This demonstrates that the relationship between fields of study and their connection to particular career pathways is an increasingly important determinant of future earnings. Sometimes less education in a high-paying field of study is worth more than more education in a low-paying field of study. This is why more than 40 percent of people with bachelor's degrees make more than people with graduate degrees; 28 percent of associate's degrees lead to higher earnings than the average bachelor's degree; and many certificate holders make more than an average worker with an associate's degree or a bachelor's degree.[79]

In response to the rising value of education related to specific careers, many support more specific education, both within degree programs and in the form of programs that offer non-credit customized training and non-degree credentials, such as certificates, industry-based certifications, and badges. The current advocates of specific education tend to emphasize the growing economic mission of education. Specific education in particular majors or fields of study adds economic value by preparing individuals with particular occupational skills that prepare them to enter high-skill, in-demand career pathways.

There is a wide and growing variation in the lifetime economic value of specific fields of study. The growth of earnings associated with specific education, and the growing variation in earnings among specific fields, reflects both the increasing relative value of education beyond high school and increasing texture in the relationship between postsecondary education and the economy. Transparency regarding the connection between postsecondary programs and labor markets has become more important as people seek to choose among a growing diversity of both postsecondary programs of study, and modes of delivery aligned with an increasingly complex set of credentials and career pathways. Some indicators of that growing diversity include:

- the number of career fields identified by the U.S. Census Bureau increased from 270 to 840 between 1950 and 2010;[80]
- the number of colleges and universities grew from 1,850 to 4,720 between 1950 and 2014;[81] and
- the number of different programs of study offered by postsecondary education and training institutions grew from 410 to 2,260 between 1985 and 2010.[82]

In this new environment, programs and curricula matter more, and institutions matter less. The economic value of postsecondary education and training has less to do with institutional brands and more to do with growing differences, in both cost and labor-market value, among an expanding array of programs in specific fields.

Measuring Up: Creating Standards for Educational Adequacy

Education is the preferred response in the United States to social and economic change, as opposed to expansion in other aspects of the welfare state.[83] Education empowers individuals as responsible agents in dealing with change, and it minimizes government control. It also plays an important role as an arbiter in balancing market forces with democratic commitments to equal opportunity.

College offers individuals the opportunity to attain entry into the middle class. At the same time, however, it perpetuates socioeconomic inequalities, including vastly divergent economic and life outcomes between racial, ethnic, and class groups in American society.[84] Regardless of whether postsecondary education comes under the label of college, K–14, or career and technical education (CTE), it is clear that today people need access to affordable education and training beyond high school, and that the economy needs more educated workers to fill its new high-skill jobs and to carry out the next cycle of innovation and growth.

A new consensus is gradually emerging as we enter the initial decades of the twenty-first century. We agreed, beginning with the *A Nation at Risk* report, that every American should have access to a solid general education in the K–12 system and at least some level of postsecondary education or training. There is a general recognition that while the postwar divide between college preparation and vocational preparation is not acceptable, attention to career pathways still should be an element of the K–12 system. The new consensus points toward a K–16 system that is heavy on general education in elementary school, and that through middle school, high school, and college, gradually increases exposure to specific careers and direct preparation for them.

At the postsecondary level, these forces take us back to the same set of choices that Conant and his generation faced in contemplating who gets specific and general education in a society beset, at its very core, by race, class, and gender inequality. The evolution of the American education system has shifted much of the tracking issue from high school to postsecondary education. In Conant's day, the issue was who gets the gold-standard mix of general and specific education in high school. College access was generally presumed to be the province of the elites. In our time, the issue is who gets the gold-standard mix of general and specific education at the postsecondary level.

Currently in the United States, the need for a strong and universal general education through high school is widely accepted. After high school, however, a disproportionate share of the least advantaged get specific education in sub-baccalaureate fields, while advantaged students go on to the bachelor level. The most advantaged students then go on to elite specific training in graduate and professional school. As a result, the least advantaged get their most intense specific training in two-year colleges, and the advantaged experience their most intense, specific learning in graduate and professional school.[85]

Defining adequacy in this evolving system is no small feat. Having no basis in the U.S. Constitution, the notion of adequacy, as a legal concept, rests on the gradual accretion of vague guarantees in state constitutions. The failure of nerve on the part of the Supreme Court in rejecting the plaintiff's plea for adequacy in *San Antonio v. Rodriguez* still frustrates efforts to establish a core political or legal commitment to build upon.

But higher education needs an outcome standard for adequacy. We argue that in a democracy with a market economy and little support for an extensive social safety net—as is the case in the United States—the means necessary for individual human flourishing comes, for the vast majority of citizens, from paid work. We argue that economic self-sufficiency is a necessary, though not sufficient, measure of the provision of an adequate education.[86]

We also favor establishing a labor-market standard for adequate outcomes, because the relationship between education and labor markets is especially important in the United States, due to our relatively modest welfare state and greater reliance on individual responsibility, both of which make the relationship between education and economic outcomes especially powerful. In work-based societies such as our own, the inability to get or keep jobs affects human flourishing and successful family formation, as well as political participation and healthy engagement with the civil society, culture, and community. As the psychologist Abraham Maslow observed in establishing his hierarchy of human needs more than seven decades ago, people must have their basic physiological and safety needs satisfied before they can devote their time and efforts to higher-level pursuits that culminate in the self-actualization, central to human flourishing.[87] As educational requirements increase on the job, the education system is asked, more and more, to take responsibility both for human flourishing and employability. If educators cannot fulfill their economic mission to help youths and adults become successful workers, they also will fall short in their cultural and political missions to create good neighbors, good citizens, and lifelong learners.

While labor market outcomes are not sufficient to assess educational adequacy alone, we argue that the focus on economic self-sufficiency, as a necessary condition for educational adequacy, is critical to advancing our discussion of adequacy. To date, this discussion has sidestepped the fact that people need education, and so they seek it out for the purposes of pursuing economic opportunity. For this reason, we argue that assessment of a program must start by measuring whether it provides economic self-sufficiency. We argue this for several reasons:

- First, economic self-sufficiency offers a readily measurable threshold of labor market outcomes that program graduates are expected to achieve, instead of just common outcomes based on proxy measures. There are currently no standard measures of learning across different postsecondary settings. The Lumina Foundation's Degree Qualification Profiles for associate's, bachelor's and master's degrees, which includes a process of "tuning" for specific fields of study, represents the most substantive effort to establish common outcomes at the program level for what students should know and be able to do.[88] While these efforts have led to more standardized definitions of learning outcomes, we are a long way from measuring learning in higher education programs concretely and consistently.

- Second, the use of labor market outcomes as a standard provides a uniform incentive for all types of postsecondary education programs, without discouraging local experimentation or the innovation and customization of educational delivery, curriculum development, or faculty relations. In the end, it doesn't matter how the education is delivered, so long as it enables individuals to become self-sufficient and be able to cover the costs of obtaining it.

- Third, an economic self-sufficiency standard puts the focus on programs of study,[89] rather than general institutional performance or overall attainment levels.

- Fourth, labor market outcomes are an actionable policy lever that resonates at the state and federal level, as has been demonstrated by Gainful Employment regulations at the federal level and by states' incorporation of labor-market outcomes in performance-based systems for funding public colleges.

During the Obama administration, we saw the implementation of Gainful Employment regulations that reflected a growing concern that some postsecondary programs were not a wise investment for students. While the Trump administration is expected to scale back these regulations, other policy efforts at the state and federal levels seek to measure return on investment (ROI) through outcomes. These efforts will continue to move the conversation in the direction of labor market outcomes and economic value of higher education.[90]

Another argument for shifting focus to economic outcomes is that the policy process has already accepted them as a legitimate goal. Data connecting college programs to careers are increasingly available in statewide longitudinal data systems that connect student transcript data to earnings and career pathways. A few states—including Florida, Texas and Washington—began to connect postsecondary education transcript data and Unemployment Insurance (UI) wage records starting in the 1980s. Since 2007, the federal government has spurred further connections between K–12 education, postsecondary education, and wage record data systems by providing more than $700 million in grant funding for such efforts to forty-seven states and the District of Columbia.[91] As a result, forty-seven agencies in forty-two states currently link or plan to link postsecondary education records with workforce data relayed by wage records.[92] States vary substantially in terms of access to their data, the quality of their data, and their data infrastructure and tools. Some states will need to make more progress in terms of the accessibility and usefulness of their Statewide Longitudinal Data Systems (SLDS) data before those data can be applied toward assessments related to an economic self-sufficiency standard for different postsecondary programs of study.

Thus, while acknowledging numerous complexities, considerations, and necessary adjustments for real-world application, we propose a concrete foundational earnings standard that would signal *economic self-sufficiency* of postsecondary education and training programs. Our proposed standard is this: For a program to provide economic self-sufficiency, it should lead to earnings of above *$35,000 per year ten years after completing the program* along with a *sufficient earnings premium* over an average high school graduate during the course of those ten years to cover the *total costs* of the program. (The total costs must include net price and opportunity costs, as measured by foregone earnings for the period of enrollment.)

We propose an earnings standard rather than family income because education influences individuals' economic opportunity, and earnings is the best expression of that opportunity. While we recognize that family income, in some ways, better reflects individuals' economic conditions, the relationship between one's education and family income is far less direct or clear than the relationship between education and earnings. While a family of four will need more resources than a family of one to reach the middle class, and a family may have sources of income outside of job-based earnings, the relationship between education and decisions involving family formation, childbearing, and non-earning income is not strong or clear enough to include these factors in an educational adequacy standard.

We use an earnings floor of $35,000 here for a number of reasons. Primarily it is the entry point to the middle class.[93] This earnings floor is the minimum necessary to enter the middle four deciles of earnings as defined by full-time full-year workers aged 25 through 64, which we believe is a good place to start. (This, of course, does not preclude someone from earning in the top three deciles.) Furthermore, middle-class family income has been defined as starting at $50,000, which roughly equates to our earnings at the individual level.[94]

Further, a $35,000 annual earnings level is slightly above average living wages across different parts of the country. This earnings level is approximately three times the poverty level for one person. It leaves a person with approximately $1,800 per month after rent of $800 per month and food costs of $350, the "high or liberal" menu cost estimate of the U.S. Department of Agriculture (USDA).[95] Taken together, these various metrics underpin our selection of $35,000 as a floor earnings level in beginning a conversation about economic self-sufficiency.

We present a simplified approach to give the reader a concrete grasp of how these principles can be applied to delineate economic self-sufficiency standard, underpinning educational adequacy. At the same time, we acknowledge that, to apply our concept of economic self-sufficiency to the real world, practitioners and policymakers will have to address numerous complexities and make adjustments appropriate to their local jurisdictions, institutions, and objectives. The report ends with discussion of some of these complicating issues, and suggests that a number of them can only be resolved with very subjective decisions or through social consensus.

For an Education Program to Be Adequate, Its Benefits Must Outweigh Its Costs

Our assessment of economic self-sufficiency is intentionally focused on labor market outcomes. It does not consider other outcomes of postsecondary education, such as learning or preparation for civic engagement, which are nonmonetary and, in many cases, currently difficult to measure. However, we recognize that these factors play an important role in higher education. Economic self-sufficiency is only part of the broad concept of educational adequacy, but we hold that it is a necessary and critical component.

For the purposes of defining that component, this report conceptualizes educational adequacy and economic self-sufficiency as follows:

$$Educational\ Adequacy = f\ (Economic\ Self\text{-}Sufficiency,$$
$$Nonmonetary\ Benefits,\ Consumer\ Benefits,\ Experiential\ Utility)$$

$$Economic\ Self\text{-}Sufficiency = Earnings\ Premium_{10\ years} -$$
$$(Direct\ Costs + Opportunity\ Costs)\ |\ Earnings > \$35,000/year$$

Economic self-sufficiency captures labor market benefits of postsecondary education that are important for many students and families and are the focus of this report.[96] These include an increased chance of employment, higher earnings, and a greater likelihood of working full-time and full-year, which grants access to employer-sponsored benefits, such as health insurance, retirement savings, and paid time off.

Nonmonetary benefits are not easily quantifiable, but make up an important part of the value provided by colleges to society and citizens. The nonmonetary benefits of college include: longer life expectancy; better health; lower likelihood of engaging in criminal behavior; greater political participation; a greater sense of civic responsibility; support for democratic institutions; stronger social cohesion; greater tolerance for others with a lower likelihood of involvement in socioeconomic and ethnic conflicts; more innovation; an enhanced propensity for lifelong learning; and an improved ability to deal with ethical issues raised by new technologies.[97]

Consumer benefits derive from educated individuals becoming better-informed consumers. As a result of information-processing and decision-making skills developed through higher education, such individuals make better researched, more informed, more reasoned decisions about what to purchase and how much to pay for it.[98]

Experiential utility represents the value students obtain from the college experience itself. This is what economists call the consumption—rather than investment—aspect of college. This encompasses the enjoyment and personal growth students get from social interaction with other students, from interaction with faculty, from the opportunity to satisfy their intellectual curiosity through lectures, discussions, and research, from opportunities to participate in extracurricular activities, and from access to recreational facilities, libraries and other campus amenities.

Earnings premium$_{10\,years}$ is the amount by which postsecondary program graduates' earnings exceed high school graduates' earnings, evaluated over the first ten years after graduation (the duration of the standard repayment period for federal student loans).[99] It represents the additional amount that college graduates are paid as the result of attaining a postsecondary credential and the skills that such a credential encompasses.

Direct costs are charges that students and/or their parents have to pay for their education either at the time of taking courses or through student loan borrowing, captured in net price.

Opportunity costs result from students giving up other things they could have done with their time if they were not attending college. Opportunity costs are captured in forgone earnings (based on wages of similarly aged workers with a high-school diploma) during the period when students attend college.

An Adequate Education Must Allow Graduates to Attain Middle-Class Earnings, and Cover Its Costs

The two-part economic self-sufficiency test we present in this report consists of the following criteria:

- *Part 1:* Are graduates of a postsecondary education program able to earn family-sustaining wages greater than $35,000 per year for full-time, full-year (FTFY) workers?[100]
- *Part 2:* Are graduates able to earn a sufficient premium over an average high school wage in the first ten years after completing the program to cover the costs (direct and opportunity) of the program?

This dual test would be applied to *graduates* who work full-time, full-year. Their earnings would be averaged at the *program level*, acknowledging the importance of fields of study and program completion to labor market outcomes.[101] Graduates are used as the base for this standard because graduates have received a credential, a tangible outcome. This model offers the flexibility to use other bases, such as examinations of all students ten years after separation from the institution, or all students who have taken enough coursework to meet a certain minimum credit threshold. Practitioners can choose to use other bases as appropriate, given data availability and local dynamics. But this report does not extend its analysis to non-completers, because they did not receive a credential. The logic is simple:

consider how clinical trials for drugs do not include results for participants who received an incomplete dosage, and whose condition therefore
does not properly reflect effectiveness of treatment. Likewise, inclusion of
non-completers—some of whom never complete a single course and or
may only attempt one course at a community college—would not accurately reflect educational adequacy of the analyzed programs of study. This
is not to say that completion rates are not important or that institutions
should not be held accountable for promoting completion of credentials.
We simply feel that it would be a stretch to hold programs and institutions
accountable for labor market outcomes of students who barely studied any
of the programs' offerings.

Any endeavor to establish an appropriate threshold for standard outcomes needs a starting point. In this case, we propose as the first part of
our two-part economic self-sufficiency threshold, the family-sustaining
earnings test, annual earnings greater than $35,000. As we stated earlier,
the $35,000 per year is not a random figure. It is the thirtieth percentile
of earnings for prime-age (25–64), FTFY workers—an entry point into
middle-class standards of living.[102]

The assumptions for calculating the second part of our test are more
complicated, because educational programs vary widely in cost. While
an associate's degree and a bachelor's degree may both get students to the
earnings level of $35,000 per year, a bachelor's degree has higher costs—the
direct costs of tuition, fees, and other charges; and the opportunity costs,
because it takes longer, typically twice the time, to earn a bachelor's degree
as opposed to an associate's degree. The opportunity cost we use in this
report is based on standard time to completion (two years for an associate's
degree, four years for a bachelor's degree) and on the assumption that students are studying full-time and not working while in school. We acknowledge that these ideal conditions are not met in the majority of student cases
today. Often, students combine work and studies at the same time and, as a
result, take longer to complete. The earnings of these students from working while in college somewhat balance out the opportunity costs associated

with taking longer to graduate; so our standard assumptions remain viable for demonstration purposes. However, practitioners seeking to apply the model will need to adjust time-to-completion and employment factors based on the circumstances of a majority of students at local institutions.

The second part of the two-part economic self-sufficiency test is whether graduates of a specific program earn enough of a premium over high school graduates' earnings in the first ten years after graduation to cover the costs of the program. For example, we find that, on average, the earnings premium for an associate's degree holder over a high school graduate is $9,000 per year. Over ten years, those earnings premiums add up to $90,000. The average net price for a community college is $7,000, which, over two years, adds up to direct costs of $14,000. In addition, the foregone annual earnings, based on median wages of high school graduates, are $24,000 per year, for a total of $48,000.[103] This translates to a total cost for an associate's degree of $62,000. Since the total earnings premium over ten years ($90,000) is more than the total costs of the program ($62,000), the average associate's degree program fulfills the second part of the economic self-sufficiency test (see Table 1).

Table 1. Economic Self-Sufficiency Ten-year Cost Payoff Estimates for Average Associate's and Bachelor's Degrees

	Annual earnings premium	Earnings premium over ten years	Annual net price	Direct cost	Forgone annual earnings	Opportunity cost	Total cost
Associate's degree	$9,000	$90,000	$7,000	$14,000	$24,000	$48,000	$62,000
Bachelor's degree	$24,000	$240,000	$17,700	$70,800	$24,000	$96,000	$166,800

Note: For illustrative purposes, these simplified examples do not consider interest on the debt, the value of alternative investments, nor the present value of future earnings streams; these factors would need to be included in the concrete evaluation of economic self-sufficiency for specific academic programs of study. The earnings used in estimating earnings premium are full-time, full-year (FTFY) earnings for workers aged 25–59. The earnings used to estimate forgone annual earnings are FTFY earnings for workers aged 18–24, with a high school diploma as their highest educational attainment.

Source: Georgetown University Center on Education and the Workforce analysis of *Current Population Survey* data, 2015 and *Digest of Education Statistics* tables, table 331.30, 2015.

The bachelor's degree generally takes twice as long to complete as an associate's degree, which means that the opportunity cost for a typical bachelor's degree program is double that for an associate's degree program ($96,000 versus $48,000). We find that the direct costs for a bachelor's degree programs are also more than $10,000 extra per year, based on the average net price at four-year colleges and universities ($17,700 versus $7,000), resulting in an average total cost of $166,800 for a bachelor's degree (compared to $62,000 for an associate's degree). Thus, the earnings premium for bachelor's degree holders has to be higher to cover the costs in ten years. For an average bachelor's degree, we find that the earnings premium is higher: $24,000 a year over high school graduates, which adds up to $240,000 over ten years (see Table 1). Since the accumulated earnings premium of $240,000 is more than the direct and opportunity costs of $166,800, we find that an average bachelor's degree program also fulfills the second part of the economic self-sufficiency test.

While, on average, associate's and bachelor's degrees provide a sufficient earnings premium over ten years following graduation to cover the costs of the program, the ability of individual programs to meet this dimension of economic self-sufficiency standard depends on the relationship between the program's net price and the annual earnings of its graduates. The higher the net price for a program, the greater the earnings that graduates need to attain economic self-sufficiency standard (see Figures 1 and 2).

Spending Levels Affect Educational Quality, but Alone Do Not Guarantee Educational Adequacy

The growing importance of postsecondary education has raised the question of appropriate funding levels for public institutions in general, and community colleges specifically. The takeaway lesson from the higher return on investment earned by pursuing a bachelor's degree rather than an associate's degree might be that the more resource-intensive the

Figure 1. AA Average Adequate Annual Earnings Based on Annual Net Price

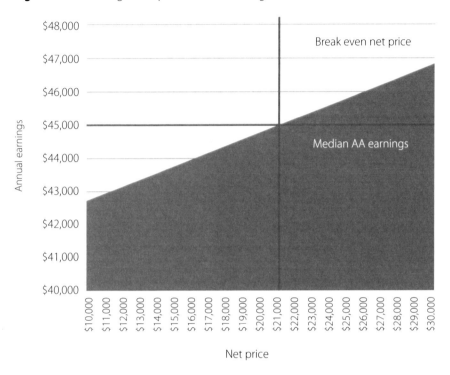

Note: For illustrative purposes, these simplified examples do not consider interest on the debt, the value of alternative investments nor the present value of future earnings streams, these factors would need to be included in the concrete evaluation of economic self-sufficiency for specific academic programs of study. The earnings used in estimating earnings premium are full-time, full-year (FTFY) earnings for workers aged 25–59. The earnings used to estimate forgone annual earnings are FTFY earnings for workers aged 18–24, with a high school diploma, as their highest educational attainment.

Source: Georgetown University Center on Education and the Workforce analysis based on Current Population Survey data, 2015 and Digest of Education Statistics tables, table 331.30, 2015.

program, the better. In some ways, this is true, but the level of spending is a very simplified metric: how money is spent may be as important as how much is spent. Furthermore, programmatic variations at otherwise similar institutions—as well as other factors—can lead to vastly different outcomes, raising questions of how to best value postsecondary institutions and programs.

Figure 2. BA Average Adequate Annual Earnings Based on Annual Net Price

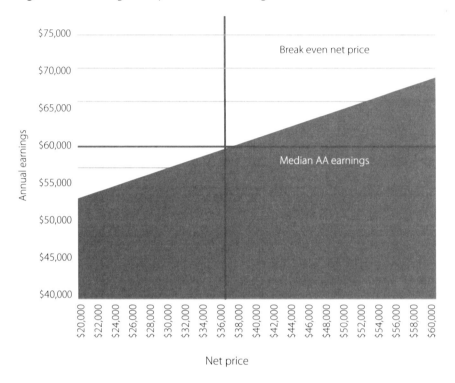

Note: For illustrative purposes, these simplified examples do not consider interest on the debt, the value of alternative investments nor the present value of future earnings streams, these factors would need to be included in the concrete evaluation of economic self-sufficiency for specific academic programs of study. The earnings used in estimating earnings premium are full-time, full-year (FTFY) earnings for workers aged 25–59. The earnings used to estimate forgone annual earnings are FTFY earnings for workers aged 18–24, with a high school diploma, as their highest educational attainment.

Source: Georgetown University Center on Education and the Workforce analysis based on Current Population Survey data, 2015 and Digest of Education Statistics tables, table 331.30, 2015.

Better-Funded Colleges Seem to Offer Better Results

The correlation between spending levels and quality of outcomes is fairly well established. The 468 most selective four-year colleges, which spend more than twice as much per student on instruction compared to open-access two- and four-year colleges ($13,400 versus $6,000), have substantially higher completion rates (82 percent versus 49 percent) and greater graduate degree attainment among their graduates (35 percent versus 21 percent), and their graduates have higher annual earnings ten years after graduation ($67,000 versus $49,000).[104] Yet, whether these disparities in outcomes are primarily the result of differences in spending is a subject of debate in the field.

Researcher Stacy Dale at Mathematica and Princeton economist Alan Krueger, looking at a very narrow group of highly selective schools, suggest that the majority of positive outcomes are explained by self-selection of students with higher abilities into the selective schools, and not by the schools themselves. This study suggests, though, that selectivity has positive impact on minority students, possibly implying that higher resources benefit those who have been without support historically.[105] This argument about self-selection, often attributed to American economist Andrew Michael Spence in the context of signaling,[106] is widely debated, but intuitively sensible in terms of selective institutions. Students from privileged backgrounds are less likely to benefit from marginal differences in resources, while for disadvantaged students the differences are not small (cumulatively) and, hence, resources have an impact. On the other hand, recent research suggests that two-thirds of differences in graduation rates can be attributed to the variance in resources.[107]

Stanford economist Raj Chetty and colleagues show that colleges that spend more per student are better at moving students from the bottom quintile of (parental) household income to the top quintile. Colleges in the bottom quartile of instructional spending per student spend on average $1,900 per student and have a 12 percent success rate in moving students from the bottom quintile of household income to the top quintile, with average earnings for all former students of $31,000 at ten years after first enrollment (based on College Scorecard data). On the other hand, colleges in the top quartile of instructional spending per student spent on average $10,000 per student, and have a 31 percent success rate in moving students from the bottom quintile of household income to the top quintile, with average earnings of $45,000 at ten years after first enrollment.[108]

Still, the relationship between spending and outcomes is not linear or clear-cut. Community colleges in the top quartile of instructional spending compared to those in the bottom quartile of instructional spending do not have significantly different success rates of moving students from the bottom quintile of household income to the top quintile. Simply stated, the relationship between costs and outcomes is not strong enough to tell policymakers where best to spend the next dollar. On the other hand, at least when it comes to addressing economic performance, an outcomes criterion is quite clear.

Shifting Focus from Postsecondary Institutions to Programs of Study Adds to the Complexity of Determining What It Costs to Provide Adequate Education

The key to the value of postsecondary education lies in learning and earning at the program-of-study level. While more education on average yields more pay, what a person makes depends on what that person takes—that is, their college major.[109] Sometimes less education in an in-demand field offers higher value than more education in another field. Twenty-eight percent of associate's degree holders make more than an average bachelor's degree holder.[110]

The value of programs of study varies substantially, based on the alignment between particular curricula and regional labor market demand.[111] The costs of delivering different programs of study also vary substantially. A highly technical program that requires the acquisition and maintenance of expensive equipment and the employment of faculty with particular skills will cost a college more to administer than a program that typically involves only classroom instruction. Some colleges charge students differently based on program of study, whereas others do not. In some states, public colleges are not allowed to charge students differently by program of study, even when there is a wide variation in the costs to deliver those programs.

A High Degree of Variation in Postsecondary Education Makes Estimating Costs Challenging

As the Supreme Court majority stated in its opinion in the *San Antonio v. Rodriguez* (1973) decision:

> On even the most basic questions in this area the scholars and educational experts are divided. Indeed, one of the major sources of controversy concerns the extent to which there is a demonstrable correlation between educational expenditures and the quality of education.[112]

Today, there is not much more consensus or clarity on the impact of expenditures on educational outcomes, at least when it comes to postsecondary education. In comparison to K–12 education, postsecondary education has much greater variability in how different programs are organized and delivered, little standardization in curriculum, and almost no standardized proficiency tests or standardized exit exams.[113] That is why we define an adequate education in terms of a common metric of labor market outcomes that cuts across fields.

It is difficult to guide policymakers and administrators as to where precisely to invest the next dollar in order to achieve the greatest impact on the provision of an adequate postsecondary education.

Comparing two community colleges, for example, can provide an illustration of how similar institutional costs can have very different outcomes. In 2000, Richland Community College in Illinois and Collin County Community College in Texas both spent around the same amount ($1,892 to $1,893) per FTE (full-time equivalent) student. However, a decade later, those who attended Richland Community College earned a median wage of $26,900 per year, whereas those who attended Collin County Community College earned $35,400 per year.[114] In part, demand-side factors arising from differences in local economies may have contributed to these divergent labor market outcomes. It is important for practitioners and policymakers to consider local economic conditions when applying an economic self-sufficiency standard. Nonetheless, researchers can do their best with the data to provide an estimated minimum level of funding required to achieve adequate outcomes (defined above as earnings over $35,000 ten years out and sufficient earnings premium over ten years to cover program's costs) for specific programs in specific institutions. Overall, however, the complexity of providing higher education, combined with variation obtained by regional labor markets, makes it a daunting, if not impossible task, to derive a single, general figure of cost that could be meaningfully applied to all programs.

The wide variation of institutions and programs in higher education makes estimating the costs of reaching a commonly defined labor market outcome particularly difficult. There are 2,260 different postsecondary programs of study across different types of institutions,[115] 910 community colleges among 4,583 two- and four-year colleges and universities,[116] a variety of delivery modes (classroom, online, lab, field experience), and new innovations, such as competency-based education and co-requisite remediation. Any meaningful estimate of a cost figure will need to, at a minimum, be at the program level. Connecting cost to a defined labor market outcome of $35,000 will be much more politically salient than simply asking for more funds for an ill-defined goal. Policymakers want to know what they are likely to get for their investments.

Employment and earnings metrics that show how graduates of postsecondary education programs perform in the labor market are standard outcomes measurable across different public postsecondary-education institutions, programs of study, credential types, and delivery methods. With the help of more than $700 million in grants from the federal government, states have developed Statewide Longitudinal Data Systems (SLDS), many of which connect students' K–12 and postsecondary educational experiences with their subsequent employment and earnings. These systems provide the necessary information to compare employment and earnings outcomes across the postsecondary education spectrum. By setting a common adequacy of outcomes standard—expressed in labor market metrics—colleges will have an incentive to experiment and innovate in order to use the financial support received as efficiently as possible.

Investments in Specific Practices and Interventions at Community Colleges Have Been Shown to Improve Outcomes

Some postsecondary investments are more promising than others. In terms of improving outcomes, the following investments have substantial potential: more structured programs, smaller class sizes, student success courses, redesigned developmental coursework, more full-time faculty, expanded tutoring and academic support services, and expanded access to guidance through more counselors and coaches.[117] For example, one comprehensive program, the Accelerated Study in Associate Programs (ASAP) at the City University of New York (CUNY), combined many of these promising elements, including a highly structured learning environment, comprehensive advising, enhanced career services, and additional tutoring and financial support. The result was a near doubling in the three-year graduation rate for students in the program, compared to control group of CUNY students who did not participate (40 percent versus 22 percent).[118] Even though the program cost 60 percent more per student, it actually brought down the cost-per-awarded–degree, due to its significant success in increasing the graduation rate.[119]

Another report, by the Center for Community College Student Engagement, found a positive relationship between 13 "high impact" practices and intermediate student outcomes, such as completing at least one developmental course with a grade of C or better; completing at least one gateway course with a grade of C or better; and persisting in the program through enrollment in subsequent academic terms and subsequent academic years.[120] The "high impact" practices considered in the report included student-success courses, accelerated developmental education, proper orientation, tutoring and supplemental instruction, experiential learning beyond the classroom, alerts and interventions, and structured group learning experiences.[121]

Other research highlighting promising investments includes:

- a review of evidence on the negative effect of lack of structure in community colleges and promising programs that add structure to community college programs;[122]
- a Tennessee-focused study that found positive impact on persistence from exposure to redesigned developmental math courses;[123]
- a study finding that the California Acceleration Project had a positive impact by providing accelerated developmental programs in math and English;[124] a randomized trial involving women in college that charted improvements in grades and academic standards as a result of academic support services and financial incentives for good grades;[125]
- a separate, randomized experiment that found that student coaching has positive impact on persistence and completion;[126]
- a six-state evaluation of a performance-based scholarship demonstration project, which showed that performance-based scholarships can be an effective investment in improving academic performance of participating low-income students, both during the program and several years after the program ends;[127] and
- research that suggests that another promising, comprehensive approach to improving student outcomes is program redesign, with the goal of accelerating entry into and completion of programs, guided by research-supported principles such as instructional program coherence, student engagement, contextualized instruction, and the integration of student support services.[128]

While none of these studies directly link investment in inputs to labor-market outcomes providing students with economic self-sufficiency after program completion, they offer a solid starting point for researchers, practitioners, and policymakers seeking to connect adequate outcomes with practices and interventions that could lead to them.

It Costs More to Provide Postsecondary Education That Leads to Adequate Outcomes
for Disadvantaged Students, Disproportionately Served by Community Colleges

Community colleges fundamentally serve a different population of students than the one served by four-year public and private universities. Community colleges enroll a disproportionate number of students who are older, working class, black or Latino, or the first generation in their family to go to college; have limited proficiency in English; and who need substantial remediation because of poor preparation in K–12. Students from the bottom two socioeconomic (SES) quartiles account for three out of five students at community colleges.[129] At such institutions, low-SES students outnumber high-SES students two-to-one, and blacks and Latinos account for one-third of all students.[130] Nearly two-thirds of students enter community college academically unprepared for college-level coursework.[131] These populations present a greater challenge for educators, and it takes more resources to help these students attain outcomes that meet a standard of educational adequacy.[132]

Students can face many types of disadvantages. Attempting to capture and adjust for each of these would add substantially to the complexity of determining appropriate funding levels for each community college. In addition, states differ in the way they provide services to disadvantaged groups, with the political environments of different jurisdictions determining which disadvantages are recognized in adjustments of funding levels.

Nevertheless, one specific indicator may be used to adjust funding for many types of disadvantages, without triggering political argument over which specific disadvantages should be recognized by a state. Standardized test scores, while reflecting socioeconomic inequities, also reflect academic preparation for college-level work. Aggregated at the institution level, such scores can serve as a proxy for the degree of disadvantage among a college's students, and can be the primary basis for risk adjustments that account for differences in student populations.

The relationship between college preparation and socioeconomic disadvantages within a community is well established.[133] Many of the socioeconomic disadvantages start in early childhood, and they tend to exhibit a pattern of geographic concentration or residential segregation, affecting some communities more than others.[134]

The K–12 education system tends to perpetuate and exacerbate these disadvantages rather than mitigate them.[135] In most states, students enroll in K–12 schools based on where they live, and funding for local schools primarily is driven by local property taxes. The geographic segregation by race, ethnicity, and class generally results in students from white wealthy families attending well-funded, high quality schools with other students from white wealthy families; while students from disadvantaged backgrounds attend poor quality, underfunded schools with disproportionate enrollments of disadvantaged students. This dynamic—of distribution and perpetuation of privilege and disadvantage—gives us the ability to consistently and systematically identify communities with higher concentrations of disadvantaged students, and the community colleges that serve them. It lets us sidestep the political and practical complications that arise from getting caught up in specific states' debates over which populations should be considered disadvantaged and which students should be classified as part of those populations.

Remaining Considerations

Our simplified approach in applying an economic self-sufficiency standard to postsecondary education programs does not take into account several key considerations. To establish a sound educational adequacy framework, researchers will need to address the following issues:

1. Our model is based on the on-time student who graduates and finds full-time employment. How should the measurement of adequacy be modified to address the many students who do not complete their programs in the typical time expected, do not complete

at all, do not enter the workforce, or do not obtain a full-time, full-year position with benefits? Has the highly educated homemaker who does not work but supports a well-to-do household received an adequate education?

2. The $35,000 floor in our model is a national standard that does not account for regional differences in the cost of living. Practitioners and policymakers will have to apply necessary adjustments based on regional price parities to set an appropriate adequate earnings floor for their state or area. These tools are widely available (see Appendix: Expanding on Additional Considerations for Researchers).

3. The effect of education on labor market outcomes varies substantially with age and experience. Researchers and practitioners need to recognize that different educational paths may lead to different earnings trajectories.

4. Occupational choice and field of study have a tremendous impact on people's earnings. Numerous jobs are socially necessary, but do not offer high pay. How do we assess labor market outcomes for graduates entering intellectual and caring professions (ICP)?

5. Should we be using a risk-adjustment model that factors in different outcomes expectations based on demographic and social variables in order to adjust performance expectations?

6. Should education returns be color- and gender-blind? Does adequacy fail if education does not reduce social inequities in the labor market?

7. How do we measure the labor market outcomes of nontraditional students with previous labor market participation?

8. How do we measure the outcomes for students who attend multiple institutions or major in more than one program?

9. Considering that we need to wait out a ten-year post-graduation period to properly assess the earnings of graduates, how do we deal with the long delay in getting feedback on institutional performance?

10. How do we measure how nonmonetary benefits contribute to the overall value of higher education?

Conclusion

These issues present a number of complex challenges in determining a benchmark for educational adequacy. Higher education is a complex endeavor. Outcomes are affected by many interconnected elements. Oversimplification that emphasizes the importance of some elements and ignores others will lead to skewed incentives and undermine the holistic nature of higher education. That said, the difficulties we face in grappling with such challenges should not become an excuse for failing to improve the higher education system and hold state and local governments accountable for their higher education policies and expenditures.

In setting out educational adequacy standards, practitioners and policymakers should not strive for perfection, but rather use the best available metrics and methods, with the expectation of continuous refinement and improvement as new information, data, and technologies become available. This approach should be focused on outcomes and afford local administrations the flexibility to determine the most appropriate set of inputs necessary to produce adequate outcomes. Economic self-sufficiency, at the program of study level, must have a central role in this practical approach to setting educational adequacy standards.

Appendix

https://s3-us-west-2.amazonaws.com/production.tcf.org/app/uploads/ 2018/04/01160708/TCF_EducationalAdequacyAppendix.pdf

Notes

1. Arthur Wise, "Educational adequacy: A concept in search of meaning," *Journal of Education Finance* 8, no. 3 (1983): 300–15.

2. Anthony Carnevale, Tamara Jayasundera, and Andrew Hanson, *Career and Technical Education: Five Ways that Pay Along the Way to the BA* (Washington, D.C.: Georgetown University Center on Education and the Workforce, 2012).

3. Anthony Carnevale, Nicole Smith, and Jeff Strohl, *Recovery: Job Growth and Education Requirements through 2020* (Washington, D.C.: Georgetown University Center on Education and the Workforce, 2013).

4. Anthony P. Carnevale, Jeff Strohl, Ban Cheah, and Neil Ridley, *Good Jobs that Pay without a BA* (Washington, D.C.: Georgetown University Center on Education and the Workforce, 2017).

5. See Table A1 in the Appendix to this report, https://s3-us-west-2.amazonaws.com/production.tcf.org/app/uploads/2018/04/01160708/TCF_EducationalAdequacyAppendix.pdf.

6. Experience with the federal No Child Left Behind Act in K–12 education illustrates the perils of simply pronouncing end goals without providing schools with adequate resources to reach those aims. See, e.g. William D. Duncombe, Anna Lukemeyer, and John Yinger, "Dollars without Sense: The Mismatch between the No Child Left Behind Act Accountability System and Title I Funding," in *Improving on No Child Left Behind: Getting Education Reform Back on Track*, ed. Richard D. Kahlenberg (New York: The Century Foundation Press, 2008).

7. Alfred Marshall, quoted in Thomas Humphrey Marshall and Thomas Burton Bottomore, *Citizenship and Social Class*, vol. 2 (London: Pluto Press, 1992), 4–5.

8. Alfred Marshall, cited in Arthur Cecil Pigou, *Memorials of Alfred Marshall* (London: Macmillan, 1925), 105.

9. John H. Holland, *Complexity: A Very Short Introduction*. New York: Oxford University Press, 2014.

10. A. Alesina, E. Glaeser, and B. Sacerdote, "Why doesn't the US have a European-style welfare system?" Harvard Institute for Economic Research, discussion paper no. 1933, 2001.

11. "American Public Education: An Origin Story," *Education News*, April 16, 2013.

12. Claudia Goldin, *The Race between Education and Technology* (Cambridge, Mass.: Harvard University Press, 2008), 195; Claudia Goldin, "The Human-Capital Century and American Leadership: Virtues of the Past," *Journal of Economic History* 61, no. 2 (June 2001).

13. Claudia Goldin and Lawrence F. Katz, "Why the United States led in education: Lessons from secondary school expansion, 1910 to 1940," NBER working paper 6144, National Bureau of Economic Research, 1997; A. Alesina, E. Glaeser, and B. Sacerdote, "Why doesn't the US have a European-style welfare system?" Harvard Institute for Economic Research discussion paper no. 1933, 2001.

14. In *San Antonio v. Rodriguez* (1973) 411 U.S. 1, The U.S. Supreme Court found that the U.S. Constitution does not provide a right to education.

15. Paul Starr, *The Creation of the Media: Political Origins of Modern Communications* (New York: Basic Books, 2005).

16. Robert H. Wiebe, *Self-rule: A Cultural History of American Democracy* (Chicago: University of Chicago Press, 1995).

17. "Morrill Act," *Primary Documents in American History*, Library of Congress, 2017, https://www.loc.gov/rr/program/bib/ourdocs/Morrill.html.

18. Ibid.

19. John Dewey, *Experience and Education* (New York: Simon and Schuster, 2007).

20. David D. Marsh and Judy B. Codding, *The New American High School* (Thousand Oaks, Calif.: Corwin Press, 1999).

21. Association for Career and Technical Education (ACTE), "History of CTE," https://www.acteonline.org/general.aspx?id=810#.Ws5sIojwaUk.

22. Claudia Goldin, "America's graduation from high school: The evolution and spread of secondary schooling in the twentieth century," *Journal of Economic History* 58, no. 2 (1998): 345–74.

23. *120 years of American Education: A Statistical Portrait*, ed. Thomas D. Snyder (Washington, D.C.: National Center for Education Statistics, 1993).

24. Vincent Tompkins, "Smith-Hughes Act of 1917—Primary Source," in *American Decades Primary Sources: 1910-1919*, vol. 2, ed. Vincent Tompkins (Farmington Hills, Mich.: Gale, 2000).

25. George, B. Vaughan, *The Community College Story* (Washington, D.C.: American Association of Community Colleges, 2006).

26. Richard J. Altenbaugh, *Historical Dictionary of American Education* (Westport: Greenwood Publishing Group, 1999).

27. Thomas Humphrey Marshall, "Citizenship and Social Class," in *Contemporary Political Philosophy: An Anthology*, ed. Robert E. Goodin and Philip Pettit (Oxford, U.K.: Blackwell Publishing, 1997), 311.

28. Ibid.

29. Ibid.

30. Thomas Humphrey Marshall, "Citizenship and Social Class," in *Citizenship: Critical Concepts*, vol. 2, ed. Bryan S. Turner and Peter Hamilton (London: Routledge, 1994), 33–35.

31. Ibid.

32. James G. Hershberg, *James B. Conant: Harvard to Hiroshima and the Making of the Nuclear Age* (Stanford, Calif.: University Press, 1993).

33. Ibid.

34. Ibid.

35. Ibid.

36. Ibid., 707.

37. Ibid., 11.

38. Ibid., 723.

39. James Bryant Conant, *Slums and Suburbs: A Commentary on Schools in Metropolitan Areas* (New York: McGraw-Hill, 1961).

40. Ibid.

41. James Bryant Conant, *Education in a Divided World: The Function of the Public Schools in Our Unique Society* (London: Oxford University Press, 1948).

42. *The Adams-Jefferson Letters: The Complete Correspondence Between Thomas Jefferson and Abigail and John Adams*, ed. Lester J. Cappon (Chapel Hill: University of North Carolina Press, 2012).

43. Ibid.

44. *Brown v. The Board of Education of Topeka* (1954), 347 US 453, p. 493.

45. *San Antonio v. Rodriguez* (1973) 411 U.S. 1, p. 35.

46. *Rose v. Council for Better Education* (1989) 790 S.W. 2d 186.

47. The National Commission on Excellence in Education, *A Nation at Risk: The Imperative for Educational Reform: A Report to the Nation and the Secretary of Education* (Washington, D.C.: United States Department of Education, April 1983).

48. Goldin, *The Race between Education and Technology*.

49. Trudy A. Suchan, Marc J. Perry, James D. Fitzsimmons, Anika E. Juhn, Alexander M. Tait, and Cynthia A. Brewer, "Chapter 10. Education," in *Census Atlas of the United States*, Series CENSR-29 (Washington, D.C.: U.S. Census Bureau, 2007).

50. Ibid.

51. Audrey Watters, "How Sputnik Launched Ed-Tech: The National Defense Education Act of 1958," *Hack Education: The History of the Future of Education Technology*, June 20, 2015, http://hackeducation.com/2015/06/20/sputnik.

52. Gamson, David A., Kathryn A. McDermott, and Douglas S. Reed. "The Elementary and Secondary Education Act at Fifty: Aspirations, Effects, and Limitations." RSF (2015).

53. Anthony Carnevale and Stephen Rose, *The Economy Goes to College: The Hidden Promise of Higher Education in the Postindustrial Service Economy* (Washington, D.C.: Georgetown University Center on Education and the Workforce, 2015); Anthony Carnevale and Stephen Rose, *The Undereducated American*(Washington, D.C.: Georgetown University Center on Education and the Workforce, 2011).

54. Anthony P. Carnevale, Tamara Jayasundera, and Artem Gulish, *America's Divided Recovery: College Haves and Have-Nots* (Washington, D.C.: Georgetown University Center on Education and the Workforce, 2016).

55. Ibid.

56. Georgetown University Center on Education and the Workforce analysis of Current Population Survey data, 1970, 2015.

57. Carnevale and Rose, *The Undereducated American*; Anthony Carnevale, Stephen Rose, and Ban Cheah, *The College Payoff: Education, Occupations, Lifetime Earnings* (Washington, D.C.: Georgetown University Center on Education and the Workforce, 2011).

58. Anthony Carnevale, Nicole Smith, and Jeff Strohl, *Help Wanted: Projections of Jobs and Education Requirements through 2018* (Washington, D.C.: Georgetown University Center on Education and the Workforce, 2010); Anthony Carnevale, Nicole Smith, and Jeff Strohl, *Recovery: Job Growth and Education Requirements through 2020* (Washington, D.C.: Georgetown University Center on Education and the Workforce, 2013).

59. Anthony Carnevale, Tamara Jayasundera, and Andrew Hanson, *Career and Technical Education: Five Ways that Pay Along the Way to the BA* (Washington, D.C.: Georgetown University Center on Education and the Workforce, 2012).

60. Gardner et al., *A Nation at Risk*.

61. Ibid.

62. Ibid.

63. Katherine L. Hughes, Thomas R. Bailey, and Melinda J. Mechur, "School-to-Work: Making a Difference in Education: A Research Report to America," Institute on Education and the Economy, Teachers College, Columbia University, 2001, http://www.tc.columbia.edu/iee/STWrelease.HTM.

64. U.S. Department of Education, National Center for Education Statistics, *High School and Beyond Longitudinal Study of 1980 Sophomores* (HS&B-So:80/82), 1982, and *2009 High School Transcript Study (HSTS)*, 2009.

65. National Center for Education Statistics (NCES), *Data Point: Trends in CTE Coursetaking*, NCES2014-901, Washington, D.C.: U.S. Department of Education, 2013, https://nces.ed.gov/pubs2014/2014901.pdf.

66. U.S. Department of Education, National Center for Education Statistics, *2009 High School Transcript Study (HSTS)*, 2009.

67. The American Diploma Project, *Ready or Not: Creating a High School Diploma That Counts* (Washington, D.C.: Achieve, Inc., 2004), https://www.achieve.org/files/ReadyorNot.pdf; Andrew Porter, Jennifer McMaken, Jun Hwang, and Rui Yang, "Common core standards the new US intended curriculum," *Educational Researcher*40, no. 3 (2011): 103–16.

68. Carnevale and Rose, *The Economy Goes to College.*

69. The high school summit included the mantra that "every student in high school should graduate both proficient and prepared for the real demands of work and postsecondary learning" that survives in the rhetoric of reform in the current "common core" curriculum. In fact, the connection to work through job specific vocational education typical of Conant's comprehensive high school has all but disappeared in American high schools in favor of career exposure through limited coursework in career and technical education. The more significant commitment was "every student should be proficient and prepared for . . . postsecondary learning." Achieve, Inc. and National Governors Association, 2005 National Education Summit on High Schools, Washington, D.C., February 2005.

70. Margaret Spellings, *A test of leadership: Charting the future of US higher education*, U.S. Department of Education, 2006.

71. "Remarks of President Barack Obama—Address to Joint Session of Congress," The White House, February 24, 2009, https://obamawhitehouse.archives.gov/the-press-office/remarks-president-barack-obama-address-joint-session-congress.

72. Anthony Carnevale and Jeff Strohl, *Separate & Unequal: How Higher Education Reinforces the Intergenerational Reproduction of White Racial Privilege* (Washington, D.C.: Georgetown University Center on Education and the Workforce, 2013).

73. The National Leadership Council for Liberal Education and America's Promise, *College Learning for the New Global Century* (Washington, D.C.: Association of American College and Universities, 2009).

74. Ron Brownstein, "Why Some Cities and States Are Footing the Bill for Community College," *The Atlantic*, April 20, 2017.

75. *The LEAP Vision for Learning: Outcomes and Employers' Views* (Washington, DC: Association of American Colleges and Universities, 2017).

76. Louis E. Vila, "Non-Monetary Benefits of Education," *European Journal of Education* 35, no. 1 (2000, March): 21–32; Paul H. Buck and James Bryant Conant, *General Education in a Free Society* (Cambridge, Mass.: Harvard University Press, 1945); The National Leadership Council for Liberal Education and America's Promise, *College Learning for the New Global Century*; Cliff Adelman, Peter Ewell, Paul Gaston, and Carol Geary Schneider, *The Degree Qualifications Profile: A Learning-Centered Framework for What College Graduates*

Should Know and Be Able to Do to Earn the Associate, Bachelor's or Master's Degree (Indianapolis, Ind.: Lumina Foundation, 2014).

77. Thomas Bailey and Clive R. Belfield, "Community college occupational degrees: Are they worth it?" *Preparing Today's Students for Tomorrow's Jobs in Metropolitan America*, ed. Laura W. Perna (Philadelphia: University of Pennsylvania Press, 2012): 121–48.

78. Eric A. Hanushek, Guido Schwerdt, Ludger Woessmann, and Lei Zhang, "General Education, Vocational Education, and Labor-Market Outcomes over the Lifecycle," *Journal of Human Resources* 52, no. 1 (2017): 48–87; Dirk Krueger and Krishna B. Kumar, "Skill-specific Rather than General Education: A Reason for US–Europe Growth Differences?" *Journal of Economic Growth* 9, no. 2 (2004): 167–207; Eric D. Gould, "Rising wage inequality, comparative advantage, and the growing importance of general skills in the United States," *Journal of Labor Economics* 20, no. 1 (2002): 105–47.

79. Carnevale, Rose, and Cheah, *The College Payoff*.

80. Ian D. Wyatt and Daniel E. Hecker, "Occupational changes during the 20th Century," *Monthly Labor Review* 129 (2006): 35, and U.S. Department of Labor, Bureau of Labor Statistics, Occupational Employment Statistics, 2015, https://www.bls.gov/oes/.

81. National Center for Education Statistics (NCES), *Digest of Education Statistics*, U.S. Department of Education, 2015–2016, table 317.10, https://nces.ed.gov/programs/digest/.

82. National Center for Education Statistics (NCES), Integrated Postsecondary Education Data System (IPEDS), Classification of Instructional Programs (CIP) Resources, U.S. Department of Education 2010, http://nces.ed.gov/ipeds/cipcode/resources.aspx?y=55.

83. W. Norton Grubb and Marvin Lazerson, *The Education Gospel* (Cambridge, Mass.: Harvard University Press, 2009); Anthony Carnevale, "Discounting Education's Value," Chronicle Review 53, no. 5 (September 22, 2006): B6.

84. Anthony Carnevale and Jeff Strohl, *Separate & Unequal*; Anne Case and Angus Deaton, "Mortality and morbidity in the 21st century," *Brookings Papers on Economic Activity*, 2017.

85. Anthony Carnevale and Jeff Strohl, *Separate & Unequal*.

86. Due to the lack of an extensive social safety net, attainment of adequate education is more important in the United States than in other developed countries. For example, Case and Deaton find that unlike in Europe, where mortality rates declined for all education groups, in the United State mortality rates for non-college-educated whites actually increased between 1998 and 2015; Anne Case and Angus Deaton, "Mortality and morbidity in the 21st century."

87. Abraham Harold Maslow, "A theory of human motivation," *Psychological Review* 50, no. 4 (1943): 370.

88. Cliff Adelman, Peter Ewell, Paul Gaston, and Carol Geary Schneider, *The Degree Qualifications Profile: A Learning-Centered Framework for What College Graduates Should Know and Be Able to Do to Earn the Associate, Bachelor's or Master's Degree* (Indianapolis, Ind.: Lumina Foundation, 2014).

89. Melguizo, et al. demonstrate one potentially promising approach to evaluating labor market outcomes at the program level. Tatiana Melguizo, Gema Zamarro, Tatiana Velasco, and Fabio J. Sanchez, "The Methodological Challenges of Measuring Student Learning,

Degree Attainment, and Early Labor Market Outcomes in Higher Education," *Journal of Research on Educational Effectiveness* 10, no. 2 (2017): 424–48.

90. A number of bills to make student unit record data available at the federal level have also been introduced in Congress, including S.1195—*Student Right to Know Before You Go Act of 2015*, sponsored by Ron Wyden (D-OR), Marco Rubio (R-FL) and Mark Warner (D-VA), and S1121—*College Transparency Act* (2017), sponsored by Orrin Hatch (R-UT), Elizabeth Warren (D-MA), Bill Cassidy (R-LA.) and Sheldon Whitehouse (D-RI).

91. John Armstrong and Christina Whitfield, *The State of State Postsecondary Data Systems: Strong Foundations 2016* (Boulder: State Higher Education Executive Officers Association, 2016), http://www.sheeo.org/sites/default/files/publications/SHEEO_Strong-Foundations2016_FINAL.pdf.

92. Ibid.

93. Georgetown University Center on Education and the Workforce analysis of *Current Population Survey (CPS), Annual Socioeconomic Supplement* data, 2016. The $35,000 is based on 2016 dollars and earnings distribution and would need to be adjusted over time with substantive changes in inflation and earnings distribution.

94. Harry J. Holzer, the John LaFarge, Jr. S.J. Chair and Professor at the McCourt School of Georgetown University, uses individual median earnings of $36,000 as one of the factor to arrive at $50,000 family income standard. The fact that these standards equate was discussed in unpublished email with Dr. Holzer.

95. The cost of a liberal food menu plan is an average for unmarried men and women, 19–50 years of age from "Official USDA Food Plans: Cost of Food at Home at Four Levels, U.S. Average, May 2017," U.S. Department of Agriculture, 2017.

96. Rachel Fishman, *2015 College Decisions Survey: Part I: Deciding to Go to College* (Washington, D.C.: New America, 2015); Kevin Eagan, Ellen Stolzenberg, Abigail Bates, Melissa Aragon, Marian Ramirez Suchard, and Cecillia Rios-Aguilar, *The American Freshman: National Norms Fall 2015* (Los Angeles: Higher Education Research Institute, University of California, 2016).

97. Louis E. Vila, "Non-Monetary Benefits of Education," *European Journal of Education* 35, 1 (2000, March): 21–32; John Gaventa and Gregory Barrett, "Mapping the outcomes of citizen engagement," *World Development* 40, no. 12 (2012): 2399–410.

98. Jamie Merisotis and J. Wellman, "Reaping the benefits: Defining the public and private values of going to college," Institute for Higher Education, 1998; Lusardi, Annamaria, and Olivia S. Mitchell, "How ordinary consumers make complex economic decisions: Financial literacy and retirement readiness," NBER working paper no. 15350, National Bureau of Economic Research, 2009.

99. "The Standard Repayment Plan is the basic repayment plan for loans from the William D. Ford Federal Direct Loan (Direct Loan) Program and Federal Family Education Loan (FFEL) Program," U.S. Department of Education, Office of Federal Student Aid, https://studentaid.ed.gov/sa/repay-loans/understand/plans/standard.

100. There is no accepted level that delineates self-sustaining earnings. We chose $35,000 per year ($17 per hour for a full-time job) as a floor, where jobs above this level pay a median $52,000. The easiest explanation for this floor is that it is the thirtieth percentile

of the full-time full-year earnings distribution, which serves as the entry point to the "middle" of the earnings distribution, the central four deciles ($35,000–$65,000). This threshold is consistent with the living wage levels. It is also consistent with $50,000 family income threshold to be considered middle class (Harry J. Holzer, "Building a New Middle Class in the Knowledge Economy," Progressive Policy Institute, 2017, http://www.progressive policy.org/wp-content/uploads/2017/04/PPI_MiddleClassJobs.pdf). A $35,000 annual wage is three times the poverty level for one person. This earnings level leaves a person with approximately $1,800 per month after food costs of $350, the "high or liberal" menu cost estimate of the U.S. Department of Agriculture (USDA), and rent of $800 per month. (The cost of a liberal food menu plan is an average for unmarried men and women, 19–50 years of age from U.S. Department of Agriculture, "Official USDA Food Plans: Cost of Food at Home at Four Levels, U.S. Average, May 2017," 2017).

101. Anthony Carnevale, Ban Cheah, and Andrew Hanson, *The Economic Value of College Majors* (Washington, D.C.: Georgetown University Center on Education and the Workforce, 2015).

102. Georgetown University Center on Education and the Workforce analysis of *Current Population Survey (CPS), Annual Socioeconomic Supplement* data, 2016.

103. The forgone wages are based on based on starting (18–24 year olds) full-time, full-year (FTFY) earnings of high school graduates. Georgetown University Center on Education and the Workforce analysis of *Current Population Survey*, March Supplement, 2016.

104. Carnevale and Strohl, *Separate & Unequal*.

105. Stacy Berg Dale and Alan B. Krueger, "Estimating the payoff to attending a more selective college: An application of selection on observables and unobservables," *Quarterly Journal of Economics* 117, no. 4 (2002): 1491–527.

106. Andrew Michael Spence, *Market Signaling: Informational Transfer in Hiring and Related Screening Processes* (Cambridge, Mass.: Harvard University Press, 1974).

107. John Bound and Sarah Turner, "Cohort crowding: How resources affect collegiate attainment," *Journal of Public Economics* 91, no. 5 (2007): 877–99.

108. Raj Chetty, John Friedman, Emmanuel Saez, Nicholas Turner, and Danny Yagan, "Mobility Report Cards: The Role of Colleges in Intergenerational Mobility Data," July 2017, http://www.equality-of-opportunity.org/assets/documents/coll_mrc_slides.pdf. The earnings ten years after first enrollment are from the U.S. Department of Education, the *College Scorecard*, linked to other institution-level data.

109. Anthony P. Carnevale, Tanya I. Garcia, and Artem Gulish, *Career Pathways: Five Ways to Connect College and Careers* (Washington, D.C.: Georgetown University Center on Education and the Workforce, 2017).

110. Carnevale, Rose, and Cheah, *The College Payoff*.

111. Carnevale, Garcia, and Gulish, *Career Pathways*.

112. *San Antonio v. Rodriguez* (1973) 411 U.S. 1.

113. The adequacy of inputs is based on equalizing expenditures among school districts that meet the set performance standards according to student scores on standardized proficiency tests. Sarah Archibald and Allan Odden, "A Summary of Previous Research in Wisconsin on School Finance Adequacy," 2005, https://www.researchgate.net/

publication/242278298_A_Summary_of_Previous_Research_in_Wisconsin_on_School_Finance_Adequacy.

114. Chetty, Friedman, Saez, Turner, and Yagan, *Mobility Report Cards.*

115. National Center for Education Statistics (NCES), Integrated Postsecondary Education Data System (IPEDS), Classification of Instructional Programs (CIP) Resources, U.S. Department of Education 2010.

116. National Center for Education Statistics (NCES), *Digest of Education Statistics* tables, U.S. Department of Education, 2015–2016, table 317.10.

117. The Century Foundation Task Force on Preventing Community Colleges from Becoming Separate and Unequal, *Bridging the Higher Education Divide: Strengthening Community Colleges and Restoring the American Dream* (New York: The Century Foundation Press, 2013).

118. Susan Scrivener, Michael J. Weiss, Alyssa Ratledge, Timothy Rudd, Colleen Sommo, and Hannah Fresques, *Doubling Graduation Rates: Three-year Effects of CUNY's Accelerated Study in Associate Programs (ASAP) for Developmental Education Students* (New York: MDRC, 2015).

119. Ibid.

120. Center for Community College Student Engagement, *A Matter of Degrees: Practices to Pathways: High impact practices for community colleges* (Austin: The University of Texas at Austin, 2014).

121. Ibid.

122. Judith Scott-Clayton, "The Shapeless River: Does a Lack of Structure Inhibit Students' Progress at Community Colleges?" CCRC Working Paper no. 25, Community College Research Center, 2011.

123. Angela Boatman, "Evaluating Institution Efforts to Streamline Student Remediation: The Causal Effects of Tennessee Developmental Course Redesign Initiative," National Center for Postsecondary Research, 2012.

124. Craig Hayward and Terrence Willett, *Curricular Redesign and Gatekeeper Completion: A Multi-College Evaluation of the California Acceleration Project* (Sacramento: The Research and Planning Group for California Community Colleges, 2014).

125. Joshua Angrist, Daniel Lang, and Philip Oreopoulos, "Incentives and services for college achievement: Evidence from a randomized trial," *American Economic Journal: Applied Economics* 1, no. 1 (2009): 136–63.

126. Eric Bettinger and Rachel Baker, "The Effects of Student Coaching in College: An Evaluation of a Randomized Experiment in Student Mentoring," NBER Working Paper 16881, National Bureau of Economic Research, 2011.

127. Alexander K. Mayer, Reshma Patel, Timothy Rudd, and Alyssa Ratledge, *Designing Scholarships to Improve College Success: Final Report on the Performance-Based Scholarship Demonstration* (New York: MDRC, 2015).

128. Davis Jenkins, "Get with the Program: Accelerating Community College Students' Entry into and Completion of Programs of Study," CCRC Working Paper no. 32, Community College Research Center, Columbia University, 2011.

129. Anthony Carnevale and Jeff Strohl, "How Increasing College Access Is Increasing Inequality, and What to Do About It," in *Rewarding Strivers: Helping Low-Income Students Succeed in College*, ed. Richard Kahlenberg (New York: The Century Foundation Press, 2010).

130. The Century Foundation Task Force on Preventing Community Colleges from Becoming Separate and Unequal, B*ridging the Higher Education Divide*.

131. Thomas R. Bailey and Shanna Smith Jaggars, "When college students start behind," 2016.

132. The Century Foundation Task Force on Preventing Community Colleges from Becoming Separate and Unequal, *Bridging the Higher Education Divide*.

133. Regina Deil-Amen and Ruth Lopez Turley, "A review of the transition to college literature in sociology," *Teachers College Record* 109, no. 10 (2007): 2324–366; Jennifer Engle, "Postsecondary access and success for first-generation college students," *American Academic* 3, no. 1 (2007): 25–48; Watson Scott Swail, Alberto Cabrera, and Chul Lee, "Latino Youth and the Pathway to College," Pew Hispanic Center, 2004.

134. Douglas Massey, "The age of extremes: Concentrated affluence and poverty in the twenty-first century," *Demography* 33, no. 4 (1996): 395–412; National Academies of Sciences, Engineering, and Medicine, *Information Technology and the U.S. Workforce: Where Are We and Where Do We Go from Here?* (Washington, D.C.: National Academies Press, 2017), doi:10.17226/24649. Lauren Krivo, Heather Washington, Ruth Peterson, Christopher R. Browning, Catherine A. Calder, and Mei-Po Kwan, "Social isolation of disadvantage and advantage: The reproduction of inequality in urban space," *Social Forces* (2013): 141–64.

135. John T. Yun and Jose F. Moreno, "College Access, K–12 Concentrated Disadvantage, and the Next 25 Years of Education Research," 2006.

Policy Strategies for Pursuing Adequate Funding of Community Colleges

RICHARD D. KAHLENBERG, ROBERT SHIREMAN,
KIMBERLY QUICK, and TARIQ HABASH

Community colleges are uniquely situated to address a paramount national challenge: reducing economic inequality. Students who complete an associate's degree have higher rates of employment and significant earnings gains over those with only a high school degree or a general equivalency diploma (GED).[1] With 86 percent of high school graduates going on to further postsecondary education and training,[2] experts are increasingly emphasizing the central importance of high-quality programs that provide ample support to ensure that a high percentage of entrants graduate and enhance their lives and careers. As institutions that serve all students regardless of background and preparation and are located close to where students live and work, community colleges are pivotal in efforts to reduce economic inequality and restore the American Dream—but can only succeed if they are adequately funded.

"Adequate funding" may not have bumper sticker appeal. But the idea is simple and compelling: To help restore social mobility in America, policymakers must provide community colleges the resources necessary to successfully educate the country's aspiring middle class.

This report proceeds in four parts. First, it discusses the need to reform funding of community colleges in order help students succeed. Second, it outlines the current barriers to reform—the lack of research on how much funding community colleges need; the overreliance on tuition dollars and local funding; the haphazard ways in which money is allocated; and the political forces that shape funding decisions. Third, it suggests some reason for optimism: emerging political trends and the existence of alternative models of funding for equity, including K–12 funding formulas in certain states, and higher education funding in countries such as England and Ireland. Fourth, it makes recommendations for a better model of funding community colleges that includes state-level and federal-level reforms. In particular, the report discusses the ways in which proposals for adequately funding community colleges could dovetail with three ongoing trends in higher education: the adoption of state higher education goals, the desire for greater accountability, and the free college movement.

The Need for Reform

Currently, the performance at resource-strapped community colleges is often disappointing.[3] As discussed further below, community colleges frequently do a good job of enrolling disadvantaged students—something elite four year colleges often fail to do. "We serve the top 100 percent of students," notes one community college leader.[4] But there is enormous room for growth in the outcomes that colleges are able to help these students achieve. While more than four out of five first-time beginning community college students say they wish to earn at least a bachelor's degree,[5] only about one out of thirteen students transfer and complete this goal within six years;[6] moreover, only about a third of students earn even just a certificate or associate's degree from the community college.[7]

Among students who go to community college with the eventual goal of getting a bachelor's degree, studies that carefully control for academic and demographic factors find a substantial "community college penalty"—a reduced chance of earning a bachelor's degree—if a student begins at a two-year rather than a four-year institution.[8] For instance, C. Lockwood Reynolds, an economist now at Kent State University, estimated, after applying appropriate controls, that beginning at a two-year college reduces one's ultimate chances of receiving a bachelor's degree by 30 percentage points.[9]

These results are not surprising, given the resource differentials and the complications of transfer, but they are disappointing. Individuals who are trying to better their lives and move out of poverty into the middle class rely on community colleges, yet these schools frequently are not able to provide students with the support they need and deserve. What is holding back students entering community colleges?

Community Colleges Enroll the Most Disadvantaged Students, Yet Receive the Fewest Resources

The prevailing impulse by policymakers in response to poor results is to impose accountability mechanisms on them. For instance, a number of states have shifted toward systems that fund institutions based in part on student progress. But these approaches are unlikely to be effective unless colleges have the resources necessary to provide quality instruction and support, given the needs of the students who typically enroll. We often hear the mantra that community colleges need to do more with less; but if we truly care about improving the promise and performance of two-year schools, we need to investigate, empirically, the importance of resources rather accepting the current level of funding as optimal.

Today, higher education tends to shower the greatest resources on wealthy and high-achieving students with the fewest educational needs, and devotes the fewest resources to economically disadvantaged students with the greatest educational needs.[10] At the most selective four-year colleges, students from the wealthiest socioeconomic quartile outnumber those from the poorest quartile by 14 to 1, yet at community colleges

Figure 1. Socioeconomic Distribution at Colleges by Selectivity, 2006

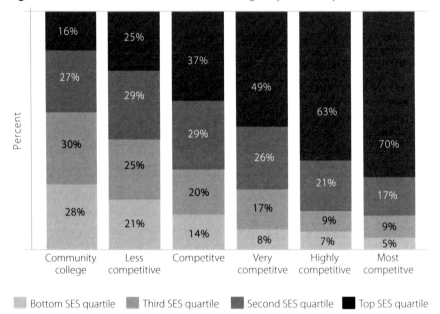

Bottom SES quartile   Third SES quartile   Second SES quartile   Top SES quartile

Source: Anthony P. Carnevale and Jeff Strohl, "How Increasing Access Is Increasing Inequality, and What to Do about It," in Richard D. Kahlenberg (ed), Rewarding Strivers: Helping Low-Income Students Succeed in College (Century Foundation Press, 2010), 137, Figure 3.7.

disadvantaged students outnumber those from the richest quarter by 2 to 1 (see Figure 1).[11]

Stanford University professor Raj Chetty and his colleagues found a similar pattern using a more granular set of data that examined where students from various slices of the income distribution attended college. Students from low-income and moderate-income families were much more likely to attend community colleges than students from higher income families (see Figure 2).

Researchers generally agree that disadvantaged students have the greatest challenges attending college—less access to preparation from high-quality K–12 schooling, greater likelihood of food insecurity during college, and the like. Indeed, researchers estimate that wealthy parents invest about $6,600 per year on enrichment activities for their children, nine times the

Figure 2. Where Today's Twenty-Five-Year-Olds Went to College, Grouped by Their Parents' Income

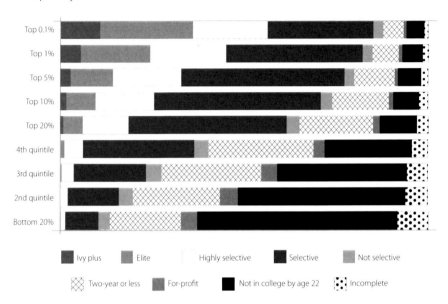

Source: Gregor Aisch, Larry Buchanan, Amanda Cox, and Kevin Quealy, "Some Colleges Have More Students from the Top 1 Percent than the Bottom 60. Find Yours," New York Times, January 18, 2017 (adapted from Source: "Mobility Report Cards: The Role of Colleges in Intergenerational Mobility," The Equality of Opportunity Project).

amount ($750) that low-income parents spend.[12] Multiplied over eighteen years, that $5,850 annual difference amounts to $105,300. Differential access to K–12 schooling opportunities compound those inequalities.

Students who suffer through the inequities of the K–12 education system find that these challenges are exacerbated even further in higher education. As shown in Figure 3, private research universities spend five times as much per student per year ($71,597) as community colleges do ($14,090), and public research universities almost three times as much ($39,783).[13]

Much of the difference in aggregate spending, of course, is connected to different functions associated with different types of universities and colleges. Research universities are charged not only with educating students, but also with conducting basic research that advances human understanding of the world. But inequalities in per student expenditures

Figure 3. Per-Pupil Total Operating Expenditures, FY 2013

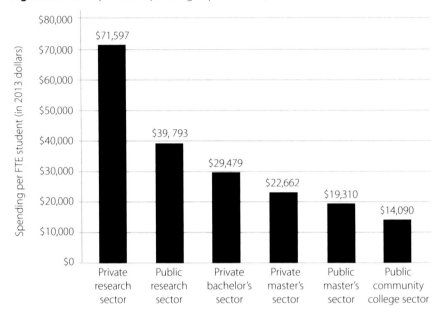

Source: Donna M. Desrochers and Steven Hurlburt, "Trends in College Spending 2003–2013," Delta Cost Project and the American Institutes of Research, January 2016, 24–27.

persist even when one separates out the research function of universities and focuses exclusively on educational instruction.[14] These differences remain substantial after excluding spending on sponsored research and auxiliary enterprises, with private research sectors spending up to three times more than the amount spent by public community colleges in education and related spending.[15]

Moreover, research by George Washington University's Sandy Baum and her coauthor Charles Kurose finds that inequalities in spending remain even when one accounts for the common assumption that the first two years of college are less costly than the third and fourth.[16]

Even more troubling, these disparities in resources are growing. Educational spending per public four-year college student increased by 16 percent between the 2003–04 academic year and 2013–14; by contrast, during this same time period, per student community college funding increased just 4 percent.[17]

Sometimes, the inequity in public spending is generated by explicit policy. In Maryland, for example, state law imposes unequal funding by requiring that full-time equivalent community college students should be funded at 25 percent the level of students at four-year colleges.[18] Moreover, the bottom-line inequality in spending has grown over time. In the period from 2003 to 2013, funding in real terms increased by $5,413 per FTE student at public research universities, while public community colleges saw an increase of just $1,044 in real funding.[19]

It is important also to note that there is substantial inequality in funding within the two-year sector, in part because community colleges typically receive some local funding, which tends to reflect the wealth of neighborhoods. In a 2006 paper, scholars Alicia C. Dowd and John L. Grant found that the intrastate variation in state and local community college appropriations (as measured by the ratio of the community college appropriation at the ninetieth and tenth percentiles of funding in each state) in half the states studied ranged from 2.0 to 2.8. These levels "are considered high in comparison to K–12 finance inequities," the authors concluded.[20] A 2018 analysis of spending on community colleges by Tammy Kolbe and Bruce Baker, likewise, found "substantial differences in per-FTE spending within states. The extent of variation was on par with levels that have raised alarm bells when evaluating fiscal equity among K–12 school districts."[21]

Money—Well Spent—Can Make a Difference in Higher Education and Have Big Payoffs in Economic Growth

To meet the goals of providing equal educational opportunity to students and improving efficiency, we need to examine resource inequities. "Supporting the success of community college students requires much more than adequate funding for the students and their institutions," as Sandy

Baum and Charles Kurose noted in a paper for The Century Foundation. "But without adequate funding, significant progress is unlikely."[22]

At the most basic level, evidence suggests that higher state per-pupil appropriations to community colleges do generally correlate with higher completion rates; high-spending states such as Wyoming, Alaska, and North Dakota all have above-average completion rates.[23] More importantly, careful research by leading economists suggests that community college funding increases cause improved outcomes. David Deming and Christopher Walters, for example, found in an August 2017 study for the National Bureau of Economic Research examining the impact of postsecondary spending between 1990 and 2013 "positive and statistically significant causal impacts of spending on degree completion."[24] The authors found larger impacts of spending in two-year institutions than four-year institutions.[25] An increase in spending in year t resulted in increased awards of certificates and degrees of 14.5 percent in year t + 1 and 14.6 percent in year t + 2.[26] It is possible, the authors suggest, that increased spending means increased course offerings, shorter waiting lists, better student guidance, and smaller class sizes.[27] So powerful were the results, Deming and Walters suggested that the federal government place more emphasis on providing financial support for higher education institutions rather than efforts to reduce tuition costs through financial aid, because access without support is insufficient to raise attainment.[28]

In addition, there is evidence that certain investments are particularly likely to pay off:

- **Full-time faculty.** Much—though not all—relevant research finds that having more full-time faculty on staff leads to improved outcomes for students.[29] Yet today, as a way of saving money, community colleges are much more likely to rely on inexpensive adjuncts and other part-time instructors. Only 31 percent of faculty members at public community colleges are full-time, compared with 42 percent at public research universities and 50 percent at private research universities. (Graduate assistants are counted as part-time in this analysis.)[30] Investing in more full-time community college faculty could result in improved outcomes for students.

- **Extra tutoring, small class size, intensive advising, and generous financial aid.** There is strong evidence that investing in extra tutoring, small class sizes, intensive advising, and generous financial aid at community colleges can have big payoffs. At a typical community college, classes are crowded and student–adviser ratios can be as high as 1,500 to 1. But at the City University of New York's Accelerated Study in Associate Programs (ASAP), students are provided with the tutoring, class size, advising, and effective financial aid more typical of wealthy four-year colleges. These benefits, provided within a highly structured environment in which students must attend classes full time, have been found by the nonprofit research institute MDRC in a randomized trial to nearly double the three-year graduation rates of students (to 40 percent compared with a control group's 22 percent).[31] The program costs 60 percent more per student—about $16,300 more per pupil over three years—yet by boosting results, it actually reduced the amount spent for each college degree awarded by more than 10 percent.[32] More generally, research also finds that investments in smaller class sizes and more counselors in community colleges can improve student outcomes.[33]

- **High-impact practices.** The Center for Community College Student Engagement has found a positive relationship between thirteen "high-impact" practices—orientation, accelerated developmental education, first year experiences, student success courses, learning communities, academic goal setting and planning, experiential learning beyond the classroom, tutoring, supplemental instruction, proper assessment and placement, registration before classes start, alerts and interventions, and structured group learning experiences—and positive student outcomes.[34] Numerous other studies find positive results from redesigned developmental education, academic support services, and other interventions.[35] We mention these examples of productive spending not to suggest that a straightjacket be imposed on community college presidents to spend resources in a particular way, but rather to illustrate that these practice often require increased investments.

Rigorous research on the four-year college sector has also found that resources can have a powerful influence on outcomes for students. John Bound of the University of Michigan, Michael Lovenheim of Cornell, and Sarah Turner of the University of Virginia, for example, found in an important 2010 study that declining completion rates over time were due primarily to declines in resources per student.[36]

Research evaluating the importance of resources in the K–12 level is also particularly relevant to the community college arena given the similar demographic populations served by the two sectors. In a 2017 analysis, Bruce Baker, after analyzing national and state-specific studies, concluded: "The preponderance of the evidence shows that resources do matter."[37] Likewise, in a February 2018 study of California's K–12 funding increases, Rucker Johnson of the University of California, Berkeley, and Sean Tanner of WestEd, looking at the effects of the Local Control Funding Formula, "found strongly significant impacts of LCFF-induced increases in district revenue on average high school graduation rates for all children." In particular, they found that "a $1,000 increase in district per-pupil revenue from the state experienced in grades 10–12 leads to a 5.3 percentage-point increase in high school graduation rates, on average, among all children."[38]

A better-funded system of community colleges could have a big payoff for society at large. In 2012, annual average earnings for associate's degree holders were $12,000 (51 percent) more than for high-school graduates with no college. The present value of those net additional lifetime earnings is $246,000.[39] While some believe that it is appropriate to put the cost burden of education primarily on students, because they will reap private gains from education, in fact there is a long line of research suggesting that there are enormous spillover benefits to expanding higher education opportunities for society as a whole. The higher earnings of community college graduates can fuel more economic growth and more tax revenue for states. The present value of lifetime taxes paid by an individual with an associate's degree is estimated to be $201,341 compared with $136,654 for a high school graduate.[40] And people with associate's degrees reduce state expenditures on public assistance. The poverty rate of an associate's degree holder (7.7 percent) is half the rate of high school graduates with no college (15.3 percent).[41] Associate's degree holders receive about $22,000 less in lifetime public assistance as high school graduates, in present value terms.[42] A 2014 study found that, overall, the benefit to taxpayers of investing in community colleges exceeded the costs by a factor of 2.5 to 1.[43]

The Current System of Funding Makes All of Higher Education Less Cost Effective

The current approach—inequitable investments in low-income and low-achieving students—creates powerful inefficiencies, in that it leads far too many students to drop out before completion. It simply is inefficient to enroll students in programs that are not adequately supported with institutional resources.[44]

According to research from the National Student Clearinghouse Research Center, the outcomes of students entering community college show that, six years later, only 29.8 percent have completed a two-year degree, and 7.7 percent have completed a four-year degree. In other words, as Figure 4 shows, six years after beginning college, 62.5 percent have not received a degree of any type (15.2 percent are still enrolled, but 47.3 percent are no longer enrolled).[45]

Granted, there can be valuable learning gained from taking courses without receiving a credential. However, to the extent that enrolling students hope for a benefit in terms of their earning potential, the evidence of wage gains from attending some college without receiving a certificate or degree is mixed.[46]

Figure 4. Six-Year Outcomes for Community College Students

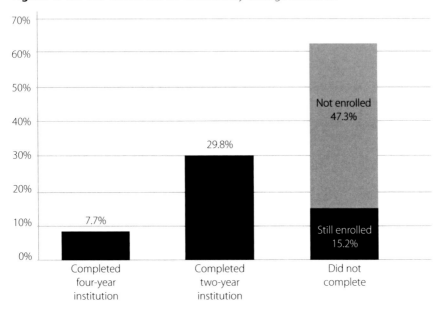

Source: National Student Clearinghouse Research Center, Signature Report: Completing College: A National View of Student Completion Rates—Fall 2011 Cohort, December 2017, 14, Figure 8.

The underfunding of the community college sector may also be cost inefficient to the extent that it pushes students toward for-profit colleges and online learning—neither of which has a particularly good track record for students. After a two-year investigation of thirty for-profit companies, the U.S. Senate Committee on Health, Education, Labor, and Pensions reported in 2012 that while community colleges and for-profit two-year programs have similar retention rates, "the cost of the for-profit programs makes those programs riskier for students and Federal taxpayers." The committee noted: "While 96 percent of those attending a for-profit college borrow to attend, just 13 percent of community college students do so."[47]

Furthermore, students who are swayed to enroll at a for-profit rather than a community college may be incurring debt with little to show for it. On average, students attending for-profit programs earn no more than if they had not attended college at all, according to one recent study.[48]

Likewise, low-income and less prepared students show worse outcomes when enrolling online.[49] When community colleges push their students into online classes to save money, retention rates fall.[50]

Barriers to Reform

Given the considerable evidence suggesting that increased resources could improve outcomes in community colleges, why do inadequate levels of funding persist? Four explanations stand out: (1) scholars have failed to generate sufficient research on the true cost of a high quality community college education; (2) an overreliance on local funding and tuition dollars undercuts resources at open access institutions; (3) state funding is often allocated in a haphazard or poorly designed fashion; and (4) unfortunate political structures support inequitable funding schemes. This section explores each barrier to reform in turn.

Inadequate Research on the True Cost of a High Quality Community College Education

Although there is evidence that additional investment in community colleges could improve completion, equity, and quality, there is inadequate research on the appropriate level of spending necessary to meet those goals. Relatedly, how much more do low-income and ill-prepared students need, compared with other students, to produce acceptable outcomes? The K–12 system—which has greater experience educating disadvantaged students and has higher completion rates than higher education—has a much stronger research basis for answering those questions than does higher education.[51]

The Century Foundation Working Group on Community College Financial Resources, whose report opens this volume, creates a framework for how K–12 costing out analysis might be applied to community colleges. To guide the group's work, The Century Foundation (TCF) commissioned a few background papers that are also contain in this volume. In the first, Bruce Baker of Rutgers University and Jesse Levin of the American Institutes of Research tackle the question of how K–12 costing out analysis might apply to community colleges. They note the absence of rigorous analyses of what it costs to provide an adequate community college education. They also observe that models are widely employed at the K–12 level to conduct such cost analyses. While acknowledging critical differences between higher education and K–12 schooling, they make recommendations on how K–12 costing methodologies could be adapted to community colleges.[52]

In the second background paper, Anthony Carnevale, Jeff Strohl, and Artem Gulish of Georgetown University analyze the appropriate metrics by which to judge community college performance. In order to determine the costs of an adequate community college program, one must first identify clearly defined goals for the program. The authors propose that, in order to be "adequate," a community college education should not only provide a reasonable likelihood of completion, but also produce skills for gainful employment that allow for the full flourishing of individuals. Specifically, the authors propose a two-part test for economic self-sufficiency: (1) "a program must leave its graduates earning more than $35,000 per year ten years after they have completed it"; and (2) "over that ten-year period, that program also must provide its graduates with a sufficient earnings premium, compared to the earnings of workers with only a high-school diploma, to cover the program's total cost to the student."[53]

Barriers to Equity Baked Into the Current Systems Funding Community Colleges

Even if researchers are able to articulate a defensible number for what it costs to provide an adequate education—and for the premium needed to educate disadvantaged students well—three other barriers to equitable funding exist, related to where money comes from, how it is allocated, and the political structures that control the system.

Where the Money Comes From: The Overreliance on Local Funds and Tuition

The funding of community colleges is based on a hybrid model that draws a piece from four-year colleges (with some reliance on tuition dollars) and another piece from K–12 education (with some reliance on local appropriations). In some ways, however, this in-between position results in the worst of all worlds. The reliance on local funds is regressive, since wealthier districts supply more funds to community colleges in rich areas; and the reliance on tuition dollars means the burden of funding education can be shifted from the state to the individual—which is precisely what legislators have done in recent years, as the student population has grown more diverse.

Originally, tuition was not a major source of community college funding. Many of the early community colleges—at the time usually referred to as "junior" colleges—began as extensions of K–12 education systems and followed the K–12 model that is 100 percent funded by state or local appropriations. Under this system, the enrollment of each additional student creates a need for coverage of 100 percent of the marginal institutional costs, either by spreading existing resources over a larger number of students, or by adding more funding. This relationship has shifted over time as the proportion of state and local funding of two-year colleges declined from 64 percent to 52 percent and funding through tuition revenue increased from 22 percent to 33 percent (see Figure 5).

The shift was facilitated by federal financial aid. Tuition support that was available first from the GI Bill after World War II, and then from federal student aid programs in the 1960s and 1970s, encouraged public institutions to join private colleges in the use of tuition revenue as a way to pay to costs of greater student enrollment. From an institutional standpoint, increasing enrollment without charging tuition would place the added financial burden squarely on the state or local government, while switching to charging tuition would bring in per-student funds from the federal government, at least for some students. The problem with this model is that not all students can afford to pay, as they face not only tuition expenses,

Figure 5. Funding Sources and Enrollment at Two-Year Public Institutions in the United States

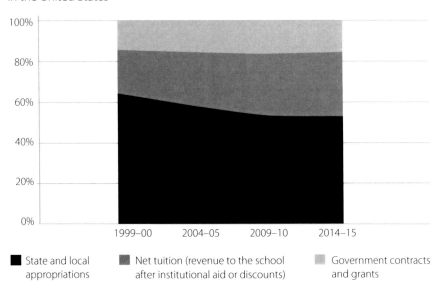

State and local appropriations

Net tuition (revenue to the school after institutional aid or discounts)

Government contracts and grants

Source: Compiled February 2017 by author from Jennifer Ma and Sandy Baum, "Trends in College Pricing 2012," College Board, October 2012; Jennifer Ma, Sandy Baum, Matea Pender, and Meredith Welch, "Trends in College Pricing 2017," College Board, October 2017 and U.S. Department of Education, National Center for Education Statistics, Higher Education General Information Survey (HEGIS), "Fall Enrollment in Colleges and Universities" surveys, 1967 through 1985; Integrated Postsecondary Education Data System (IPEDS), "Fall Enrollment Survey" (IPEDS-EF:86–89); IPEDS Spring 2001 through Spring 2016, Fall Enrollment component; and Enrollment in Degree-Granting Institutions Projection Model, 2000 through 2026.

but also the costs of housing, food, transportation, books and, frequently, supporting families.

The burden on students to provide tuition dollars for public higher education creates greater hardships in some states than others. The use of tuition charges as a revenue source varies enormously across the states. Some states appropriate four or five times as much as their public institutions receive in net tuition, while in other states it is the opposite: tuition support is two, three, or four times the appropriations.[54] (See Figure 6).

On the other hand, there is logic to the idea that charging tuition allows institutions to serve more students. After all, if every student must be fully financed by tax revenue, then a given amount of tax revenue can only finance a certain number of students. A student who pays tuition that at

Figure 6. Net Tuition Revenues Relative to Total Appropriations for Public Higher Education, by State, Fiscal Year 2014

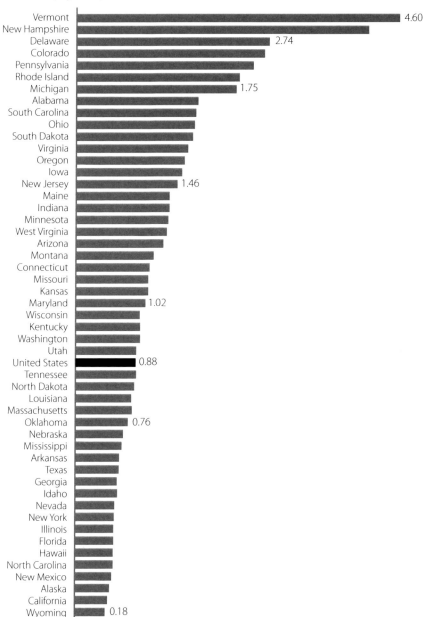

Source: National Center for Education Statistics, "Integrated Postsecondary Education Data Syste," 2014.

least equals the marginal institutional cost is increasing the capacity of the institution by one. If every student paid half of the cost of running the institution, on average, then twice as many students could be served compared to if there was no tuition.

But the increased reliance on tuition dollars, especially at open access community colleges, is also deeply problematic. Since state lawmakers see tuition as a viable alternative source of revenue for their colleges, when state tax revenues are tight, higher education may appear to be among the least problematic places to reduce state spending. As a result, higher education is frequently among the first areas to suffer cuts when states face budget shortfalls.[55]

More troubling still, there is evidence that recent disinvestment in public higher education may be related to the growing demographic diversity of the student population. Although conservative complaints about higher education focus on liberalism, Ronald Brownstein of *The Atlantic* makes the case that the changing demographics of the student body seems a more likely explanation for conservative enthusiasm to cut higher education budgets. There has been a "clear determination . . . to shift the burden from the community collectively to families individually precisely as the student body is reaching historic levels of diversity."[56] As the nation's population becomes blacker and browner, this challenge may become even more acute.

How Funding Is Allocated: Too Often Haphazardly or Poorly

In theory, state funding of community colleges could compensate for inequities in local funding, but few states fully do so. State funding is often haphazard, sometimes not even based on a formula at all. And, to the extent that states have adopted formulas in recent years, the predominant trend is toward poorly designed performance metrics.

As recently as 2012, there were seventeen states that did not have any set formula that drives funding to the state's community colleges, according to a study by SRI International.[57] Since that study was conducted, a subset of those states have adopted performance-based formulas. The bulk of states that do not have funding formulas typically base the next year's funding on the prior year's funding, adjusting it by a percentage across the board. Other non-formula states adjust funding based on legislative priorities.

In the states that do use formulas, most use various measures of enrollment of state residents or so-called performance funding (which has not generally been found to produce better results for students.).[58] SRI International did not find any state that allocated formula funds to community colleges specifically for financial aid, though California now has such a program.[59]

Even in states where there is a formula based on enrollment—so that college can establish a budget and ensure that there is an adequate number of instructors and classroom space—it is usually based on a *prior* year's enrollment. In other words, in any particular year, the colleges are not necessarily able to get more money for the school year by enrolling more students; nor are they faced with a budget cut if their enrollment drops from the previous year. The increased or decreased allocation comes in a later year.

When a state decides to make funding available for additional enrollment, it frequently does so as a percentage increase to all of its colleges. While an "equal percentage" may seem like an equitable approach, consider what would happen if it was applied in the K–12 context: budget growth would be unrelated to need, such that shrinking communities would have stable funding for their emptying schools, while communities with population growth would soon have five-year olds without a school nearby to attend. Such a lack of kindergarten access would be obvious and would be addressed, but in higher education, the lack of adequate access spurs little response.

The strong presumption in favor of funding community colleges according to their historical enrollment levels can mean that geographic areas end up being under-served by their community colleges because those colleges are not able to grow commensurate with local needs. A study of California colleges used counts of adults without a college degree as an indicator of need, and found that access was higher by a factor of three or four in some areas of the state compared to others.[60] To address inadequate access in particular geographic areas, California revised its formula for allocating "growth" funds so that the formula includes consideration of the number of adults who lack a college degree, are unemployed, or are in poverty, compared to the community college enrollment of the population in the area. Those districts with larger gaps between need and current enrollment are allocated more growth.[61]

Unfortunate Political Structures that Support Current Inequitable Funding Mechanisms

Current funding levels for community colleges are the result of important political realities that must be recognized. Scaling investments to meet adequate levels of funding for community colleges faces three critical political challenges associated with political power realities, state budget constraints, and declining support for higher education as registered in public opinion research.

First, current institutional funding disparities—both those between four-year universities and community colleges and those between community colleges themselves—result in part from inequitable access to political power.[62] State representatives—who are more likely to have attended or sent their children to four-year institutions—may also be more likely to respond to the interests of wealthy donors, who support investments in these schools rather than community colleges.[63] While higher education funding should not be a zero-sum game, where two- and four-year institutions compete against one another for limited resources, community colleges must receive the necessary resources to deliver high-quality opportunities to all students.

Second, state policymakers determining community college funding face budget constraints. States slashed their higher education budgets during the Great Recession, but even today, slow revenue growth—which economists attribute to a number of factors, including falling agricultural commodity and energy prices, but also state decisions to enact costly tax cuts and reticence to raise additional revenue streams—poses challenges to meeting adequacy funding goals. A December 2017 report from National Association of State Budget Offices indicates that state budget expenditures saw the lowest year-over-year increase in the post-recession era, with twenty-six states enacting budgets with general spending increases under 2 percent, and fifteen states enacting budget reductions. Even when considering investments that fuel economic growth in the long run, state legislators are often reticent to raise taxes needed to pay for them;[64] combined with the fact that most states have balanced budget requirements, it is difficult for states to increase education spending absent a bond initiative or a revenue windfall. Indeed, according to American Association of State Colleges and Universities analysis of state higher education policy issues in 2018, political uncertainty, stagnant state revenue growth, competing state priorities, and upcoming election cycles will be the primary determinants of state higher education policy priorities.[65]

Finally, public support of and confidence in institutions of higher education have increasingly fallen amongst Republicans and conservatives. According to a 2017 survey by Pew Research Center, 58 percent of Republicans and Republican-leaning independents believe that colleges and universities have a negative effect on the way things are going in the country, while just 36 percent say their effect is positive. Strikingly, Republicans' attitudes towards college were positive as recently as 2014, when a 54 percent majority of Republicans and Republican-leaners said that colleges were having a positive effect.[66] This suggests views may be fluid. Some of this hostility may stem from a belief that, due to rising prices, quality higher education has become an increasingly inaccessible and elitist project.

In some ways, this critique is fair. As noted above, whereas high-socioeconomic-status students outnumber low-socioeconomic-status students at the most competitive four year institutions, the reverse is true in community colleges; that is, society's resources increasingly are being dedicated to quality higher education for the wealthy only.[67] Research also demonstrates that the income gap in degree attainment has widened.

According to research by University of Michigan economists Martha J. Bailey and Susan Dynarski, children of wealthy families are six times as likely to graduate from college as those from poor families.[68]

However, disinvestment in higher education is the wrong reaction to these trends, as it tends to reinforce this inaccessibility rather than alleviate it. Community colleges are often the campuses doing the most to offer diverse options to underserved populations and the working class.

Reasons for Optimism for a Path Forward

Although the current funding system—and the political dynamics underlying it—is deeply troubling, some reasons for optimism exist. This section outlines five areas where political trends give reason for hope that community college funding can be reformed. It also looks to K–12 funding in certain states, and to higher education funding in places such as Ireland and England, as sources of inspiration.

New Positive Political Trends Offer Levers for Change

Several political opportunities are available to elevate the need for adequate funding for community colleges related to workforce development, populism, local control, the free college movement, and even performance funding.

- **Workforce development.** As noted above, several states—particularly conservative states—that have increased their commitment to higher education have done so (in part) by tying higher education investments to workforce development. Tennessee's Reconnect program allows adults to access last-dollar scholarships to community colleges. Kentucky used a $100 million bond initiative to distribute funding for targeted workforce development grants, and Arkansas approved limited free community college based on workforce needs. Lifting up community colleges as gateways to workforce opportunities continues to resonate.[69]

- **Populism.** Investment in community colleges counters the growing conservative narrative that higher education is elitist by supporting lower-tuition, open access institutions that more likely serve predominantly disadvantaged populations. Community colleges completely bypass the anger directed at elite four-year schools, which are often portrayed as gated communities with very high entrance fees. A 2018 Demos poll found that 85 percent of Americans have a favorable view of community colleges compared with 66 percent who have such a view of private four-year colleges.[70] Likewise, a 2018 poll from New America found that 83 percent of Republicans and 81 percent of Democrats say community college is worth the cost. Adam Harris, writing about the poll in *The Atlantic*, noted "Despite lukewarm feelings about higher education generally, 80 percent of Americans have a positive view of the institution near them—that often means community colleges."[71]

- **Local control.** Unlike four-year institutions, community colleges are geographically dispersed and rooted in myriad communities throughout states. These realities give them political breadth, and also appeal among conservatives, who like the idea of institutions that serve the particular needs of local communities. Likewise, community college graduates are more likely to stay and work near their alma mater than graduates of four-year colleges, who frequently decamp to far flung regions of the country.[72]

- **Connecting to free college.** The free community college movement has also gained traction nationally—including in "red" states like Tennessee. Designing those proposals in a way that makes clear that adequacy-level funding is an important pillar presents a viable possibility in some states.[73] Similarly and relatedly, even as state budgets have not rebounded with the strength needed to reinvest in education funding at pre-Recession levels, states have started to reverse their per FTE cuts and are putting some (though limited) money back into higher education. In those states, reinvestment conversations could be benchmarked to adequacy funding metrics.

- **Performance funding.** Finally, there may be a chance to insert the need for adequacy funding into the ongoing, often bipartisan conversations around so-called performance-based funding. There is little evidence that performance-based funding improves performance, and considerable evidence that it can work against needy students and incentivize inefficient gaming of measures.[74] But the instinctual political appeal of the concept creates the opportunity for discussions in which the issue of funding adequacy can be a core element. Providing policymakers with evidence about practices that would improve student success, and what those practices cost, opens a door to increased funding whether or not performance becomes part of a funding formula.

Alternative Funding Models That Give Hope for More Equitable Funding of Higher Education

While inadequate funding of community colleges is a longstanding problem, other models—including parts of the U.S. K–12 system of funding, and the funding of higher education in foreign countries such as Ireland and England—offer alternative visions for how U.S. higher education could be financially supported.

U.S. K–12 Education

In thinking through alternative funding systems, the K–12 system is a reasonable model to consider (even acknowledging key differences between the community college and K–12 systems). This suggestion might seem odd at first blush. Top American colleges and universities rank among the best in the world, and higher education is routinely cited as a model for our elementary and secondary schools. But completion rates in higher education are poor: only about half of all full-time students graduate, compared with nine of ten in our K–12 system. Moreover, our K–12 system has much more experience and success educating a broad cross-section of students.

In learning how to educate growing numbers of low-income and minority students, higher education could learn much from what has worked to address funding inequalities in our K–12 schools.

To be sure, there are important differences between K–12 and higher education that need to be acknowledged. (See text box.) Having said that, certain funding principles at the K–12 level may apply to the community college sector.

The Differences between K–12 and Higher Education: Who Is Served

The factors that go into a spending-per-student figure in public K–12 education are far simpler than the factors that affect public higher education. In a K–12 system, the number of students who need a seat in a classroom is a given: it is the number of youth in the geographic area covered by the school district. There may be complications over which school a student is assigned to, and some spillage into private schools, but the school district or state is ultimately responsible for finding a seat for, essentially, every person between the ages of about five and about eighteen.

The K–12 education system has an obligation to serve everyone. Postsecondary education is completely different. There is no fixed set of people who must be enrolled, nor a common understanding of what they should be studying or how long they should persist. For community colleges, there is no naturally defined who or what; those are politically determined, and a considerable amount of choice is left to individual students.

How many people enroll in a community college, and who they are, depends on the kinds of courses and programs that are offered, when and where the classes are held, the admissions requirements and procedures, the type of outreach that is done, the pricing and aid models, transportation and parking, and numerous other design factors. Those factors are generally not at play in K–12 enrollment, except in how some of them might affect dropout rates.

Translating the analyses of adequacy in K–12 education into a similar analysis of community college funding is complicated by the lack of an exogenous denominator (who is to be served). Without a consideration of who is and is not enrolling, an analysis could determine that the enrolled students in a particular community are being served phenomenally well, even though the education is available to very few of the people who need it.

Roughly speaking, K–12 public schools receive their funding from three sources: local revenues (45 percent), state revenues (45 percent), and federal revenues (10 percent).[75] Local sources tend to reflect the wealth of communities and give rise to large inequalities; but, over time, federal and state sources have sought to ameliorate those inequalities.

Beginning in 1965, Title I of the Elementary and Secondary Education Act began providing "compensatory" funding on the premise that schools with concentrations of poverty deserve greater resources. To discourage local school districts from using federal funds for disadvantaged children to displace what the district might have otherwise spent on such students, the federal government requires that federal funds must supplement rather than supplant local efforts.[76]

Historically, state K–12 funding has not been particularly progressive, and it remains highly inequitable in many states. But over time, a series of state lawsuits has brought greater progressive change in some states. In the first phase, progressive litigators brought lawsuits to ensure that an equal amount of money be spent on low-income and high-income students. But these cases were soon replaced by a desire for "adequate" funding to reach a particular substantive outcome. These adequacy lawsuits were more far reaching in two respects: (1) they sought not just equal inputs in spending, but a substantive level of educational results for all students (such as numeracy and literacy in order to be good citizens); and (2) they recognized that to reach those results, more money must be devoted to disadvantaged students than to advantaged students.[77] Today, at the state level, thirty-seven K–12 funding formulas recognize that students with greater needs deserve greater resources.[78] (See Figure 7.)

To establish the appropriate funding premium for low-income students in K–12 education, adequacy studies have been commissioned in several states to cost out the funding necessary to achieve a given result.[79] A 2008 review of thirteen studies found that the extra cost of educating socioeconomically disadvantaged students ranged from 22.5 percent to 167.5 percent more than other students with no needs that would require

Figure 7. K–12 State Funding for Low-Income Students or
Compensatory Education

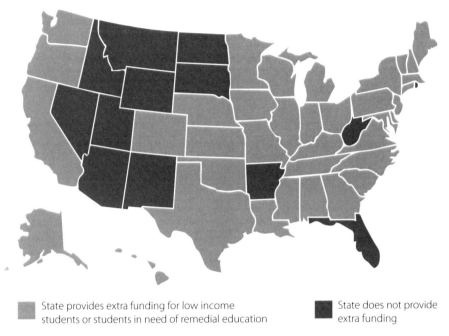

State provides extra funding for low income students or students in need of remedial education

State does not provide extra funding

Source: Deborah A. Verstegen, "How Do States Pay for Schools? An Update of a 50-State Survey of Finance Policies and Programs," Association for Education Finance and Policy Annual Conference, San Antonio, Texas, March 15, 2014, 8.

additional educational supports, such as being designated as an English learner, identified as eligible for special education services, and the like.[80] In a 2015 analysis, the Education Trust said a 40 percent premium should be considered "conservative," given some research finding that it costs twice as much to educate low-income students to the same standards as more-affluent students.[81] Although many inequities remain in our K–12 system of funding, when federal and state and local resources are considered, high-poverty districts spent an equal or greater amount on students than wealthier districts in forty-five states in 2012.[82]

None of this is to suggest we should celebrate "mission accomplished" on K–12 funding equity. But a few states—such as New Jersey and Massachusetts—can be considered models.[83]

To be sure, there are myriad differences between K–12 and higher education, which Baker and Levin's paper acknowledge. To begin with, in higher education, the costing-out process is more complicated than in K–12 because the goalposts vary by institution. Whereas public primary and secondary education institutions within a state have similarly defined expectations and goals for all students, often measured by standardized test scores and graduation requirements, higher education goals are more varied, and measures of success are less firmly established. At certain community colleges, the main goal is to educate students to master a technical skill in order to become certified in a trade. Other community colleges focus on associate's degrees and transfer to four-year institutions. Similarly, four-year liberal arts colleges have different goals than research universities. To complicate matters further, different degree programs within institutions that generate different types of degrees have different cost structures—science instruction with expensive labs and lower class sizes, for example, may be more costly than instruction in history.

Nevertheless, as Baker and Levin's paper demonstrates, it is possible to derive reasonable estimates of costs associated with the instructional goals at a given type of institution (in our case, community colleges). States have already been grappling with these questions as they employ so-called outcome-based higher education funding, meaning they provide some portion of funding based on student outcomes.[84] As part of this process, states have necessarily devised standards of success that offer benchmarks to which higher education "adequacy" funding can be tied. Better research is needed to inform these policies.

International Models of Funding for Higher Education

Some international models attempt to incentivize matriculation of non-traditional and low-income students through funding counsels. The countries that employ these models typically have more centralized funding than U.S.-based higher education institutions, and place the responsibility of higher education funding more on the public than on the individual (though they have been shifting toward the latter recently). In particular, the categories of need identified in Ireland's and England's funding schemes can provide valuable insights into potential U.S. funding models, as well as both systems' acknowledgement that serving higher levels of need necessitates greater resources.

Ireland: Funding Using "Access Weighting"

In Ireland, national policy priorities include widening access to institutions of higher education, enhancing performance outcomes, and providing greater flexibility in provision. One method to achieve these objectives—particularly the goal of increased access—is weighting public investments in higher education toward institutions that serve those from lower socioeconomic backgrounds and underrepresented minorities.[85]

Ireland frames this funding policy as necessary to achieve its clearly stated goals. The nation is seeking a 72 percent higher education participation target by 2020, which will require significant increases in participation of underrepresented groups. (According to national benchmarks, all socioeconomic groups should have entry rates of at least 54 percent by this date as well.)[86]

The Higher Education Authority (HEA) identifies "access students"—those populations targeted by the National Access Plan's funding scheme—as learners falling into three categories: (1) mature students, defined as those aged twenty-three and older prior to first undergraduate entry; (2) students with disabilities; and (3) students from working-class backgrounds. In addition, Ireland is tracking data on students from specific minority ethnic and cultural backgrounds, though specific targets do not apply to these groups.

In September 2004, the OECD National Review of Higher Education in Ireland highlighted the need for the HEA to acknowledge within its funding formula "the additional costs of recruiting and retaining students from disadvantaged backgrounds." The HEA responded with a funding model that included a 33 percent bump in the weighting provided to institutions per "access" student from a target population. However, institutions receiving those additional resources have the flexibility to use them for activities beyond the access office, including but not limited to teaching and research.

Ireland is currently evaluating the effectiveness of its access weighting model, but early determinations have been generally positive. The already high tertiary education attainment rate among individuals ages thirty through thirty-four grew from an initial 27.5 percent in 2000 to 52.3 percent in 2015. All groups in Irish society have experienced increased levels of higher education participation and attainment, including students considered socioeconomically disadvantaged, students with disabilities, and nontraditionally aged students.

Having said that, when providing feedback, some universities and institutes of technology suggested that the scheme failed to sufficiently focus on pre-entry access support for schools and communities, and some schools questioned whether the 33 premium given to an access student is an adequate reflection of the additional costs to support that student. Some respondents also called for better application of access weightings to part-time students.[87]

England: Funding Premium for Students in Low-Income Postal Codes

England maintains a similar commitment to bolstering access and retention through institutional funding schemes.[88] In 2016–17, England allocated participation access funding to recognize the additional costs of supporting students in three areas: (1) students from disadvantaged backgrounds, (2) students with disabilities, and (3) those students for whom retention might be a concern. These funds are allocated to institutions rather than to students, categorized within funds for teaching.[89] As in Ireland, schools in England maintain a great deal of autonomy regarding how they choose to spend any additional funds received.

To inform teaching grant allocations, the Higher Education Funding Council for England (HEFCE) uses the Higher Education Statistics Agency (HESA) individualized student record in concert with the Higher Education

Students Early Statistics survey (HESES). Together, along with supplemental but equivalent data returns on full economic costs (FECs), these sources provide data on the number of students per institution, their aggregated academic activity (full-time or part-time and program choice), and student characteristics that could be used to determine targeted allocations.

One such target program is the National Collaborative Outreach Programme (NCOP), a new geographically focused, national scheme distributed to twenty-nine local consortia. NCOP targets locales where students have the qualifications and potential to succeed in higher education, but where entry rates remain very low. This program aligns with national goals to double the proportion of disadvantaged young people entering higher education between 2009 and 2020, and raise the number of students from black and minority ethnic communities studying in higher education by 20 percent by that same date.[90] The HEFCE recognizes that "some students need more support than others to see their courses through to completion, because of factors to do with their background or circumstances."

The HEFCE was dismantled in March 2018; however, evaluators continue to study many of its initiatives. Overall, young student participation rates in England have risen since the 1990s, with most of the increase—six percentage points—occurring since the mid-2000s. Large differences in participation rates of advantaged and disadvantaged young people remain, with the gap suspended at around forty percentage points. However, both advantaged and disadvantaged areas saw sizable participation increases of +16 percent and +52 percent, respectively. While not all of this growth can be directly attributed to postal code weighting, HEFCE believes that it was a factor in this progress.[91]

Proposal for a Better Model

What is to be done? Building on lessons learned from the adoption of equitable K–12 funding mechanisms in certain states and from higher education funding models used in some other countries, we recommend changes at both the state and federal levels. In short, this section recommends that:

- states use research to tie funding directly to the accomplishment of specific state education goals;
- states adopt a bargain by which increased funding is connected to smart accountability schemes;
- states couple new free college initiatives with commitments to ensure that the community college education being provided is adequately funded to provide high-quality opportunities; and
- the federal government forge a new partnership with states in which states that commit to providing adequate community college funding will receive matching federal grants.

State-Based Strategies

In states, we advocate a strategy for investing appropriate funds into community college educations to benefit all students, and especially those who are disadvantaged. Our key aim is to provide the resources that these students need and deserve to succeed. We begin with the premise that we want to achieve two objectives:

- **Improve college access.** Community colleges should provide opportunities for entry to students from all backgrounds to the types of programs they would like to pursue in the geographic areas in which students are located; and
- **Improve college quality to support success.** Community colleges should provide opportunities for success in these programs and regions, with a recognition that vulnerable students will need more, not fewer, resources in order to be successful.

We believe a funding formula that recognizes student needs is critical. In some respects, California's new Student Focused Funding Formula, adopted in 2018, represents an important model. For the 2018–19 school year, 70 percent of funding is based on overall enrollment, 20 percent is based on how many low-income and first-generation students are enrolled, and 10 percent is for rewarding student success. By 2020–21, the ratios evolve to 60–20–20. The student success portion of the formula (which looks at course completion, degrees and certificates awarded, and attaining a regional living wage) includes an equity component which provides a bonus for community colleges which succeed with low-income and first-generation students.[92]

In order to reach the objectives of college access and quality to support success, we think it may be possible to harness three existing trends in higher education if—and only if—policies are implemented with a focus on equity:

- **Setting state goals.** Many scholars have noted that K–12 reform—and investment of resources—accelerated when states began to articulate clearly defined goals and standards. State litigation for "adequate" spending, for example, faced a dilemma because courts would be reluctant to establish by themselves standards of what students should know and be able to do. But once states began defining the standards, litigants could point to those state-established standards as a benchmark against which spending could be judged to be adequate or inadequate.[93] Ireland's system of higher education, which is weighted in favor of institutions serving disadvantaged students and sets clear goals as part of its National Plan for Equity of Access, provides a model for this.[94] Forty-one states have created goals to increase educational attainment, according to the Lumina Foundation.[95] How can the existence of state goals, or the setting of further state goals, be shaped to promote adequate resources for community colleges?

- **Pursuing accountability.** Many states have tied funding to accountability schemes. One of the most popular strategies is to fund colleges by "performance" or "outcomes," a policy that we believe has a mixed and as yet unproven track record.[96] The question becomes: Is there way to design an accountability system that could actually result in greater equity?

- **Providing free college.** According to Century Foundation senior fellow Jen Mishory, nineteen states have adopted statewide College Promise programs that provide free or debt-free tuition to at least a substantial subset of students. Ten of these programs have been enacted and funded since 2014.[97] As Mishory and others have noted, there are pros and cons to such programs.[98] How can this movement be harnessed to also ensure adequate funding for community colleges?

Setting State Goals—and Supporting Them with Resources

The vast majority of states have set state goals. Adopting goals is an important first step, but simply setting them does not, in and of itself, guarantee adequate and equitable funding will follow. Some states have adopted goals around increased attainment, only to face budget shortfalls that led directly to cuts in higher education funding.[99] Without committing the resources necessary to reach the goals set, we see problems with meeting those goals.[100] Strong leadership must accompany any goals to ensure that colleges are provided the resources necessary to attain the goals articulated.

It is also important that these goals be constructed in the right way to serve as a catalyst for productive and equitable reforms. In particular, we recommend three ways that state goals can promote the goal of equity and adequate resources:

- The strongest types of goals are those that set objectives for the entire state population—for example, 60 percent of state residents should have a postsecondary degree or credential—as opposed to ones that seek to have a certain completion rate for colleges (which might encourage institutions of higher education simply to cherry-pick the most advantaged students whose chances of completion, on average, are higher than those from economically disadvantaged families).

- State goals that aim for a certain number of credentials need some form of check to ensure that credentials are meaningful. To guard against grade and credential inflation, states might consider labor market outcomes as one measure of whether credentials earned are worthwhile.[101]

- To reduce the chances that racial, ethnic, or economic subgroups of students are left behind, state goals (and accountability schemes) should disaggregate data by race, ethnicity, and economic status. This type of approach has been employed at the K–12 level, and there is broad agreement among liberals and conservatives alike that disaggregated data is an important first step for reducing inequity. So too, in higher education, the Lumina Foundation has emphasized that in order to reach larger attainment goals, "we must close gaps by race, ethnicity, income, and immigration status."[102]

If done right, we think setting concrete goals for what community colleges can do for a state has the potential to help explain to the public and public officials why they need to invest, and invest equitably. If voters and policymakers only hear that community colleges want more funding, they won't have a clear idea of the benefits to be gained. The goals should articulate an animating vision for the state that might include projections around the standard of living that residents could achieve under a vibrant system of well-funded community colleges. If, for example, a plan to fund community colleges adequately is expected to increase the total number of students completing by 40,000 individuals, researchers can project the concrete economic benefits to the state.

The goals should also make plain to state voters why equity in funding is paramount. Every state should want to improve performance across the economic distribution of students, but the reality in most states is that the biggest gains are possible among disadvantaged students, for two reasons. First, because of opportunity gaps, disadvantaged students have the most potential to dramatically increase success rates. Second, in many states, disadvantaged students and students of color represent a growing share of the population.

Pursuing Accountability—in Return for a Greater Investment in Equity

Accountability and investment are two sides of the same coin. Accountability schemes are unlikely to produce results when institutions are starved for funds. Conversely, a stronger case can be made for a major investment in education if skepticism about "throwing more money" at schools can be addressed with some type of accountability provisions.[103] Even deep-blue California policymakers, who recently decided to provide extra funding for community colleges with concentrations of disadvantaged students, included accountability measures in its new law.[104]

On one level, accountability is meant to be inherent in the process of defining adequate funding. Costing-out research determining a minimally adequate funding level already has accountability baked into its formula because the model is designed to produce a financial level at which a given result can be achieved through *the most efficient means*. Still this does not obviate the need for policy mechanisms to hold institutions accountable.

But there are good ways to promote accountability, and there are bad ways. As outlined above, we are largely skeptical of the use of performance-based funding and prefer models that are enrollment-based, equity-focused, and use authentic forms of accountability that are driven by human judgement, not mechanical formulas. The biggest critique we have of performance-based funding is that, without first providing community colleges with a base level of adequate funding, it makes little sense to punish "poorly performing" institutions by further starving them (and their students) of resources. It is students who are ultimately hurt when funding to an institution is cut. As long as community colleges are located in specific locations serving nearby populations, their future funding—which determines the number of people they can serve based on any assumption of class sizes—needs to be based largely on enrollment and on the needs of the area. Even community college funding formulas such as Tennessee's that do not use enrollment per se are using multiple factors that are all correlated with enrollment.

We recognize, however, that enrollment-based funding by itself does nothing to ensure that the people who are most in need are being enrolled. Further, enrollment-based funding, in light of low graduation or transfer rates, invites suspicions, valid or not, that faculty or institutions are not adequately focused on helping students succeed in earning a credential, transferring, or getting a job.

For a state considering its method of funding colleges, the right approach would focus, first, on access—meaning creating programs that successfully attract enrollment by the populations most in need, equitably distributed throughout the state. Second, the state would need to fund each of its schools for performance, meaning that each school needs to be able to spend enough to provide the instruction and support—including financial aid for living expenses, if needed—given its students' academic needs and financial position, and given local costs. Accountability should be assured with dashboards of quantitative measures, but also allow for flexibility to consider the context in which each college operates. We believe accountability mechanisms should include a critical role for human judgement rather than mechanical formulas.

We recognize that in many states, the rhetoric of performance-based funding is deeply entrenched. One way to satisfy that is for states to require system leaders to use outcome measures in the management of institutions: for funding, in reviewing the contracts of college presidents, in reporting requirements. The creation of performance review boards of outside experts could be used to work against fears of self-protection and insularity. We also think that schemes where institutions compete against their own past performance—rather than against other institutions—are more reasonable. Finally, to the extent that "performance based" provisions are included in funding formulas, guardrails should be included to

ensure that they actually result in more disadvantaged students being provided greater support. The Center for American Progress, for example, has
suggested that any benchmarks for performance that look at graduation
rates and labor market outcomes should be "tailored to [an institution's]
resources and student demographics."[105]

Providing Free College—but Ensuring Quality Is Central to the Movement

Alongside the creation of state goals for higher education and the implementation of accountability mechanism, a third major trend in state higher
education policy involves the provision of "free" community college.

Whatever one's position on free college, from a political and policy perspective, there are two important points in implementing such programs:
more resources are needed to cover the influx of students just to maintain
current levels of support; and even greater resources are needed to improve
quality, thereby rendering the investment in free college a wise one.

First, by providing free tuition, demand for enrollment is likely to grow,
so if the intent is to enroll more students, resources must be provided not
only to cover tuition, but also to cover the total cost of educating a growing
number of students. Without additional funding, the quality of education
provided will deteriorate.

Second, given evidence that current levels of funding are inadequate,
the new investment in community colleges not only will have to prevent
backsliding, but also should enhance per-pupil funding to make the most
of the new public investment in making college free. To get the most bang
for the buck, policymakers should ensure that these program are not only
free but have the resources necessary to enable students to succeed.

High quality education is something that many of the early proponents
of free college insisted upon.[106] In this sense, the free college movement
could create an important opportunity. If free college gets more students in the door, it becomes important to policymakers and the public
to ensure that this growing population of students is well served, so that
the new investment by the state reaps rewards. Providing free tuition to a

community college that is inadequately funded and provides few returns for students would be a poor investment.

As many proponents of free college have suggested, the goal must be not only that tuition is free to students, but that funding is provided for supports to increase the likelihood of student success.[107] For example, a student who is homeless, or hungry, or has no child care support for off-spring he or she has, is much less likely to succeed in college.[108] (30 percent of community college students have dependent children.)[109] Just as policy-makers have long recognized that certain K–12 pupils need publicly supported transportation to get to school and free breakfast and lunch while on campus, policymakers need to acknowledge that community colleges, as an extension of elementary and secondary public education, need to grapple with providing critical supports to particularly needy individuals. Americans understand this reality. A 2018 Demos poll found that six in ten Americans agree that full-time public college students who work part-time should not have to go into debt to pay for "books, groceries, transportation, and rent."[110]

In a joint statement, Complete College America, the College Promise Campaign, and Achieving the Dream suggested college and states deliver a "Promise with a Purpose." College promise programs are "empty" if "newly accepted students don't go on to complete their chosen credential," the groups suggested. In order to be built for completion, students need, among other things, "proactive advising" and "financial affordability supports."[111]

A Federal–State Partnership

A new federal-state partnership should be created to provide community colleges the resources they need. The federal government has a long history of supporting federal–state partnerships in higher education, going back to the 1862 Morrill Act establishing land grant colleges. Under the subsequent 1890 Morrill Act, which established eighteen land-grant institutions for African Americans, the federal government committed to funding as long as states matched the federal contribution dollar for dollar.[112] Federal–state partnerships are common in a variety of fields, such as unemployment insurance, health care, and K–12 education.[113]

In recent years, a number of think tanks and public policy research organizations have suggested creating federal–state partnerships in higher education.[114] In 2015, the Obama administration offered an intriguing proposal in which the federal government would cover three-quarters of the cost of a community college education, with states required to provide the remaining quarter in order for its residents to qualify. The program did not move forward in the Republican-controlled Congress.[115]

A new federal–state partnership for community colleges deserves another look, for two reasons. First, the federal government can be an important source of new funding for community colleges. As long as states are constrained to what is seen as a zero-sum game within the realm of education (with four-year colleges, community colleges and K–12 schools competing for their share of a small pie of state resources), the politics of boosting community college funding are challenging. A new influx of federal funds could create a very different political environment.

Second, a matching funds program in which the federal government provides new dollars only if states agree to increase their own investments can provide a strong incentive for states to commit new resources necessary to support community colleges. In the K–12 arena, federal funding under the Elementary and Secondary Education Act has provided a modest amount of revenue but has given federal policy makers considerable leverage in encouraging states to enact a variety of forward-looking policies.

Federal–state partnerships in the health care sphere are also instructive. Medicaid is a voluntary program that all states eventually adopted because of the federal matching funds made available. Likewise, the expansion of Medicaid funding, most recently under the Affordable Care Act (ACA), is encouraging in some (though not all) respects. While it is true that many conservative governors turned down federal dollars under the ACA, it is notable that a number of moderate and conservative governors agreed to take federal money, even though doing so required a modest expansion of state investments. Among the "red" and "purple" states that have adopted Medicaid expansion are Alaska, Arizona, Arkansas, Indiana, Kentucky, Louisiana, Montana, North Dakota, Ohio, and West Virginia. All told, thirty-three states (including Washington, D.C.) have adopted Medicaid expansion programs even though twenty-six states have Republican control of the executive and legislative branches.[116]

In some ways, a matching funding program for community colleges could be even more attractive to state legislators and governors than Medicaid funding. One key difference, of course, is that because Medicaid is an entitlement program whose budgetary commitments are open-ended, community college funding can be more easily circumscribed and involves a more predictable set of financial commitments. In addition, community college educations are not means-tested in the way that Medicaid is, so states may experience relatively greater political pressure from middle-class constituencies to sign onto a federal–state partnership that supports two-year institutions than to those supporting Medicaid. Finally, states have comparatively stronger reasons to invest in higher education to keep talented students in-state and avoid a "brain drain," whereas the same pressure to retain low-income families using Medicaid within state boarders does not exist.[117]

We think that, in the right political environment, a federal–state partnership could be attractive to federal policymakers. Many have grown frustrated that in years past, the federal government has substantially increased funding for the Pell Grant program, only to see state public institutions increase tuition as state governments withdraw resources. Federal financial aid expenditures tripled from $50 billion to over $150 between 1995 and 2015 in constant 2015 dollars, while state appropriations per full time equivalent student fell in inflation-adjusted dollars by 28 percent.[118] A matching funds program would assure federal policymakers that states would do their part as well.

Conclusion

Any effort to devise a new and fairer system to provide adequate funding for community colleges faces an uphill battle, since the existing allocation of resources is to some degree the result of longstanding political power dynamics. Many state legislators direct public resources toward four-year institutions, similar to the ones they themselves attended, or their children or grandchildren attend. So long as higher education funding is seen as a zero sum game, four-year and two-year institutions will fight over the crumbs and community colleges will struggle.

But against those daunting odds are some reasons for optimism. To begin with, if researchers are able to ultimately apply K–12 costing out strategies to higher education, community colleges will have, for the first time, a strong research base upon which to build the case for adequate resources. This new research will supplement a wide body of scholarship suggesting that certain types of investments in community colleges pay off, and that the economic benefits of success for the broader society are powerful.[119]

In addition, many observers have begun to acknowledge that underinvesting in community colleges is foolish, and that a greater investment, well spent, can lead to significant economic growth. There is also growing recognition across the political aisle that, in today's economy, much of our workforce needs the thirteenth and fourteenth years of schooling for labor market success.

The populist mood in the country, on both left and right, could also play to the benefit of community colleges. The push for free community college makes no sense, for example, unless the quality of community college is high. And many conservatives are increasingly alienated from four-year institutions, which they regard as out of touch, and could rally around community colleges, which focus on technical, workplace-oriented education that recognizes that all work has dignity.

These populist movements can take advantage of political strengths that two-year institutions have always enjoyed but have not fully tapped into.

Community colleges are located in many more state legislative districts than four-year institutions, and could build strong alliances between businesses that employ community college graduates, civil rights groups, and unions.

Moreover, if some progress can be made on community college funding, a virtuous cycle could ensue. If community colleges can be better funded, they will become academically stronger, thereby attracting more middle-class students. This development, in turn, will strengthen the political capital of these institutions.[120]

Likewise, success at the state and local level could give rise to a new federal matching program to encourage states to invest in adequate community college funding. An infusion of new federal funds, in turn, could help reduce the fighting between four-year and two-year institutions over scarce state resources. Armed with new information on what level of funding is required to meet our goals, state and federal legislators may finally realize that the old ways of doing business will no longer suffice.

Notes

1. Tom Hilliard, "Mobility Makers," Center for an Urban Future, November, 2011, 4, https://nycfuture.org/pdf/Mobility_Makers.pdf.

2. James Rosenbaum, Caitlin Ahearn, Kelly Becker and Janet Rosenbaum, *The New Forgotten Half and Research Directions to Support Them* (New York: William T. Grant Foundation, 2015).

3. We use the term "performance" rather than "outcomes" because overall performance includes how well a community college recruits students as well as how well students are served once enrolled. Performance better captures the fact that community colleges do not have a captive clientele in the same way that K–12 schools do. For an adult to decide to enroll at a community college requires the college to cater to the interests and needs of that adult, a task that can be particularly challenging with disadvantaged populations. Performance also includes students making progress toward their goals and society's goals, marked by earned credentials.

4. Nick Anderson, "'We serve the top 100 percent': California community college chief responds to Trump," *Washington Post*, February 16, 2018 (quoting Eloy Ortiz Oakley, chancellor of the California community college system), https://www.washingtonpost.com/news/grade-point/wp/2018/02/16/we-serve-the-top-100-percent-california-community-college-chief-responds-to-trump/?noredirect=on&utm_term=.12854ad991a9.

5. 81.4 percent, to be precise. Laura Horn and Paul Skomsvold, *Community College Student Outcomes 1994–2009* (Washington, D.C.: U.S. Department of Education, Institute of Education Sciences and National Center for Education Statistics, November 2011), Table 1 (2003–04 cohort).

6. 13.4 percent. D. Shapiro, A. Dundar , F. Huie, P.K. Wakhungu, X. Yuan, A. Nathan, and Y. Hwang, *Tracking Transfer: Measures of Effectiveness in Helping Community College Students to Complete Bachelor's Degrees*, Signature Report No. 13 (Herndon, VA: National Student Clearinghouse Research Center, September 2017), Figure 4.

7. National Student Clearinghouse Research Center, "Signature Report: Completing College: A National View of Student Completion Rates—Fall 2011 Cohort," December, 2017. Some estimates are more optimistic. See Kevin Carey, "Revised Data Shows Community Colleges Have Been Underappreciated," *New York Times*, October 31, 2017, https://www.nytimes.com/2017/10/31/upshot/revised-data-shows-community-colleges-have-been-underappreciated.html.

8. The Century Foundation Task Force on Preventing Community Colleges from Becoming Separate and Unequal, *Bridging the Higher Education Divide: Strengthening Community Colleges and Restoring the American Dream* (New York: The Century Foundation Press, 2013), 31–32.

9. C. Lockwood Reynolds, "Where to Attend? Estimating the Effects of Beginning at a Two-Year College," University of Michigan, Ann Arbor, October 25, 2006, cited in William G. Bowen, Matthew M. Chingos, and Michael S. McPherson, *Crossing the Finish Line: Completing College and America's Public Universities* (Princeton, New Jersey: Princeton University Press, 2009), 134.

10. See, e.g., Richard D. Kahlenberg, "How Higher Education Funding Shortchanges Community Colleges," The Century Foundation, May 28, 2015, https://tcf.org/content/report/how-higher-education-funding-shortchanges-community-colleges/.

11. The Century Foundation Task Force on Preventing Community Colleges from Becoming Separate and Unequal, *Bridging the Higher Education Divide: Strengthening Community Colleges and Restoring the American Dream* (New York: The Century Foundation Press, 2013), 17.

12. Robert Putnam, *Our Kids: The American Dream in Crisis* (New York: Simon & Schuster, 2015), 125–126.

13. Donna M. Desrochers and Steven Hurlburt, *Trends in College Spending 2003–2013* (Washington D.C.: American Institutes for Research, 2016), 24–27.

14. Richard D. Kahlenberg, "How Higher Education Funding Shortchanges Community Colleges," The Century Foundation, May 28, 2015, Figure 2, p. 3, https://tcf.org/content/report/how-higher-education-funding-shortchanges-community-colleges/, citing Donna M. Desrochers and Steven Hurlburt, *Trends in College Spending 2003–2013* (Washington D.C.: American Institutes for Research, 2016), Figure S2, 19–21.

15. Donna M. Desrochers and Steven Hurlburt, *Trends in College Spending 2001–2011* (Washington, D.C.: American Institutes for Research, 2014), Figure S2, 19–21.

16. Sandy Baum and Charles Kurose, "Community Colleges in Context: Exploring Financing of Two and Four-Year Institutions," in The Century Foundation Task Force

on Preventing Community Colleges from Becoming Separate and Unequal, *Bridging the Higher Education Divide: Strengthening Community Colleges and Restoring the American Dream* (New York: The Century Foundation Press, 2013), 97 and 102.

17. Harry J. Holzer and Sandy Baum, *Making College Work: Pathways for Success for Disadvantaged Students* (Washington, D.C.: Brookings Institution Press, 2017), 178.

18. Christopher M. Mullin and David S. Honeyman, "The Funding of Community Colleges: A Typology of State Funding Formulas," *Community College Review* 35, no. 2 (October 2007): 113–27, at 117. See also Christopher M. Mullin, *Doing More with Less: The Inequitable Funding of Community Colleges* (Washington, D.C.: American Association of Community Colleges, September 2010), 6.

19. Donna M. Desrochers and Steven Hurlburt, "Trends in College Spending: 2003-2013," Delta Project on Postsecondary Education Costs, Productivity, and Accountability, American Institutes for Research, 2016, figure A3, 24–27, http://www.air.org/system/files/downloads/report/Delta-Cost-Trends-in-College%20Spending-January-2016.pdf. Some may argue that the current system—which allocates many more resources to four-year institutions—is efficient because the most funds are spent developing the talents of those students (of whatever race and class) who succeeded at the K–12 level, won slots at four-year colleges, and supposedly will contribute the most to society in the future. Students who have been less successful in society's meritocratic race, the argument runs, should be educated more cheaply in the community college system. In fact, educational opportunities in primary and secondary schooling are vastly unequal, so we can have little confidence that the "meritocratic" winners by the end of high school are indeed society's most able. Moreover, many highly able low-income students "undermatch," attending community colleges even though they have the academic credentials to attend selective four-year colleges. See Caroline Hoxby and Christopher Avery, "The Missing 'One-Offs': The Hidden Supply of High-Achieving, Low-Income Students," Brookings Papers on Economic Activity, Brookings Institution, Spring, 2013, 1–50, http://www.brookings.edu/~/media/projects/bpea/spring-2013/2013a_hoxby.pdf.

20. Alicia C. Dowd and John Grant, *Equity and Efficiency of Community College Appropriations: The Role of Local Financing* (Ithaca, NY: Cornell Higher Education Research Institute, January 2006), 2, 15.

21. Tammy Kolbe and Bruce D. Baker, "Fiscal Equity and America's Community Colleges," *The Journal of Higher Education*, May 18, 2018, 24.

22. Sandy Baum and Charles Kurose, "Community Colleges in Context: Exploring Financing of Two and Four-Year Institutions," in The Century Foundation Task Force on Preventing Community Colleges from Becoming Separate and Unequal, *Bridging the Higher Education Divide: Strengthening Community Colleges and Restoring the American Dream* (New York: The Century Foundation Press, 2013), 74.

23. Richard D. Kahlenberg, "Community of Equals?" *Democracy Journal*, Spring, 2014, https://democracyjournal.org/magazine/32/community-of-equals/.

24. David J. Deming and Christopher R. Walters, "The Impact of Price Caps and Spending Cuts on U.S. Postsecondary Attainment," National Bureau of Economic Research, Working Paper 23736, August, 2017, 3.

25. David J. Deming and Christopher R. Walters, "The Impact of Price Caps and Spending Cuts on U.S. Postsecondary Attainment," National Bureau of Economic Research, Working Paper 23736, August, 2017, Table 4.

26. David J. Deming and Christopher R. Walters, "The Impact of Price Caps and Spending Cuts on U.S. Postsecondary Attainment," National Bureau of Economic Research, Working Paper 23736, August, 2017, 16.

27. David J. Deming and Christopher R. Walters, "The Impact of Price Caps and Spending Cuts on U.S. Postsecondary Attainment," National Bureau of Economic Research, Working Paper 23736, August, 2017, 21. See also David J. Deming, "Increasing College Completion with a Federal Higher Education Matching Grant," The Hamilton Project, April, 2017, 2. See also Tammy Kolbe and Bruce D. Baker, "Fiscal Equity and America's Community Colleges," *The Journal of Higher Education*, May 18, 2018, 4 (re: Deming's findings having particular power at the community college level.)

28. David J. Deming and Christopher R. Walters, "The Impact of Price Caps and Spending Cuts on U.S. Postsecondary Attainment," National Bureau of Economic Research, Working Paper 23736, August, 2017, 22.

29. Juan Carlos Calcagno, Thomas Bailey, Davis Jenkins, Gregory Kienzl, and Timothy Leinbach, "Community College Student Success: What Institutional Characteristics Make a Difference?" *Economics of Education Review* 27, 2008, 632–45 and 644. See also Jane Wellman, "Financial Characteristics of broad access public institutions," Background paper prepared for the Stanford Conference on Mapping Broad Access Higher Education, December 1–2, 2011, 21–22 (citing three research studies).

30. Donna M. Desrochers and Jane V. Wellman, "Trends in College Spending 1999–2009," Delta Project on Postsecondary Education Costs, Productivity, and Accountability, 2011, 30, https://www.deltacostproject.org/sites/default/files/products/Trends2011_Final_090711.pdf.

31. Richard D. Kahlenberg, "Community of Equals? Few elites give much thought to community colleges. But they educate 44 percent of our undergraduates—and they need help," *Democracy Journal*, Spring, 2014.

32. Susan Dynarski, "How to Improve Graduation Rates at Community Colleges," New York Times, March 11, 2015; and Katherine Mangan, "Program's Extra Support for Community-College Students Is Paying Off," *Chronicle of Higher Education*, February 26, 2015.

33. The Century Foundation Task Force on Preventing Community Colleges from Becoming Separate and Unequal, *Bridging the Higher Education Divide: Strengthening Community Colleges and Restoring the American Dream* (New York: The Century Foundation Press, 2013), 35–40. See also David J. Deming, "Increasing College Completion with a Federal Higher Education Matching Grant," The Hamilton Project, April, 2017, 6, suggesting "A number of recent high-quality studies find large impacts of student supports and mentoring on persistence and degree completion."

34. "A Matter of Degrees: Practices to Pathways," Center for Community College Student Engagement, 2014.

35. See Anthony P. Carnevale, Artem Gulish, and Jeff Strohl, "Educational Adequacy in the Twenty-First Century," The Century Foundation, May 2, 2018, 24-25, https://tcf.org/content/report/educational-adequacy-twenty-first-century/.

36. See John Bound, Michael F. Lovenheim, and Sarah Turner, "Why Have College Completion Rates Declined? An Analysis of Changing Student Preparation and Collegiate Resources," *American Economic Journal: Applied Economics*, volume 2, issue 3, 2010, 129-57. See also David J. Deming, "Increasing College Completion with a Federal Higher Education Matching Grant," The Hamilton Project, April, 2017, 12.

37. See Bruce D. Baker, "How Money Matters for Schools," Learning Policy Institute, December, 2017, p. 14. See also Bruce D. Baker, "Does Money Matter in Education?" Albert Shanker Institute, 2nd edition, 2016, i.

38. Rucker C. Johnson and Sean Tanner, "Money and Freedom: The Impact of California's School Finance Reform," Learning Policy Institute, Research Brief, February, 2018, p. 9.

39. Philip Trostel, "It's Not Just the Money: The Benefits of College Education to Individuals and Society," Lumina Foundation, Issue Papers, October 14, 2015, 9 and 14, https://www.luminafoundation.org/files/resources/its-not-just-the-money.pdf.

40. Philip Trostel, "It's Not Just the Money: The Benefits of College Education to Individuals and Society," Lumina Foundation, Issue Papers, October 14, 2015, 41.

41. Philip Trostel, "It's Not Just the Money: The Benefits of College Education to Individuals and Society," Lumina Foundation, Issue Papers, October 14, 2015, 14–15.

42. Philip Trostel, "It's Not Just the Money: The Benefits of College Education to Individuals and Society," Lumina Foundation, Issue Papers, October 14, 2015, 45–46. See also Walter W. McMahon, "The External Benefits of Education," MS No. 1226, available at https://www.researchgate.net/publication/286620724_The_External_Benefits_of_Education.

43. See Richard D. Kahlenberg, "Community of Equals?" *Democracy Journal*, Spring, 2014, https://democracyjournal.org/magazine/32/community-of-equals/.

44. See Tatiana Melguizo and Keith Witham, "Funding Community Colleges for Equity, Efficiency, and Student Success: An Examination of Evidence in California," The Century Foundation, June 14, 2018, https://tcf.org/content/report/funding-community-colleges-equity-efficiency-student-success-examination-evidence-california/.

45. "Completing College: A National View of Student Completion Rates—Fall 2011 Cohort," National Student Clearinghouse Research Center, December 2017, 14, Figure 8. This research is consistent with the 2004/2009 Beginning Postsecondary Student Longitudinal Study (BPS), which found that only 34.5 percent of students who started in a two-year college earned a degree or certificate (from their starting institution or another school) within six years (8.5 percent earned certificates, 14.4 percent earned associate's degrees, and 11.6 percent earned bachelor's degrees.) See The Century Foundation Task Force on Preventing Community Colleges from Becoming Separate and Unequal, *Bridging the Higher Education Divide: Strengthening Community Colleges and Restoring the American Dream* (New York: The Century Foundation Press, 2013), 30.

46. Compare James Rosenbaum, Caitlin Ahearn, Kelly Becker, and Janet Rosenbaum, *The New Forgotten Half and Research Directions to Support Them* (New York: William T.

Grant Foundation, 2015), 5 (which says there is "no earnings payoff" from having "some college," absent a credential) with P. R. Bahr, "The labor market returns in earnings to community college credits and credentials in California," Center for the Study of Higher and Postsecondary Education, School of Education, University of Michigan, 2015, https:// umich.app.box.com/v/Bahr-2014-earnings1 (which finds "the return to students who are not awarded credentials can be as large as, or larger than, the return to students who are awarded credentials, depending upon the coursework that students complete").

47. *Bridging the Higher Education Divide: Strengthening Community Colleges and Restoring the American Dream* (New York: The Century Foundation Press, 2013), 38.

48. Stephanie Riegg Cellini and Nicholas Turner, "Gainfully Employed? Assessing the Employment and Earnings of For-Profit College Students Using Administrative Data," *Journal of Human Resources*, January 30, 2018, http://jhr.uwpress.org/content/ early/2018/01/31/jhr.54.2.1016.8302R1.abstract. See also Stephanie Riegg Cellini, "Gainfully Employed? New evidence on the earnings, employment, and debt of for-profit certificate students," Brookings Institution, February 9, 2018, available at https://www.brookings. edu/blog/brown-center-chalkboard/2018/02/09/gainfully-employed-new-evidence-on- the-earnings-employment-and-debt-of-for-profit-certificate-students/.

49. Susan Dynarski, "Online Courses Are Harming the Students Who Need the Most Help," *New York Times*, January 19, 2018, https://www.nytimes.com/2018/01/19/business/ online-courses-are-harming-the-students-who-need-the-most-help.html/.

50. Ashley A. Smith, "Survey shows participation in online courses growing," *Inside Higher Ed,* April 21, 2015.

51. The Century Foundation Task Force on Preventing Community Colleges from Becoming Separate and Unequal, *Bridging the Higher Education Divide: Strengthening Community Colleges and Restoring the American Dream* (New York: The Century Foundation Press, 2013), 11.

52. Bruce Baker and Jesse Levin, "Estimating the Real Cost of Community College," The Century Foundation, October 23, 2017, https://tcf.org/content/report/estimating-real- cost-community-college/.

53. Anthony P. Carnevale, Artem Gulish, and Jeff Strohl, "Educational Adequacy in the Twenty-First Century," The Century Foundation, May 2, 2018, 2, https://tcf.org/content/ report/educational-adequacy-twenty-first-century/.

54. These data refer to state public higher education as a whole and are not limited to community colleges. David Baime and Sandy Baum, "Community Colleges: Multiple Missions, Diverse Student Bodies, and a Range of Policy Solutions," Urban Institute, August 18, 2016, https://www.urban.org/research/publication/community-colleges-multiple-missions- diverse-student-bodies-and-range-policy-solutions/view/full_report.

55. Jennifer A. Delaney and William R. Doyle. "State Spending on Higher Education: Testing the Balance Wheel over Time." *Journal of Education Finance* 36, no. 4, 2011, 343–368.

56. Ronald Brownstein, Reply to "Letters: Why Have States Cut University Funds?" *The Atlantic*, May 15, 2018. https://www.theatlantic.com/letters/archive/2018/05/letters- american-higher-education-hits-a-dangerous-milestone/560081/.

57. "States' Methods of Funding Higher Education," SRI International, August 2012 (Revised), 50, https://www.sri.com/sites/default/files/brochures/revised-sri_report_states_methods_of_funding_higher_education.pdf (Finding twenty-seven states.) Today, the number is nine (author's cross referencing SRI report with National Conference of State Legislature's report on performance funding, available at http://www.ncsl.org/research/education/performance-funding.aspx). The nine states are: Alaska, Delaware, Maine, Nebraska, New Hampshire, Rhode Island, Vermont, West Virginia, and New Jersey.

58. See e.g. Nicholas Hillman, "Why Performance-Based College Funding Doesn't Work College Completion Series: Part Four," The Century Foundation, May 25, 2016, https://tcf.org/content/report/why-performance-based-college-funding-doesnt-work/.

59. The legislature allocated funds designed to encourage students to enroll full-time and to complete. Laura Szabo-Kubitz, "Financial Aid Gains in the 2017–18 Budget," The Institute for College Access & Success, June 2017, https://ticas.org/blog/financial-aid-gains-2017-18-california-state-budget-agreement.

60. Need was assessed based on Census counts of adults with associates or bachelor's degrees, with access based on community college enrollment by the students' zip code. California Competes, "Educating Julio: Identifying and Addressing Community Colleges' 'Unmet Need'," April 2014, http://californiacompetes.org/assets/general-files/Educating-Julio.pdf.

61. A case could have been made for a major redistribution, but no such case was made. In fact, after the legislature adopted the outlines of the new formula, the negotiations inside the system led to a formula that still provided a growth substantial boost based on historical enrollment. The details of the formula for 2016–17 can be found here: http://extranet.cccco.edu/Portals/1/CFFP/Fiscal_Services/Budget_Workshop/2016/5b%20Explanations%20for%20Growth%20Formula%20(2016%20Budget%20Workshop).pdf.

62. Nicholas Carnes, *White-Collar Government: The Hidden Role of Class in Economic Policy Making* (Chicago: University of Chicago Press, 2013).

63. "State Legislators 2015 Highest Degree Attained," National Conference of State Legislatures Legislator Demographics Survey, available at http://www.ncsl.org/Portals/1/Documents/About_State_Legislatures/Education.pdf. Nationally, the survey found that at least 73 percent of state legislators held a bachelor's or advanced degree, with only 4 percent possessing less than a bachelor's, and 23 percent missing data. Pew, who helped conduct the survey, also points out that lawmakers with business backgrounds hold the biggest share of seats.

64. "Summary: Fall 2017 Fiscal Survey of the States," The National Association of State Budget Officers, December 14, 2017, available via https://www.nasbo.org/mainsite/reports-data/fiscal-survey-of-states/fiscal-survey-archives.

65. Thomas L. Harnisch and Dylan Opalich, "Higher Education State Policy Issues for 2018," AASCU Government Relations and Policy Analysis Division, January 2018, www.aascu.org/policy/publications/policy-matters/Top10Issues2018.pdf.

66. Hannah Fingerhut, "Republicans skeptical of colleges' impact on U.S., but most see benefits for workforce participation," Pew Research Center, July 20, 2017, http://www.

pewresearch.org/fact-tank/2017/07/20/republicans-skeptical-of-colleges-impact-on-u-s-but-most-see-benefits-for-workforce-preparation/.

67. The Century Foundation Task Force on Preventing Community Colleges from Becoming Separate and Unequal, *Bridging the Higher Education Divide: Strengthening Community Colleges and Restoring the American Dream* (New York: The Century Foundation Press, 2013), 5.

68. Martha J. Bailey and Susan M. Dynarski, "Inequality in Postsecondary Education," in *Whither Opportunity? Rising Inequality, Schools, and Children's Life Chances*, ed. Greg J. Duncan and Richard J. Murnane (New York: Russell Sage Foundation, 2011).

69. In some states, reference to a numerical goal—such as adequate funding necessary to ensure that most community college students receive a salary of at least $35,000—may prove a catalyst for political support. See Anthony P. Carnevale, Artem Gulish, and Jeff Strohl, "Educational Adequacy in the Twenty-First Century," The Century Foundation, May 2, 2018, 24-25, https://tcf.org/content/report/educational-adequacy-twenty-first-century/.

70. Jonathan Voss, vice president, Lake Research, presentation at "Higher Ed 2020: College Affordability Ideas for the Next Congress and Beyond," The Century Foundation, September 26, 2018. https://tcf.org/content/event/higher-ed-2020-college-affordability-ideas-next-congress-beyond/.

71. Adam Harris, "The Higher Education Nearly All Americans Love," *The Atlantic*, May 21, 2018.

72. Richard Florida, "The U.S. Cities Winning the Battle Against Brain Drain," City Lab, March 15, 2016.

73. See e.g. Sara Goldrick-Rab and Nancy Kendall, "F2CO: Redefining College Affordability—Securing America's Future with a Free Two Year College Option," The Education Optimists, April 2014, 18; and Jen Mishory, "The Future of Statewide College Promise Programs," The Century Foundation, March 6, 2018, https://tcf.org/content/report/future-statewide-college-promise-programs/.

74. Robert Kelchen, "Do Performance-Based Funding Policies Affect Underrepresented Student Enrollment?" *The Journal of Higher Education*, Volume 89, Issue 5, 2018, 702-727; Paul Fain, "Negative Findings on Performance-Based Funding," *Inside Higher Ed*, December 18, 2017 (referencing studies by Amy Li and Nick Hillman); Tiffany Jones and Sosanya Jones, "Can Equity Be Bought? A Look at Outcomes-Based Funding in Higher Education," Ed Trust, November 6, 2017, https://edtrust.org/the-equity-line/can-equity-bought-outcomes-based-funding/.

75. Lauren Musu-Gillette and Stephen Cornman, "Financing education: National, state, and local funding and spending for public schools in 2013," National Center for Education Statistics, January 25, 2016. https://nces.ed.gov/blogs/nces/post/financing-education-national-state-and-local-funding-and-spending-for-public-schools-in-2013.

76. See e.g. "Fact Sheet: Supplement-not-Supplant under Title I of the Every Student Succeeds Act," U.S. Department of Education, https://www.ed.gov/news/press-releases/fact-sheet-supplement-not-supplant-under-title-i-every-student-succeeds-act.

77. See Richard D. Kahlenberg, *All Together Now: Creating Middle-Class Schools through Public School Choice*(Washington, D.C.: Brookings Institution Press, 2001), 177–178.

78. Deborah A. Verstegen, "How Do States Pay for Schools? An Update of a 50-State Survey of Finance Policies and Programs," Association for Education Finance and Policy Annual Conference, San Antonio, Texas, March 15, 2014, 8, https://schoolfinancesdav.files. wordpress.com/2014/04/aefp-50-stateaidsystems.pdf.

79. The Century Foundation Task Force on Preventing Community Colleges from Becoming Separate and Unequal, *Bridging the Higher Education Divide: Strengthening Community Colleges and Restoring the American Dream* (New York: The Century Foundation Press, 2013), 17.

80. The Century Foundation Task Force on Preventing Community Colleges from Becoming Separate and Unequal, *Bridging the Higher Education Divide: Strengthening Community Colleges and Restoring the American Dream* (New York: The Century Foundation Press, 2013), 17.

81. Natasha Ushomirsky and David Williams, "Funding Gaps 2015: Too Many States Still Spend Less on Education Students Who Need the Most," The Education Trust, March 2015, 5.

82. Emma Brown, "In 23 states, richer school districts get more state and local funding than poorer districts," *Washington Post*, March 13, 2015, A18.

83. See e.g. Andrea Gabor, *After the Education Wars: How Smart Schools Upend the Business of Reform* (New York: The New Press, 2018), 129.

84. "Performance-Based Funding for Higher Education," National Conference of State Legislators, January 13, 2015.

85. The Irish Higher Education Authority allocates extra public funds—called "access weighting"—for institutions that succeed in educating larger proportions of low-income students. "National Plan for Equity of Access to Higher Education, 2008–2013," Irish Higher Education Authority, July 2008, 48. See also "National Strategy for Higher Education to 2030," Irish Department of Education and Skills, January 2011, 114–15, 122. The funding has been part of a plan to increase the proportion of economically disadvantaged students who attend college from 20 percent in 2007 to 54 percent by 2020. "External Audit of Equal Access Survey," Irish Higher Education Authority, June 2010, 7–8 and 16.

86. "External Audit of Equal Access Survey," Irish Higher Education Authority, June, 2010, 7–8 and 16.

87. "Review of the Allocation Model for Funding Higher Education Institutions," Irish Higher Education Authority, May, 2017, http://hea.ie/assets/uploads/2017/06/HEA-RFAM-Final-Interim-Report-062017.pdf.

88. England has had a similar plan in place for some time. Higher education researcher Arthur Hauptman noted in 2003: "The English funding council for a number of years has paid institutions a premium of 5 percent for students who come from postal codes with the lowest income profiles." Arthur M. Hauptman, "Using Institutional Incentives to Improve Student Performance," in *Double the Numbers: Increasing Postsecondary Credentials for Underrepresented Youth*, ed. Richard Kazis, Joel Vargas, and Nancy Hoffman (Cambridge, Massachusetts: Harvard Education Press, 2004).

89. "Guide to funding 2016–17: How HEFCE allocates its funds," Higher Education Funding Council for England, May, May 2016, http://www.hefce.ac.uk/media/HEFCE, 2014/Content/Pubs/2016/201607/HEFCE2016_07.pdf.

90. "Guide to funding 2016–17: How HEFCE allocates its funds," Higher Education Funding Council for England, May, May 2016, http://www.hefce.ac.uk/media/HEFCE, 2014/Content/Pubs/2016/201607/HEFCE2016_07.pdf.

91. "Trends in young participation in higher education," Higher Education Funding Council for England, October, 2013, http://www.hefce.ac.uk/media/hefce/content/pubs/2013/201328/HEFCE_2013_28.pdf.

92. Andrew J. Campa, "Glendale Community College prepares for new funding formula based on student success," *Los Angeles Times*, August 28, 2018, http://www.latimes.com/socal/glendale-news-press/news/tn-gnp-me-student-success-formula-20180828-story.html.

93. See e.g. Michael A. Rebell, "Educational Adequacy, Democracy, and the Courts," in Christopher Edley, Timothy Ready and Catherine Snow (eds), *Achieving High Educational Standards for All* (Washington, D.C.: National Academies Press, 2002) (noting the "link between the standards-based reform movement, which is now being implemented in virtually all of the states, and the courts' recent emphasis on adequacy . . . [S]tandards-based reforms have provided the courts with "judicially manageable" tools that allow them to devise effective remedial orders in these cases."). It is possible the litigation could be employed to provide adequate funding for community college developmental education because the substance of that education was supposed to be provided to students at the K–12 level, but the focus of this paper is on policy rather than legal strategies.

94. "National Plan for Equity of Access to Higher Education, 2008–2013," Irish Higher Education Authority, July 2008.

95. "Tracking America's progress toward 2025," Lumina Foundation, available at http://strongernation.luminafoundation.org/report/2018/#nation. For more details on twenty-nine of those state goals, see "States with Higher Education Attainment Goals," Lumina Foundation, September 16, 2018, http://strategylabs.luminafoundation.org/wp-content/uploads/2013/10/State-Attainment-Goals.pdf. As Lumina points out, "An attainment goal refers to the educational level of a state's population; a completion goal speaks to the credential completion of students enrolled at an institution or group of institutions." See "Statewide Educational Attainment Goals: A Case Study," Lumina Foundation, 2, https://www.luminafoundation.org/files/resources/01-statewide-attainment-goals.pdf.

96. Nicholas Hillman, "Why Performance-Based College Funding Doesn't Work College Completion Series: Part Four," The Century Foundation, May 25, 2016, https://tcf.org/content/report/why-performance-based-college-funding-doesnt-work/.

97. Jen Mishory, "The Future of Statewide College Promise Programs," The Century Foundation, March 6, 2018, https://tcf.org/content/report/future-statewide-college-promise-programs/.

98. Jen Mishory, "The Future of Statewide College Promise Programs," The Century Foundation, March 6, 2018, https://tcf.org/content/report/future-statewide-college-promise-programs/.

99. Jason Rosenbaum, "As State Budget Revenues Fall Short, Higher Education Faces a Squeeze, NPR, March 3, 2017, https://www.npr.org/2017/03/03/517073825/as-state-budget-revenues-fall-short-higher-education-faces-a-squeeze.

100. "Tracking America's progress toward 2025," Lumina Foundation, available at http://strongernation.luminafoundation.org/report/2018/#nation.

101. Anthony P. Carnevale, Artem Gulish, and Jeff Strohl, "Educational Adequacy in the Twenty-First Century," The Century Foundation, May 2, 2018, 24-25, https://tcf.org/content/report/educational-adequacy-twenty-first-century/. Louisiana and Florida put weight on graduate earnings in their outcome based funding models. See Harry J. Holzer and Sandy Baum, *Making College Work: Pathways for Success for Disadvantaged Students* (Washington, D.C.: Brookings Institution Press, 2017), 175.

102. "Tracking America's progress toward 2025," Lumina Foundation, available at http://strongernation.luminafoundation.org/report/2018/#nation.

103. See e.g. David Leonhardt, "The Two Biggest Problems with College," *New York Times*, June 20, 2018 (describing lack of funding and lack of accountability as the twin challenges for higher education).

104. See Tatiana Melguizo and Keith Witham, "Funding Community Colleges for Equity, Efficiency, and Student Success: An Examination of Evidence in California," The Century Foundation, June 14, 2018, https://tcf.org/content/report/funding-community-colleges-equity-efficiency-student-success-examination-evidence-california/; David L. Kirp, "If community colleges want more funding, they have to graduate more students," *Los Angeles Times*, June 22, 2018, http://www.latimes.com/opinion/op-ed/la-oe-kirp-community-college-funding-20180622-story.html.

105. See "Beyond Tuition: Promises for Affordability, Quality, and Accountability in Higher Education," Postsecondary Education Team, Center for American Progress, June, 2018, 1, https://cdn.americanprogress.org/content/uploads/2018/06/19130155/BeyondTuition-factsheet2.pdf. State formulas will have to adjust funding not only on the basis of need (such as family income) but on a variety of other factors as well. These include: accounting for student needs for housing, food, and child care not traditionally thought of as "educational" expenses; accounting for costs associated with concentrated need; accounting for differential costs associated with different programs and academic disciplines; accounting for different costs associated with geographic location; accounting for different costs associated with scale; and accounting for different costs associated with form of education (online vs. brick-and-mortar).

106. See e.g. Sara Goldrick-Rab and Nancy Kendall, "F2CO: Redefining College Affordability—Securing America's Future with a Free Two Year College Option," The Education Optimists, April 2014, 18 ("The current means-tested system demands nothing from colleges and universities in terms of program quality beyond the limited demands of accreditors. By investing in a universal system, the federal government can engage states and institutions in a conversation about what is required to ensure that students being and complete a quality education.").

107. For example, the Obama administration's 2015 America's College Promise Proposal called not only for free community college tuition but suggested "community colleges must strengthen their programs and increase the number of students who graduate [and] states must invest more in higher education and training. . . ." See "Fact Sheet—White House Unveils America's College Promise Proposal," Obama White House,

January 9, 2015, https://obamawhitehouse.archives.gov/the-press-office/2015/01/09/fact-sheet-white-house-unveils-america-s-college-promise-proposal-tuitio.

108. See e.g. Sara Goldrick-Rab, "It's Hard to Study if You're Hungry," *New York Times*, January 14, 2018, https://www.nytimes.com/2018/01/14/opinion/hunger-college-food-insecurity.html.

109. Harry J. Holzer and Sandy Baum, *Making College Work: Pathways for Success for Disadvantaged Students*(Washington, D.C.: Brookings Institution Press, 2017), 146.

110. Jonathan Voss, Vice President, Lake Research, Presentation at "Higher Ed 2020: College Affordability Ideas for the Next Congress and Beyond," The Century Foundation, September 26, 2018, https://tcf.org/content/event/higher-ed-2020-college-affordability-ideas-next-congress-beyond/.

111. "Promise with a Purpose: College Promise Programs 'Built for Completion,'" Complete College America, College Promise Campaign, and Achieving the Dream, April 30, 2018, https://completecollege.org/wp-content/uploads/2018/04/CCA015_Promisewitha Purpose_4.30.2018.pdf.

112. John Michael Lee Jr., and Samaad Wes Keys, "Land-Grant But Unequal: State One-to-One Funding for 1890 Land-Grant Universities," Association of Public and Land Grant Universities, September 2013, 1–2.

113. Jennifer Mishory, "Path to Debt-Free College: A Blueprint for Building a Successful Federal-State Partnership," The Century Foundation, September 26, 2018, 3, https://tcf.org/content/report/path-debt-free-college/.

114. See e.g. David Tandberg, Sophia Laderman, and Andy Carlson, "A Federal-State Partnership for True College Affordability," State Higher Education Executive Officers Association, June, 2017; David J. Deming, "Increasing College Completion with a Federal Higher Education Match," The Hamilton Project, April, 2017, 2.

115. "Fact Sheet: White House Unveils America's College Promise Proposal," Obama White House, January 9, 2015, https://obamawhitehouse.archives.gov/the-press-office/2015/01/09/fact-sheet-white-house-unveils-america-s-college-promise-proposal-tuitio.

116. "Status of State Action on the Medicaid Expansion Decision," Henry J Kaiser Family Foundation, April 27, 2018, https://www.kff.org/health-reform/state-indicator/state-activity-around-expanding-medicaid-under-the-affordable-care-act/?activeTab=map&currentTimeframe=0&selectedDistributions=current-status-of-medicaid-expansion-deci sion&sortModel=%7B%22colId%22:%22Location%22,%22sort%22:%22asc%22%7D. See also David J. Deming, "Increasing College Completion with a Federal Higher Education Matching Grant," The Hamilton Project, April, 2017, 6 (citing the matching program structure as having been "used successfully to boost state Medicaid spending" as discussed by Baicker and Staiger and Kane, Orzag and Apostolov).

117. For discussion of state pressure to avoid "brain drain," see Colleen Campbell, Center for American Progress, remarks at "Higher Ed 2020: College Affordability Ideas for the Next Congress and Beyond," The Century Foundation, September 26, 2018, https://tcf.org/content/event/higher-ed-2020-college-affordability-ideas-next-congress-beyond/.

118. See David J. Deming and Christopher R. Walters, "The Impact of Price Caps and Spending Cuts on U.S. Postsecondary Attainment," National Bureau of Economic Research, Working Paper 23736, August, 2017, 2.

119. Even in cases where legislators reject new research costing out the adequate spending levels required to reach a given result, an appeal can be made to equity. For example, for community college students who are required to take remedial education courses, a powerful argument can be made that they should receive funding support at the same level the state provides to high school students until those community college students reach levels of proficiency that enable them to take credit-bearing college courses. The share of students taking remedial courses in community college is large: 68 percent of community college students who entered in 2003–04 took at least one remedial class by 2009. See Harry J. Holzer and Sandy Baum, *Making College Work: Pathways for Success for Disadvantaged Students* (Washington, D.C.: Brookings Institution Press, 2017), 20.

120. See The Century Foundation Task Force on Preventing Community Colleges from Becoming Separate and Unequal, *Bridging the Higher Education Divide: Strengthening Community Colleges and Restoring the American Dream* (New York: The Century Foundation Press, 2013), 21–28.

About the Background Paper Authors

Bruce Baker is professor in the Department of Educational Theory, Policy and Administration at Rutgers Graduate School of Education in New Brunswick, New Jersey. He has been at Rutgers since 2008. Prior to Rutgers, Professor Baker was at the University of Kansas in Lawrence from 1997 to 2008. Professor Baker's specializes in the study of state school finance systems, including the estimation of education costs. He also studies teacher and administrator labor markets and his work extends from elementary and secondary education through postsecondary institutions and systems.

Anthony P. Carnevale currently serves as research professor and director of the Georgetown University Center on Education and the Workforce, a position he has held since the center was created in 2008. Between 1996 and 2006, Dr. Carnevale served as vice president for public leadership at the Educational Testing Service (ETS).

Artem Gulish is a senior analyst at the Georgetown University Center on Education and the Workforce. His areas of research include health care workforce trends; employment, education, and wage trends during the Great Recession and subsequent recovery; job opportunities for recent college graduates; labor market trends for younger and older adults; applications of education and workforce information systems; national, regional, and state forecasts of education and workforce trends; diversity in labor markets and educational institutions; trends in online job market demand; employer-provided training; competency-based education; and noncredit education at community and technical colleges.

Tariq Habash is the head of investigations at the Student Borrower Protection Center, where he leads the investigative priorities to protect student loan borrowers. Prior to joining SBPC, Tariq was a senior policy associate at The Century Foundation, working on higher education affordability, accountability, and consumer protection. His expertise and research on the predatory practices of the for-profit college industry, including the rampant use of forced arbitration, led to important student protections in federal regulations.

Richard D. Kahlenberg is director of K–12 equity and senior fellow at The Century Foundation with expertise in education, civil rights, and equal opportunity. Kahlenberg has been called "the intellectual father of the economic integration movement" in K–12 schooling and "arguably the nation's chief proponent of class-based affirmative action in higher education admissions." He is the author or editor of sixteen books.

Jesse Levin Ph.D., is a principal research economist at AIR where over the past fifteen years he has been involved in a number of projects investigating educational production, school finance and adequacy, and resource allocation. He currently directs national studies of weighted student funding systems and Title I resource allocation, both for the U.S. Department of Education, as well as a study of educational adequacy in California public schools. In addition, Levin recently directed a study of public school funding for the Maryland State Department of Education and Maryland Department of Legislative Services. He has directed high-profile educational adequacy studies in California, New Mexico, and New York, investigations of educator supply and demand in Oklahoma and Massachusetts, evaluations of state school finance systems in Hawaii, Nevada, and Pennsylvania, and researched educational resource allocation and effectiveness both within and across school districts.

Kimberly Quick is a senior policy associate at The Century Foundation working on education policy in the foundation's Washington, D.C. office.

Kimberly graduated summa cum laude from Wake Forest University in 2014 with a bachelor's degree in politics and international affairs and minors in English and American ethnic studies. Prior to joining TCF, Quick completed a fellowship at the Office of the Provost at Wake Forest, where she has helped to develop the university's communications, programming, and policy related to diversity and inclusion and student experiences. Through internships and volunteer experiences, she has also worked with the American Bar Foundation, the Federal Trade Commission, and Amnesty International.

Robert Shireman is director of higher education excellence and senior fellow at The Century Foundation working on education policy with a focus on affordability, quality assurance, and consumer protections. He served in the Clinton White House as a senior policy advisor to the National Economic Council, and in the Obama administration as deputy undersecretary of education. In 2004 he founded The Institute for College Access & Success, and in 2011 launched the policy organization California Competes.

Jeff Strohl is the director of research at the Georgetown University Center on Education and the Workforce where he continues his long involvement in the analysis of education and labor market outcomes and policy. He leads the center's research investigating the supply and demand of education and how education enhances career opportunities for today's workforce. He also focuses on how to quantify skills and how to better understand competencies given the evolving nature of the U.S. workplace.